Mentoring At-Risk Students through the Hidden Curriculum of Higher Education

Mentoring At-Risk Students through the Hidden Curriculum of Higher Education

Buffy Smith

LEXINGTON BOOKS
Lanham • Boulder • New York • Toronto • Plymouth, UK

Published by Lexington Books
A wholly owned subsidiary of The Rowman & Littlefield Publishing Group, Inc.
4501 Forbes Boulevard, Suite 200, Lanham, Maryland 20706
www.rowman.com

10 Thornbury Road, Plymouth PL6 7PP, United Kingdom

British Library Cataloguing in Publication Information Available

Library of Congress Cataloging-in-Publication Data
Smith, Buffy.
  Mentoring at-risk students through the hidden curriculum of higher education / Buffy
Smith.
      pages ; cm
  Includes bibliographical references and index.
  ISBN 978-0-7391-6566-9 (cloth : alk. paper) — ISBN 978-0-7391-8323-6 (electronic)
  1. Youth with social disabilities—Education—United States. 2. Minorities—Education
(Higher)—United States. 3. Mentoring in education—United States. 4. College
students—United States—Social conditions. 5. Universities and colleges—Sociological
aspects—United States. 6. Academic achievement—United States. I. Title.
  LC4091.S57 2013
  371.1020973—dc23   2013004769

  ISBN 978-1-4985-1580-1 (pbk : alk. paper)

Printed in the United States of America

Dedicated to my beloved mother Henreitta Smith and in loving memory of my grandmother Everlean Smith

Contents

Acknowledgments ix

Introduction xi

1. Invest Now or Pay Later 1

2. Learning at the Margins 17

3. Decoding the Hidden Curriculum 55

4. Transforming Mentoring Programs 89

5. Play to Win: Learn the Rules 111

6. Overcoming Mentoring Barriers: Do Not Give Up 127

Conclusion 143

Appendix A 147

Appendix B 155

Appendix C 161

Bibliography 165

Index 173

About the Author 177

Acknowledgments

I could not have written this book without the loving grace and mercy of God. I was blessed to have a strong supporting network of family and friends during this entire process. I would like to thank Gary Sandefur, Jane Collins, Marino Bruce, Grace Livingston, Julia H. Cradle, Carlotta Calmese, Susan Smith-Cunnien, and Barbara Townsend who have been great mentors and friends to me.

I am indebted to my beloved mother Henreitta Smith, aunts Cora Lockett and Henrine Wilson, late uncle Cleophus Smith, brother Ronald Smith, god-mothers Mary Albritton and Debra Skinner, and other relatives and friends for their unwavering love, encouragement, and support. In addition, I am blessed to have a loving and wonderful life partner Sherrie Fernandez-Williams who provided me with insightful feedback on numerous drafts of the book and for keeping me sane during the writing process. She is also a remarkable mentor.

I am extremely grateful to Sandie McNeel for editing my chapters and providing words of encouragement. I would also like to express deep gratitude to all the mentees, mentors, and mentoring program directors who participated in my study. It was an honor to interview you and I learned a lot from each of you. You have all inspired me to become a better mentor.

I want to thank other significant people who have been instrumental in bringing this book to fruition; Stephen Brookfield, Carolyn Holbrook, Priscilla Gibson, Mary Easter, Carla-Elaine Johnson, Latoya Beck, and Aundria Morgan.

Moreover, I am thankful for TRIO Educational Opportunity Programs, Ronald E. McNair Scholars Program, Association for the Study of Higher Education, and the Lumina Foundation for professional development, mentoring, and financial support.

In addition, I appreciate the willingness of both journals *African American Research Perspectives* and *Equity & Excellence in Education* for granting me permission to use sections of my previously published articles for this book. Finally, I would like to thank my editors Eric Wrona and Emily Natsios and the great production team at Lexington Books for their patience, expertise, and assistance in producing this book.

Introduction

In the United States, the stereotypes of people in low-income neighborhoods include drug dealers, pimps, gangsters, and other criminals. However, the reality is that within these same neighborhoods there are also many community-building and law-abiding families who value education and hard work. Unfortunately, these families are often ignored and/or perceived as dysfunctional because their family structure does not always fit the college educated, two-parent, White, heterosexual, and middle/high income class model. However, if we take a closer look inside these families, we would recognize that most parents/guardians, regardless of their race/ethnicity, socioeconomic background, or other social identities, have high educational aspirations for their children.

The major difference between low-income families and middle-income and high-income families is that low-income families often lack the academic cultural capital and resources to help their children achieve their college dreams. Therefore, we should not be amazed that some young people who come from low-income families grow up believing that they have a more realistic chance of becoming an entertainer or athlete than of earning a bachelor's degree. One possible reason these young people focus more on entertainment than on education is that they see more stories about celebrities who look like them going from "rags to riches" in the media than individuals who have succeeded in life by earning a college degree. In 2009, 55% of students who came from low-income families ($0-$18,000) and graduated from high school enrolled in two or four year colleges the October immediately following high school completion compared to 67% middle-income ($18,100-$86,700) and 84% high-income ($86,800 and higher) high school graduates.[1] These statistics represent the transition to college data, which underscores the idea that students who come from low-income backgrounds are less likely than their middle class and upper class peers to attend college immediately after high school, which contributes to the socioeconomic achievement gap in higher education.

Although there is a socioeconomic gap among students who attend college, there are also significant racial disparities in college graduation rates. In 2010, for example, 38.6% Whites, 19.4% Blacks, 13.5% Hispanics, and 52.5% Asians/Pacific Islanders aged 25-29 graduated with a bachelor's degree from college.[2] The evidence reveals that higher education opportunities are less accessible to low-income students and Black and Latino college students also have lower graduation rates. Many scholars have tried to explain these educational inequities by examining students' family background characteristics, their lack of academic preparation, lack of parental support, lack of financial resources, and lack of institutional support at schools.[3] Although one could argue that all of these factors contribute to racial and social class disparities in the higher education system, the focus of this book will primarily address issues of institutional support at colleges.

The low college enrollment and graduation rates of underrepresented and underserved students (e.g., low-income, first-generation, and racial/ethnic minorities) should be a national priority because we are losing global prestige and status compared to other nations with highly educated populations. In fact, according to the study by the Organization for Economic Cooperation and Development, the United States ranks 12th among other developed nations with respect to graduating young adults with at least an associate's degree. For example, the percentage of 25-34 year olds with an associate's degree or higher was 40.4% in the United States, 55.8% in Canada, 55.5% in Korea, 55.5% in the Russian Federation, 53.7 % in Japan, and 47.3% in New Zealand.[4]

President Obama and other leading educational researchers and policy makers have proposed that the United States will need to increase its overall college completion rate to 60% by 2025 in order to have a globally competitive economic advantage.[5] We can no longer afford to be complacent when a significant proportion of our young adult population do not earn college degrees in a reasonable amount of time (e.g., four to six years). Therefore, this book will focus exclusively on mentoring as one major type of institutional support that students need in order to thrive in college, particularly "at-risk" students. It is imperative for colleges and universities to rethink and restructure their mentoring programs to better serve "at-risk" students (e.g., low-income, first-generation, and students of color). The term "at-risk" has many meanings but the definition most appropriate for this study refers to students who are not adequately prepared to achieve academic success due to institutional cultural barriers.[6] I will use the terms "at-risk," underrepresented, and underserved interchangeably throughout the book. I present a new mentoring model and provide specific recommendations on how to better prepare "at-risk" students to succeed in college.

It is important that we move beyond labeling "at-risk" students as people with deficiencies who need to be "fixed"; instead, racial and social class inequities in our higher education system are a national social problem that needs to be resolved. In order to understand the complex lives and stories of the students behind the statistics I created a fictitious character named Krista as a composite of several students I have known in my professional career. Her fictional name is derived from all of the letters in the word "at-risk."

Krista is an intelligent and witty low-income, first-generation African American college student from public housing in Chicago. She is an introverted creative writer who was the editor of her high school newspaper. She loves watching movies and playing video games with her friends. Krista is the youngest of four children (two boys and two girls) and she is celebrated as the one with the most "promise" to succeed in college. Family members, teachers, neighbors, and church members have always praised Krista for her academic achievements in the past.

However, now Krista sits alone in the last row of a nearly deserted campus library and reflects on her mid-term grades during her first semester at the elite American Dream University. Krista hangs her head in shame as she reflects on her past and all of the things she had to endure over her 18 years of struggle with poverty, racism, sexism, abuse, and numerous developmental challenges related to growing up as a misunderstood, marginalized, and mistreated youth. Now she is performing poorly in her college classes and all of her previous doubts and insecurities seem so overwhelming that tears begin to roll down her cheeks. As Krista's heart aches, she softly cries out to God.

> Why did I get poor grades my first semester in college? What am I doing wrong? I studied hard but I could never earn anything above a "C." I don't know what I am doing wrong and there is no one here to guide me. I don't know who to ask for help. It is funny how I always won awards and certificates for my academic achievements in junior high and high school, but now, I can't get a "B" to save my life. What could have happened in one year that could make me so dumb? Maybe I'm fooling myself to think that I have what it takes to make it in college and graduate with a bachelor's degree in Communication Arts. I guess I should stop wasting my time and money and get a real job. However, if I quit I let my family down with their big dreams for me. Okay, God, I'm gonna try one more semester, but God, please help me to understand why I'm not succeeding in college and send me some help soon cuz my hope is fading.

Although Krista is a fictitious character, the internal dialogue and emotional and mental anguish she undergoes represents the experiences that many underrepresented college students encounter when they attend predominantly white colleges and universities in the United States. When students do not feel connected to a school, they are less likely to ask for guidance because they fear they could be judged as academically unprepared to attend the institution. Unfortunately, students do not know who to ask for help or that it is acceptable for students to be proactive in seeking out assistance when they need it. In other words, students do not know what they do not know.

Krista's story also symbolizes the retention challenges of higher education institutions. For instance, since Krista decided to enroll at the "American Dream University," one could argue the university reached its diversity recruitment objectives; however, the university is in jeopardy of not achieving its retention goals because Krista is considering leaving school without earning a degree. Her situation illuminates the problem many colleges and universities experience in retaining and graduating low-income students of color and first-generation college students.

Mentoring At-Risk Students through the Hidden Curriculum of Higher Education reveals a new mentoring model that could help institutions better serve underrepresented students. Mentors are an essential resource for "at-risk" students to thrive in college. Mentors could unveil the hidden curriculum of higher education to students, which could ultimately help them reach their full potential. The hidden curriculum represents the unwritten norms, values, and expectations that unofficially govern the interactions among students, faculty, professional staff, and administrators.[7] The hidden curriculum is revealed to students who possess the institutional cultural capital and social capital that is rewarded in higher education. Institutional cultural capital refers to the information and knowledge that individuals use to decode, interpret, understand, and navigate the culture of the school.[8] Social capital is defined as acquiring information, resources, knowledge, and skills through individuals' social relationships and social networks (see Chapter 2 for more details on the three concepts).[9] Students need to master both the hidden and formal curricula in order to thrive in college.

Krista's story reflects my experience and the educational journey of many underserved college students I have taught, advised, and mentored during my academic career. The book explores how mentoring could influence students' acquisition of institutional cultural capital and social capital, which are related to broader retention and degree completion issues in higher education.

I interviewed eight mentors and twelve mentees (including four matched mentoring pairs) at the University of Wisconsin-Madison. Each interview lasted approximately two hours. This book is based on findings from empirical research and it incorporates lessons from my teaching, advising, and mentoring experiences in higher education.

This book could be of interest to administrators, researchers, policy makers, student affairs professionals, faculty, and students who want to learn more about the types of institutional cultural capital and social capital that are transmitted and acquired within mentoring relationships. The significance of the research is that it illuminates the theoretical connections among institutional cultural capital, social capital, the hidden curriculum, and the academic mentoring process.

In addition, the book offers policy recommendations on how universities could restructure mentoring programs to reveal explicitly the hidden curriculum to underrepresented students.

In fact, the book presents underserved students with practical advice on how they could acquire institutional cultural capital and social capital from their mentors. The last chapter provides strategies for mentors on how they could assist students with understanding and navigating the culture of higher education. Overall, all higher education stakeholders could gain new insights into how to improve academic success and increase graduation rates among "at-risk" college students.

Mentoring At-Risk Students through the Hidden Curriculum of Higher Education is organized around six chapters. The story of Krista is interwoven through the majority of the chapters. In the first chapter, I define mentoring and provide a brief summary of the history and purpose of mentoring programs. I also present my methodological approach for studying the mentoring process.

In chapter two, I describe the major principles of my conceptual framework and explain how the hidden curriculum, institutional cultural capital, and social capital connect to the academic mentoring process. This chapter provides a solid theoretical foundation for restructuring mentoring programs to improve the academic success of students.

In the next chapter, I study the relationship between the hidden curriculum and the cycles of mentoring. Chapter three reveals a new mentoring model that focuses on the cycles of mentoring (i.e., advising, advocacy, and apprenticeship). My mentoring cycles offer new insights into how to assist "at-risk" students to thrive in college.

Chapter four provides best practices for restructuring mentoring programs to unveil explicitly the hidden curriculum to students. In the fifth chapter, I describe common issues that students encounter in college and offer varied approaches for handling them.

Finally, in chapter six, I provide strategies to help mentors deal with various scenarios they could encounter with their mentees. I conclude with final thoughts on how to transform colleges and universities into mentoring institutions.

Notes

1. Susan Aud, William Hussar, Grace Kena, Kevin Bianco, Lauren Frolich, Jana Kemp, and Kim Tahan, *The Condition of Education 2011* (NCES 2011-033), U.S. Department of Education, National Center for Education Statistics (Washington, DC: U.S. Government Printing Office, 2011), 68-69.

2. Aud, Hussar, Kena, Bianco, Frolich, Kemp, and Tahan, *Condition of Education 2011*, 230-231.

3a. Vincent Tinto, *Leaving College: Rethinking the Causes and Cures of Student Attrition*, 2nd ed. (Chicago: University of Chicago Press, 1993).

3b. Patricia M. McDonough, *Choosing Colleges: How Social Class and Schools Structure Opportunity* (Albany: State University of New York Press, 1997).

3c. Edward Warburton, Rosio Bugarin, Anne-Marie Nunez, *Bridging the Gap: Academic Preparation and Postsecondary Success of First-Generation Students* (NCES Report 2001-153), National Center for Education Statistics (Washington, DC: U.S. Department of Education, 2001).

3d. Annette Lareau, *Unequal Childhoods: Class, Race, and Family Life* (Berkeley: University of California Press, 2003).

3e. MaryBeth Walpole, "Emerging from the Pipeline: African American Students, Socioeconomic Status, and College Experiences and Outcomes," *Research in Higher Education* 49, no. 3 (May 2008): 237-255.

4. John M. Lee, Jr. and Anita Rawls, *The College Completion Agenda 2010 Progress Report*, College Board Advocacy & Policy Center, 2010, www.collegeboard.com (accessed August 26, 2011).

5. Dewayne Matthews, *A Stronger Nation through Higher Education*, Lumina Foundation for Education, Inc., 2010, www.luminafoundation.org (accessed August 26, 2011).

6. Timothy W. Quinnan, *Adult Students "At-Risk": Culture Bias in Higher Education* (Westport, Connecticut: Bergin & Garvey, 1997), 27-44.

7. Michael Apple, *Education and Power* (New York: Routledge, 1982).

8. Pierre Bourdieu, "The Forms of Capital," in *Handbook of Theory and Research for the Sociology of Education*, ed. John G. Richardson (New York: Greenwood, 1986), 241-258.

9. James Coleman, "Social Capital in the Creation of Human Capital," *American Journal of Sociology* 94 (Issue Supplement 1988): S95-120.

Chapter 1

Invest Now or Pay Later

In the United States, we are struggling with recovering from a great recession, high unemployment rates, numerous home foreclosures, bankruptcies, and trillions of dollars of national debt. It makes financial sense to ask the big and tough questions such as which social programs can be reduced. Some reasonable people argue that education should not be spared from the cutting blocks because we need to regain national financial prosperity. Yet other reasonable people claim that now is not the time to decrease education funding because it could have a negative impact on our school system. If we want to grow our economy, we need to produce skilled workers who can compete with highly educated and trained professionals from other developed nations.

In addition to our economic problem, we are also simultaneously experiencing an educational crisis that—unless we are intentional about resolving it—will lead to a long-term lower standard of living for the majority of Americans. Historically, higher education has been perceived as the ladder for upper mobility for the masses of people who were not lucky enough to be born into wealthy families.

The American Dream was once believed to be accessible to anyone and everyone who worked hard and earned a postsecondary education. Now Americans are working harder and longer without fair compensation and the path to higher education is becoming more expensive. If we limit our youth's educational opportunities, we are creating a social environment that could breed political, social, and economic unrest in the United States. In the Middle East, Northern Africa, and Europe, young people are engaging in angry protests because they perceive that their countries no longer promote their socioeconomic advancement. Some young people in the United States have started to publicly challenge the social hierarchy that limits opportunities to fulfill their academic and career goals (e.g., the Occupy Wall Street Movement).

Economic and Social Benefits of Higher Education

We have a chance to prevent a complete break down in our civil society if we respond with urgency to help young people earn associate's and bachelor's degrees. We know that people who increase their overall educational attainment also earn more money. College degrees have the potential to provide more financial security to students and their families. According to the United States Census, the mean earnings for all high school graduates were $31,283, associate's degree graduates $39,506, and bachelor's degree graduates $58,613. If we examine the mean earnings and educational attainment of three racial groups, Whites earned the most at all education levels. For instance, White high school graduates earned $32,126 (Blacks—$27,265, Hispanics—$27,020); White associate's degree graduates earned $40,317 (Blacks—$34,494, Hispanics—$36,830), and White bachelor's degree graduates earned $59,866 (Blacks—$46,527, Hispanics—$48,081).[1]

There are not only individual benefits but also societal benefits to earning a college degree. Some of the benefits include generating more tax revenues at local, state, and national levels. Cities and states with more highly educated residents usually have better health care centers, schools, and social services, as well as lower crime rates. Educated individuals are more likely to volunteer in their communities and become civic leaders. Overall, our democracy is stronger with a highly educated population.[2]

Currently we are operating at a deficit when we compare our students with students from other countries. According to the study by the Organization for Economic Cooperation and Development, the United States ranks twelfth among other developed nations with respect to graduating young adults with at least an associate's degree.[3] If our college graduate population continues to decline, we will not posses adequate national human capital to either demand or fill highly skilled international jobs.

President Obama and other leading education policy makers have set an ambitious goal of increasing our college completion rate from 40% to 60% (which includes two year and four year degrees) by 2025.[4] In order for this education goal to be achieved we need to intentionally help "at-risk" students earn college degrees. Many institutions have already made the commitment to support outreach academic programs (e.g., mentoring programs) that prepare "at-risk" students for postsecondary success.[5] However, underrepresented students still encounter more challenges during their college journey. For instance, only 19% of young people (20-29-year-olds) who come from families with incomes below $25,000 earn an associate's degree or higher. On the other hand, 76% of young people who come from families with incomes $76,000 or more graduate with at least a community college degree.[6]

Defining "At-Risk"

The term "at-risk" is often perceived as problematic because it presumes that there is something deficient about the students when they enter schools. Students labeled "at-risk" are typically considered by some scholars to have two or more of the following characteristics: raised in a single family household, low-income, first-generation, demonstrate poor academic performance, and other factors that put students in danger of failing in school.[7] Other scholars argue that students are placed "at risk" because of the institutional cultural barriers embedded within the higher education system.[8] In fact, many researchers believe that colleges have a responsibility to provide students with the information, resources, and knowledge they need to acculturate to the institutional academic culture of higher education.[9] Although I acknowledge the controversy surrounding the term "at-risk" I will continue to use it to emphasize that students who have been traditionally labeled as "at-risk" have the potential to *succeed* or *fail* depending on the types of institutional support they receive.

Since underrepresented students have limited knowledge about how to play and win the higher education game, it is crucial that we create mentoring programs that help students navigate their school's academic cultural environment. It is unrealistic to expect underserved students to begin college with all the essential skills needed to navigate the cultural learning environment of predominantly white middle class institutions. The fact that these students have enrolled in college despite their past family, social, economic, and academic challenges is a testimony to their resiliency and persistence to achieve academic success. Thus, one could reason that underrepresented students value education but they still need some institutional support with adapting to the academic acculturation process of higher education.[10]

As a nation, we cannot reach our 2025 college graduation benchmark if we continue to think of "at-risk" students primarily as people with personal deficiencies on the brink of academic failure. If instead institutions perceive "at-risk" students as having greater promise to succeed than to fail, schools could increase their retention and graduation rates of these underserved students. It is no longer good enough to be content with having visible diversity in our schools, we should strive to ensure that underrepresented students are fully integrated within the academic culture of colleges. Mentoring programs offer one approach for assisting students with navigating the foreign cultural terrains of the academy. Before we can create a paradigm shift in how we think about the mentoring process, it is necessary to first review the mentoring literature.

What is Mentoring?

People in the fields of business management, developmental psychology, and education all utilize the term mentoring, yet there is little agreement on a comprehensive definition of the term.[11] Although there does not appear to be a consensus on a universal definition of mentoring among many educational researchers and scholars, there are some common themes in most definitions of academic mentoring. For instance, one definition describes academic mentoring as "a form of professional socialization whereby a more experienced (usually older) individual acts as a guide, role model, teacher and patron of a less experienced (often younger) protégé. The aim of the relationship is to further the development and refinement of the protégé's skills, abilities, and understanding."[12] Another definition is that "mentoring is an intensive kind of teaching."[13] My study incorporates both definitions.

Mentoring is divided into two broad camps: informal and formal. Informal mentoring is considered "true/authentic" mentoring because it is not structured and the interaction among individuals occur naturally and spontaneously without external intervention.[14] For instance, a professor might be impressed with the insights that a student expresses in class, and as a result, she might offer that student an opportunity to work with her on one of her research projects. On the other hand, formal mentoring is considered "forced/imitation" mentoring because the initial interaction between the mentor and mentee is more structured and individuals are selected and assigned either a mentor or mentee by the director/coordinator of the mentoring program.[15] An example of this type of mentoring occurs when professors volunteer to be assigned as mentors for students in a formal mentoring program.

Numerous studies conclude that informal mentoring contributes to the overall satisfaction and success that many individuals experience in business and education.[16] One of the major underlying assumptions about informal mentoring relationships is that the "natural chemistry" that develops between mentors and mentees is essential for effective mentoring relationships. However, this presumption of "natural chemistry" as crucial to the formation of effective mentoring relationships is questionable and open for debate. For instance, one could argue that waiting for natural chemistry to occur between students and professors in the classroom would not be the most efficient and effective pedagogy, nor is it a prerequisite for students to learn or professors to teach the formal curriculum. The formal curriculum refers to the written requirements and policies that students must satisfactorily complete in order to graduate from college (see chapter 2 for more details on the concept). For example, at many colleges and universities students have to complete a specified number of credits of social science before they can graduate with a liberal arts degree.

Likewise, one could ask why "natural chemistry" should be considered a prerequisite for learning or teaching the hidden curriculum through formal academic mentoring programs. The hidden curriculum represents the unwritten norms, values, and expectations that unofficially and implicitly govern the interactions among students, faculty, professional staff, and administrators (see chapter 2). For example, there are appropriate ways to discuss grades with professors without challenging their authority, a "hidden" code of behaviors that may not be self-evident to all students. Therefore, the main objective of mentoring programs is not to foster "natural chemistry" between mentors and mentees; instead, the goal is to unveil explicitly and systematically the hidden curriculum of higher education to "at-risk" students.

Historical Context

The concept of informal mentoring has its historical roots in Greek mythology. Before going to fight in the Trojan War, Odysseus asked his trusted friend, Mentor, to serve as a "spiritual guide" or surrogate father to his son Telemachus.[17] Although one could argue that informal mentoring relationships have existed since the earliest forms of human interaction, formal institutionalized mentoring is a relatively new phenomenon in the United States. In fact, one of the first organizations in the United States to incorporate the principles of mentoring as part of their mission was the New York Association for Improving the Condition of the Poor (AICP). In 1843, the members of this organization volunteered to serve as "friendly visitors" who visited and tried to form personal relationships with the poor as a means of reducing poverty. Throughout the late 19th century, philanthropic organizations like AICP flourished because the middle classes believed that the best way they could serve the poorer classes was to form benevolent personal relationships with them. This ideology that establishing personal friendships/relationships with the poor could help solve social problems like poverty was adopted and extended by organizations like the Big Brothers and Big Sisters in the twentieth century.[18]

During the middle of the twentieth century, formal mentoring was not only perceived as a way to address issues of class inequality but it also offered hope for reducing gender and racial inequality. In the 1970s, formal mentoring gained in popularity because businesses and government agencies utilized it to assist people of color and women in their quest for upward mobility in corporate and government organizations. In order to address the racial and gender inequities that people of color and women faced in the labor market some companies and government agencies incorporated formal mentoring programs. For example, many corporations paired male senior executives with female junior executives in order to help guide, advise, and counsel them on how to negotiate such things as merit pay raises and promotions at various stages of their careers.[19]

Businesses were not the only social institutions that seized the opportunity to utilize formal mentoring programs to address social problems. Institutions of higher education also struggled with how to provide greater access and opportunities to students of color. In order to reduce racial disparities and simultaneously increase diversity in higher education, many colleges and universities established formal academic mentoring programs.[20] In fact, academic mentoring programs are becoming increasingly popular as an inexpensive strategy for increasing the recruitment and retention rates of underserved students on many college and university campuses.

The Purpose of Academic Mentoring Programs

There are numerous types of mentoring programs in higher education, which serve various populations such as new faculty, women faculty, faculty of color, and female students majoring in math, science, or other male-dominated fields. However, the majority of undergraduate mentoring programs in higher education are designed to serve underrepresented students.[21] "At-risk" students are the targeted population for many mentoring programs because numerous studies indicate that these students often experience academic and social alienation within predominantly white institutions of higher education.[22]

The reason that many mentoring programs at predominantly white institutions target underrepresented and first-generation college students is because these students have less access to informal networks with faculty and administrators, who tend to be primarily White middle class males. If students experience alienation from faculty and administrators they are less likely to pursue other academic support services (e.g., tutorial services, writing center, and math resource center) which could produce positive academic outcomes.[23] It is important to note that while many White middle class students also find it difficult to establish relationships with faculty and administrators outside of the classroom, these students often still learn the academic culture of higher education through their family's cultural and social class backgrounds.

A New Research Design

The study included four mentoring pairs (i.e., mentees and mentors who were officially matched with one another by the director of their respective mentoring program), four mentors, and eight mentees whose respective mentoring partners elected not to participate in the study. The mentees were all students of color (predominantly African-Americans), and the mentors were both White and people of color. The respondents' race, gender, and social class backgrounds were self-reported. The categories for social class backgrounds were the following: lower class, working class, lower-middle class, middle-middle class, upper-middle class, and upper class. The respondents reported that they identified their social class background based on their parents' education, income, or combinations of both socioeconomic indicators. Overall, the mentors and mentees represented varied racial, gender, and socioeconomic backgrounds, as indicated in table 1.1.

Although few studies report a direct correlation between mentoring and academic success, a growing body of literature indicates that mentoring has an indirect positive influence on the academic achievement of students.[24] These studies suggest that contact with faculty contributes to the overall academic success of students, but they do not explore in-depth the nature of this faculty-student interaction which influences students' achievement and retention. My research addresses this gap in the literature by investigating the types of institutional cultural capital and social capital that are transmitted and acquired within formal academic mentoring relationships. It is important for "at-risk" students to acquire a high degree of institutional cultural capital and social capital in order to understand and navigate the hidden curriculum. If students become more competent in the hidden curriculum, they are more likely to perform better in the formal curriculum, which could lead to increase GPAs and graduation rates.

Another major problem with previous studies on mentoring programs is that they focus too much attention on measuring how mentoring relationships influence academic success exclusively in terms of the formal curriculum, and fail to recognize the relationship between the formal curriculum and the hidden curriculum. In order to achieve academic success students need to have a mastery of the written and unwritten rules. The hidden curriculum is the invisible key that unlocks the door and provides full access for understanding and mastering the formal curriculum. Unfortunately, this key is not readily available to all students, especially to underserved students who are often unfamiliar with the academic culture of predominantly white colleges and universities.[25]

Table 1.1 Description of Respondents in Study

Total 20 Respondents
12 Mentees —11 undergraduates, 1 law student[+]
8 Mentors —1 faculty member, 7 administrators

***[The first four mentors and mentees were paired with one another]*

**Mentees

1. Hispanic woman, lower-middle class, first-generation, 3rd yr. law student,[+] (4 yrs. #) *** (Luz)
2. Black man, lower class, first-generation, senior, (4 yrs. #) *** (Jovaun)
3. Asian woman, working class, first-generation, sophomore, (1 yr. #) ***(Larenda)
4. Black man, upper-middle class, sophomore, (2 yrs. #) ***(Robert)
5. Black woman, working class, first-generation, senior, (4 yrs. #) (Henrine)
6. Black woman, working class, junior, (3 yrs. #) (Marie)
7. Asian woman, lower-middle class, sophomore, (1 yr. #) (Basema)
8. Black woman, upper-middle class, senior, (3 yrs. #) (Jay)
9. Hispanic woman, upper-middle class, sophomore, (1 yr. #) (Ana)
10. Biracial woman (Black and White), middle-middle class, first-generation, senior, (4 yrs. #) (Debra)
11. American Indian man, upper-middle class, sophomore, (1 yr. #) (Corey)
12. Black woman, middle-middle class, first-generation, senior, (3 yrs. #) (Dorothy)

**Mentors

1. Black woman, working class, first-generation, (6 yrs. #) *** (Henreitta—administrator)
2. White man, middle-middle class, (2 yrs. #) *** (Tom—administrator)
3. Hispanic woman, working class, first-generation, (1 yr. #) *** (Grace—administrator)
4. Black man, middle-middle class, (2 yrs. #) *** (Reggie—faculty member)
5. White woman, middle-middle class, (5 yrs. #) (Sherry—administrator)
6. Hispanic woman, lower-middle class, (6 yrs. #) (Cora—administrator)
7. Biracial man (Black and Middle-Eastern), middle-middle class, (5 yrs. #) (Ronald—administrator)
8. Black man, working class, (15 yrs. #) (Damon—administrator)

# indicates the number of years in the mentoring program
**self-reported information from surveys, class information based on mentors and mentees parents'/guardians' education, income, or a combination of both
+ the law student started the mentoring program when she was an undergraduate

Navigating the hidden curriculum is crucial because it influences students' academic performance and their ability to improve that performance, as well as their ability to master the formal curriculum. For example, if a professor interprets a student's behavior as disrespectful when he is discussing his grade on an exam, she will probably be less likely to provide him with strategies on how to better prepare for the next exam. What is problematic about this example is that this student could be unaware of the fact that his behavior is being interpreted as showing lack of respect for authority. Therefore, students could greatly benefit from mentoring relationships, in which mentors explicitly teach their mentees the appropriate ways to engage in conversations with faculty about grades or other concerns they have about the course.

The formal curriculum is transparent to most students, as it is what they are officially evaluated on; however, the formal curriculum is influenced by the hidden curriculum, which is not transparent to everyone. The hidden curriculum refers to the unwritten norms, values, and expectations that are known and taken for granted by the dominant social actors (e.g., White and middle class administrators, faculty, and students) within colleges and universities as a body of knowledge that is assumed to be "academic common sense" and known to "everyone" in higher education.

However, "academic common sense" operates within a specific cultural context and is not readily transparent to individuals who share different cultural and social class backgrounds, which places these individuals at an institutional disadvantage. For instance, underrepresented students are often at an academic cultural disadvantage at predominantly white colleges and universities because those institutions primarily recognize and reward the cultural capital of students from White middle class backgrounds.[26] Therefore, in order for institutions of higher education to ensure a more equal "playing field" for all their students from various diverse racial and class backgrounds, they could explore ways to explicitly and systematically make the hidden curriculum transparent to more students.

Research Questions and New Mentoring Model

In this book, I explored two research questions. First, what types of institutional cultural capital and social capital do students need in order to succeed in college (see table 1.2)? Second, what types of institutional cultural capital and social capital are transmitted and acquired within mentoring relationships (see chapters 2 and 3)?

Table 1.2 Themes About Academic Success

1. Time management (Ex. balance between school, work
   and social activities) (mentors=2 and mentees=10)#
   *[formal curriculum and hidden curriculum]**

2. Academic strategies, study skills, and resources
   (Ex. emotional and financial support) (mentors=4 and mentees=5)#
   *[formal curriculum and hidden curriculum]**

3. Networks with faculty, administrators, and peers
   (mentors=3 and mentees=5)# *[hidden curriculum]**

4. Interpersonal communication skills (Ex. be assertive, ask the
   "right" kinds of questions) (mentors=4 and mentees=4)#
   *[hidden curriculum]**

5. Openness to new cultures and ideas (mentors=1 and mentees=5)#
   *[hidden curriculum]**

6. Self-confidence (Ex. you have the "right" to be here)
   (mentors=1 and mentees=3)# *[hidden curriculum]**

7. An understanding of the academic culture of the university and how to
   navigate it (mentors=3 and mentees=0) # *[hidden curriculum]**

8. Sense of duty (Ex. work independently and don't expect
   someone to hold your hands) (mentors=1 and mentees=2)#
   *[hidden curriculum]**

9. Basic educational skills (Ex. math, reading, and writing)
   (mentors=1 and mentees=1)# *[formal curriculum]**

10. Knowledge of educational requirements and policies (mentors=1 and
    mentees=1)# *[formal curriculum]**

#The number of respondents who expressed the particular themes
*The connection between the themes and the formal curriculum and/or hidden
curriculum

In addition to addressing these two questions, I also created a new three-cycle mentoring model. The cycles of this new mentoring model are advising, advocacy, and apprenticeship. The names of each cycle represent the roles mentors and mentees are playing when institutional cultural capital and social capital are transmitted and acquired within the mentoring relationship. The names of the cycles were selected based on previous studies regarding the various roles that have been used to describe the relationship between mentors and mentees.[27]

The term "cycle" is used to describe this new academic mentoring model because it is based on the premise that mentoring is a process that produces growth over a period of time if certain actions are repeated over and over again in the same order. It is important to underscore the idea that individuals cannot advance from one cycle to the next cycle without embodying the attributes of the previous cycle(s). For instance, mentors and mentees cannot immediately move from the advising cycle into the apprenticeship cycle; they must first possess the elements of the advocacy cycle. The mentors and mentees embody the features of the cycles they occupy and they build upon those characteristics as they travel from one cycle to the next.

However, it is important to emphasize that there is not a natural progression from one cycle to the next cycle. Mentors and mentees can advance to the next cycle only when the transmission and acquisition of the institutional cultural capital and social capital has reached the maximum for that particular cycle. Likewise, if the transmission and acquisition of institutional cultural capital and social capital decrease, mentors and mentees could either remain in their current cycle or move backwards to the previous cycle(s), depending on the degree and intensity of mentoring (see Appendix A for more details on methodology).

Krista Participates in a Mentoring Program

In the introduction, Krista was devastated after receiving her mid-term grades during her first semester of college. She vowed that she would try harder next semester. However, before she could register for her second semester classes she had to meet with her academic advisor. Amanda, her advisor, is a friendly White woman in her late twenties. Amanda expresses great concern over Krista's midterm grades that average to a 2.00 GPA. Amanda reminds Krista that she is in jeopardy of losing her scholarship if she does not maintain a 3.0 GPA. Amanda engages with Krista to find out why she is having trouble in her classes. Krista states that she is studying four hours every day but she is not performing well on exams or papers. Krista tells Amanda that she is attending classes but that is not helping her earn good grades in the class. Krista exclaims, "College is a lot harder than high school."

Immediately, Amanda remarks, "You could benefit a lot from our mentoring program." Amanda asks Krista if she would be interested in participating in a mentoring program. Amanda explains that the mentoring program matches students with faculty, staff, or administrators to make sure students feel connected to the university. Amanda tells Krista she could think of it as having an academic big brother or big sister. Krista thinks the program sounds cool and agrees to sign up for the program. Amanda gives Krista a business card that lists the contact information for the mentoring program. Amanda encourages Krista to sign up for the mentoring program as soon as possible. In the meantime, Amanda recommends that she meet with all of her professors to find out how she might be able to improve her grades in each class. Finally, Amanda advises Krista to utilize the academic support services on campus, such as the writing center and math resource center.

After giving tips on how to improve her grades, Amanda gives Krista some recommendations on what classes she could register for next semester. Krista selects her course schedule and thanks Amanda for her advice. She promises that she will follow-up on all of her suggestions, including joining the mentoring program. Krista leaves her advisor and immediately walks toward the mentoring program office. As Krista is walking, she begins to have some reservations about joining the mentoring program. She quietly expresses her internal fears:

> What am I doing? Do I really want to join this program and admit to these people that I cannot succeed in school on my own? What will my professors think of me? If I join this program, they are going to think that I cannot make it here and think I was just admitted because of my race. I hate when people think I am an affirmative action case. Okay, let me think about what are the benefits for joining this program. I guess I will probably meet more students of color and we could hang out with each other, which would be great. I could have a really awesome mentor and maybe he or she would be able to help me do better in school. I hope I get a professor of color. But, if I don't, I hope the person is at least comfortable with Black people. Well, if the person is not cool I guess I could always quit the program. But, I wonder if I quit, would that have a negative impact on my relationship with my advisor? I hope not, I like my advisor. Oh well, I am here and I did promise Amanda I would join the program. I am determined to do whatever it takes to prove to myself and everyone at the school that I deserve to be at the American Dream University.

Krista knocks on the door and a middle-aged White woman opens her door with a cell phone in her hand. She points to a chair for Krista to sit down and says, "One moment, please." She talks on the phone for another minute, hangs up the phone, and officially welcomes Krista to her office. She extends her hand and says, "Hello, my name is Mary, and I am the director of the mentoring program. Welcome! What can I do for you?" Krista introduces herself and remarks that her advisor Amanda recommended that she join the mentoring program because she is having some trouble with her classes. Mary smiles and states, "Well, I am sure we will be able to find you a mentor but let me first tell you a little bit about the program." Mary explains that the purpose of the mentoring program is to help underrepresented students feel less alienated on campus. Mary briefly highlights special features of the program:

We will do our best to match you with a mentor based on the academic and social interests you list on your application and mentee profile forms. You will participate in an orientation/training session, which will provide you information on the roles and responsibilities for mentors and mentees. If the initial match is unsuccessful, we will match you with another mentor. We want this experience to be enjoyable for you and the mentor. We have several mandatory events including social events that provide opportunities for all mentors and mentees in the program to network with one another. You will also participate in our academic workshops that cover topics like time management, and note-taking skills. We have bowling and pizza parties, but the biggest benefit of the program is that you will build a relationship with a faculty or staff mentor. You can receive all these benefits and more if you are willing to commit to be in the program for at least two years and have at least two one-on-one meetings with your mentor each year.

Mary asked Krista if she had any questions. Krista did not have questions. She completed and returned the application and mentee profile forms. Mary welcomed her to the mentoring program and told Krista that she would provide her with the contact information for her mentor in a couple of weeks.

Notes

1. U.S. Census Bureau, Statistical Abstract of the United States, 2011, Table 228, 150, www.census.gov/population (accessed September 1, 2011).

2. Zachary J. Mulholland, *The Value of Education: A Comprehensive Look at the Benefits Associated with Higher Education,* Indiana University Public Policy Institute, no. 11-C16 (June 2011).

3. John M. Lee, Jr. and Anita Rawls, *The College Completion Agenda 2010 Progress Report,* College Board Advocacy & Policy Center, 2010, www.collegeboard.com (accessed August 26, 2011).

4. Dewayne Matthews, *A Stronger Nation through Higher Education,* Lumina Foundation for Education, Inc., 2010, www.luminafoundation.org (accessed August 26, 2011).

5a. Patrick T. Terenzini, Alberto F. Cabrera, and Elena M. Bernal, *Swimming Against the Tide: The Poor in American Higher Education,* College Board Research Report No. 2001-3 (New York: The College Board, 2001).

5b. Laura W. Perna, "Precollege Outreach Programs: Characteristic of Programs Serving Historically Underrepresented Groups of Students," *Journal of College Student Development* 43 (2002): 64-83.

6. Paul Osterman, *College for All?: The Labor Market for College-Educated Workers* (Washington, DC: Center for American Progress, 2008).

7a. Laura J. Horn, Xianglei Chen, and Clifford Adelman, *Toward Resiliency: At-Risk Students Who Make It to College,* Office of Educational Research and Improvement (Washington, DC: U.S. Department of Education, 1997).

7b. Timothy W. Quinnan, *Adult Students "At-Risk": Culture Bias in Higher Education* (Westport, CT: Bergin & Garvey, 1997), 27-44.

8a. Amaury Nora and Alberto F. Cabrera, "The Role and Perceptions of Prejudice and Discrimination on the Adjustment of Minority Students to College," *Journal of Higher Education* 67, no.2 (1996): 119-148

8b. Quinnan, *Adults Students "At-Risk,"* 1997, 27-44.

8c. Patricia M. McDonough, *Choosing Colleges: How Social Class and Schools Structure Opportunity* (Albany: State University of New York Press, 1997).

9a. Vincent Tinto, *Leaving College: Rethinking the Causes and Cures of Student Attrition,* 2nd ed. (Chicago: University of Chicago Press, 1993).

9b. Quinnan, *Adults Students "At-Risk,"* 1997, 27-44.

9c. Annette Lareau, "Linking Bourdieu's Concept of Capital to the Broader Field: The Case of Family-School Relationships," in *Social Class, Poverty, and Education: Policy and Practice,* ed. Bruce J. Biddle (New York: Routledge Falmer, 2001), 77-100.

10a. Paul B. Thayer, "Retention of Students from First Generation and Low Income Backgrounds," (ERIC ED446633). *Opportunity Outlook* (May 2000): 2-8.

10b. *A Shared Agenda: A Leadership Challenge to Improve College Access and Success,* Pathways to College Network: The Education Resource Institute (TERI), Boston, MA: Pathways to College Network Clearinghouse, 2004, www.pathwaystocollege.com (accessed September 2, 2011).

10c. Joel H. Vargas, *College Knowledge: Addressing Information Barriers to College,* Boston, MA: College Access Services: The Education Resources Institute (TERI), 2004, www.teri.org (accessed September 2, 2011).

11a. Sharon Merriam, "Mentors and Protégés: A Critical Review of the Literature," *Adult Education Quarterly* 33 (1983): 161-173.

11b. Charles C. Healy, "An Operational Definition of Mentoring," in *Diversity in Higher Education: Mentoring and Diversity in Higher Education,* ed. Henry T. Frierson (Greenwich, CT: JAI Press Inc., 1997), 9-22.

11c. Lillian T. Eby, Jean E. Rhodes and Tammy D. Allen, "Definition and Evolution of Mentoring," in *The Blackwell Handbook of Mentoring,* ed. Tammy D. Allen and Lillian T. Eby, Blackwell Reference Online, 2007, www.blackwellreference.com (accessed September 2, 2011).

12. Kathryn M. Moore and Marilyn J. Amey, "Some Faculty Leaders are Born Women," in *Empowering Women: Leadership Development Strategies on Campus, New Directions for Student Services,* ed. Mary Ann D. Sagaria (San Francisco: Jossey-Bass, 1988), 39-50.

13. Morris Zelditch, "Mentor Roles in Graduate Studies," in *Diversity in Higher Education: Mentoring and Diversity in Higher Education,* ed. by Henry Frierson, (Greenwich, CT: JAI Press Inc, 1997), 34.

14a. Healy, "An Operational Definition of Mentoring," 1997.

14b. Eby, Rhodes and Allen, "Definition and Evolution of Mentoring," 2007.

14c. Renée Spencer, "Naturally Occurring Mentoring Relationships Involving Youth," in *The Blackwell Handbook of Mentoring,* ed. Tammy D. Allen and Lillian T.

Eby, Blackwell Reference Online, 2007, www.blackwellreference.com (accessed September 2, 2011).

15a. Healy, "An Operational Definition of Mentoring," 1997.

15b. Eby, Rhodes and Allen, "Definition and Evolution of Mentoring," 2007.

15c. Carol A. Mullen, "Naturally Occurring Student-Faculty Mentoring Relationships: A Literature Review," in *The Blackwell Handbook of Mentoring*, ed. Tammy D. Allen and Lillian T. Eby, Blackwell Reference Online, 2007, www.blackwellreference.com (accessed September 2, 2011).

16a. Terry Cronan-Hillix, Leah K Gensheimer, W.A. Cronan-Hillix and William S. Davidson, "Students' Views of Mentors in Psychology Graduate Training," *Teaching of Psychology* 13 (1986): 123-127.

16b. Ellen A. Fagenson, "The Mentor Advantage: Perceived Career/Job Experiences of Protégés Versus Non-Protégés," *Journal of Organizational Behavior* 10 (1989): 309-320.

16c. Spencer, "Naturally Occurring Mentoring Relationships Involving Youth," 2007.

16d. Mullen, "Naturally Occurring Student-Faculty Mentoring Relationships: A Literature Review," 2007.

17a. Eby, Rhodes and Allen, "Definition and Evolution of Mentoring," 2007.

17b. Thomas E. Keller, "Youth Mentoring: Theoretical and Methodological Issues," in *The Blackwell Handbook of Mentoring*, ed. Tammy D. Allen and Lillian T. Eby, Blackwell Reference Online, 2007, www.blackwellreference.com (accessed September 2, 2011).

18a. Eby, Rhodes and Allen, "Definition and Evolution of Mentoring," 2007.

18b. Keller, "Youth Mentoring: Theoretical and Methodological Issues, 2007.

19a. Nancy Collins, *Professional Women and Their Mentors: A Practical Guide to Mentoring for the Woman Who Wants to Get Ahead.* (Englewood Cliffs, NJ: Prentice Hall, Inc., 1983).

19b. Terri A. Scandura and Ekin K. Pellegrini, "Workplace Mentoring: Theoretical Approaches and Methodological Issues," in *The Blackwell Handbook of Mentoring*, ed. Tammy D. Allen and Lillian T. Eby, Blackwell Reference Online, 2007, www.blackwellreference.com (accessed September 2, 2011).

20a. W. Brad Johnson, "Student-Faculty Mentorship Outcomes," in *The Blackwell Handbook of Mentoring*, ed. Tammy D. Allen and Lillian T. Eby, Blackwell Reference Online, 2007, www.blackwellreference.com (accessed September 2, 2011).

20b. William E. Sedlacek, Eric Benjamin, Lewis Z. Schlosser and Hung-Bin Sheu, "Mentoring in Academia: Considerations for Diverse Populations," in *The Blackwell Handbook of Mentoring*, ed. Tammy D. Allen and Lillian T. Eby, Blackwell Reference Online, 2007, www.blackwellreference.com (accessed September 2, 2011).

21a. Linda Dunphy, Thomas E. Miller, Tina Woodruff, and John E. Nelson, "Exemplary Retention Strategies for the Freshman Year," in *Increasing Retention: Academic and Student Affair Administrator in Partnership, New Directions for Higher Education*, ed. Martha M. Stodt and William M. Klepper (San Francisco: Jossey-Bass, 1987), 39-60.

21b. Clark D. Campbell, "Best Practices for Student-Faculty Mentoring Programs," in *The Blackwell Handbook of Mentoring*, ed. Tammy D. Allen and Lillian T. Eby,

Blackwell Reference Online, 2007, www.blackwellreference.com (accessed September 2, 2011).

21c. William E. Sedlacek, Eric Benjamin, Lewis Z. Schlosser and Hung-Bin Sheu, "Mentoring in Academia: Considerations for Diverse Populations," 2007.

22a. Tinto, *Leaving College: Rethinking the Causes and Cures of Student Attrition*, 1993.

22b. McDonough, *Choosing Colleges: How Social Class and Schools Structure Opportunity*, 1997.

23a. Merriam, "Mentors and Protégés: A Critical Review of the Literature," 1983.

23b. Johnson, "Student-Faculty Mentorship Outcomes," 2007.

24a. Johnson, "Student-Faculty Mentorship Outcomes," 2007.

24b. Campbell, "Best Practices for Student-Faculty Mentoring Programs," 2007

25a. Maryann Jacobi, "Mentoring and Undergraduate Academic Success: A Literature Review," *Review of Educational Research* 61, no. 4 (1991): 505-532.

25b. W. Brad Johnson, Gail Rose and Lewis Z. Schlosser, "Student-Faculty Mentoring: Theoretical and Methodological," in *The Blackwell Handbook of Mentoring*, ed. Tammy D. Allen and Lillian T. Eby, Blackwell Reference Online, 2007, www.blackwellreference.com (accessed September 2, 2011).

26. This book is based on my unpublished dissertation and the methodology and data sections come from it. Buffy Smith, *Demystifying the Higher Education System: Rethinking Academic Cultural Capital, Social Capital, and the Academic Mentoring Process*, Unpublished Dissertation, University of Wisconsin-Madison, 2004.

27a. McDonough, *Choosing Colleges: How Social Class and Schools Structure Opportunity*, 1997.

27b. Lareau, "Linking Bourdieu's Concept of Capital to the Broader Field: The Case of Family-School Relationships," 2001.

27c. Nora and Cabrera, "The Role and Perceptions of Prejudice and Discrimination on the Adjustment of Minority Students," 1996.

27d. Laura I. Rendón, "Validating Culturally Diverse Students: Toward a New Model of Learning and Student Development," *Innovative Higher Education* 19, no. 1 (1994): 33-50.

Chapter 2

Learning at the Margins

"At-risk" students present a moral dilemma for our education system because they represent the "others" in the academy.[1] These students are often perceived by members of the dominant groups in schools (e.g., teachers and administrators) to be culturally and academically deficient and as a result, they are pushed to the periphery of our schools.[2] Since many underserved students are not fully embraced and integrated into the core culture of the higher education system, it forces us to rethink our cultural belief in meritocracy.

Meritocracy implies that individuals are rewarded with upward mobility based on their talents, intellect, educational credentials, skills, merits, and hard work.[3] However, if higher education is embedded with cultural biases related to race and social class, then "at-risk" students do not have a fair chance to earn college degrees and move up the socioeconomic ladder. Simply stated, if underrepresented students have less access to privileges, resources, and power in colleges because of characteristics such as race and social class, we have to question whether the United States is a meritocratic society. In order for colleges to be a vehicle that promotes meritocracy, they have to unveil the hidden curriculum to all students, which would provide students with equal access to the institutional cultural capital and social capital they need to succeed in higher education. Although many schools have mentoring programs, my research indicates that mentors need a little more guidance on how to effectively teach the unwritten rules of higher education to their mentees.

The persistent racial and socioeconomic gap in graduation rates highlights inequalities in higher education. For instance, Whites graduate at a rate 19.2%

higher than Blacks and 25.1% higher than Hispanics.[4] An example of social class inequality is that students who come from middle-income and upper-income families (i.e., $76,000 or more) graduate 57 percentage points higher than students who come from low-income families (i.e., below $25,000).[5] When sociologists examine the disparities in educational outcomes for majority and non-majority students at predominantly white universities, they could either explain those inequities from a functionalist or conflict perspective.

Functionalists argue that the majority of the members in a society share the same values and norms that promote the overall stability of the nation. Since there is a presumed consensus about shared norms and values people generally accept inequality among groups as an indicator that some individuals, because of free-will, choose not to follow the rules of society (e.g., go to school and work hard) and as a result they perform different functions in society.[6] For example, if "at-risk" students drop out of college, functionalists would perceive them as making a rational choice that they no longer want to play by the rules of higher education and therefore they do not deserve to earn college degrees and work in middle class professions.

However, they still could serve a function that benefit society such as working in housekeeping at a hotel. The individuals are not only providing services to our nation but they also serve as an example to younger generations regarding the types of job opportunities they will have if they drop out of college. It is important to emphasize that functionalists do not promote inequality; rather, they believe society can be stable with a certain/functional level of inequities among groups. As long as society is perceived to provide equal opportunities to the majority of people, most people will not question the social order of the stratification system. After all, functionalists would point out that if former college dropouts return to school and earn their degrees, they too could have an opportunity to move up the socioeconomic ladder.

At the other end of the continuum, conflict theorists argue that there is continuous tension and conflict among dominant and non-dominant groups in society. These groups compete for privileges, power, and scarce resources (e.g., education, occupations, and housing) and therefore society is never stable. The inequality in society is the direct result of dominant groups amassing a disproportionate amount of political, social, economic, and educational privileges and power at the expense of non-dominant groups.[7] For example, if "at-risk" students drop out of college, conflict theorists would perceive them as victims of an unjust education system. It would be presumed that the students never had a fair chance to succeed in school because of their racial and social class backgrounds. Most predominantly white colleges unconsciously reward students who come from a White middle class cultural background because the majority of the staff, faculty, administrators, and students at the school come from similar backgrounds.[8] This practice is what I refer to as "cultural favoritism."

"At-risk" college students do not have the same access to upward mobility through higher education as their White middle class peers because their race and social class penalized them before they entered college and during their time in college. If these students drop out of college they are likely to remain in a lower social class because their future job outlook is very bleak, which could weaken their belief in an open, fair, and meritocratic society. According to conflict theorists, a society cannot remain stable when a large segment of the population feels disconnected and hopeless because they do not believe they have equal access to upward mobility. History has proven repeatedly that stability and gross inequities are not compatible and that it is only a matter of time before non-dominant group members protest their oppression via non-violent or violent actions.

As a nation, we should heed the warnings of conflict theorists and history; we have to think of innovative ways to transform universities into more equitable and just institutions. One approach for reforming colleges is to empower students to acquire the institutional cultural capital and social capital they need in order to master the hidden curriculum, which indirectly influences their ability and performance in the formal curriculum. In other words, if students learn how to demonstrate the cultural attitudes and behaviors that are favored by teachers and administrators they are more likely to succeed in school.

Cultural Favoritism

Most educators do not want to admit that cultural favoritism is pervasive in colleges. Cultural favoritism occurs when institutions show preference for students who express similar cultural attitudes, behaviors, norms, and values as the dominant groups in the school. Although this form of favoritism primarily operates at the unconscious level, the rewards that are given because of it increases the racial and social class disparities in higher education. Sociologist Pierre Bourdieu's theory of social reproduction provides a complex and elaborate theoretical framework for understanding how the education system creates, sustains, and reproduces inequality in society.[9] Bourdieu argues that colleges grant credentials that are largely a by-product of displaying the cultural capital of the dominant groups in higher education (e.g., White middle class and upper class staff, faculty, and administrators) and that these credentials are less likely to be based on merits or hard work.[10] He believes that individuals with power in schools are engaged in subtle behaviors that maintain and reproduce the status quo among dominant and non-dominant groups.[11] Therefore, one could interpret that Bourdieu's scholarship supports the idea that meritocracy is a myth in the United

States because cultural favoritism is embedded within our higher education system.[12]

I utilize Bourdieu's concepts of habitus, field, cultural capital, and social capital and connect them to the mentoring process.[13] In order to understand how some students enter college with a more favorable cultural background than other students; we have to examine the concept of habitus, field, cultural capital, and social capital. Habitus is a social class based socialization process that occurs from childhood to adulthood and it reflects how individuals perceive themselves and relate to other individuals in the social world.[14] Habitus is related to field because an individual's socialization process has to occur in a particular social setting. Field is a class based social setting such as a family or school. Field is related to cultural capital because individuals within the social setting compete to control and determine the meaning and worth of the cultural capital within it.[15]

Cultural capital is a popular concept in education and it has been employed to address larger questions related to social stratification in higher education.[16] In addition, many researchers have used the cultural capital concept to examine access, success, and retention issues in colleges.[17] Although cultural capital is less tangible than economic capital (e.g., money) it can provide access to economic capital.[18] Cultural capital is a cultural resource manifested through behaviors that mirror cultural dispositions, norms, knowledge, attitudes, preferences, tastes, mannerisms, abilities, competencies, and skills that individuals learn because of their habitus.[19] Habitus relates to cultural capital because it represents an individual's cumulative cultural capital. Figure 2.1 shows the relationship among habitus, field, and cultural capital.

Bourdieu describes cultural capital in three forms: embodied, objectified, and institutionalized/institutional. Embodied cultural capital reflects how individuals express the internalization of their habitus.[20] Objectified cultural capital is how individuals express their embodied cultural capital through objects such as art, books, and music.[21] Institutionalized cultural capital represents the cultural capital embedded within the institution. Institutional cultural capital refers to the quantity and quality of information and knowledge individuals have about the culture of the institution, which is manifested in their behaviors and skills.[22] Institutions reward or sanction individuals based on their institutional cultural capital (e.g., placed on academic probation or on the dean's list).

Inequality in Higher Education

As students begin college they carry with them educational advantages or disadvantages based on their habitus, which is expressed through their embodied cultural capital.[23] Students' perceived assets or liabilities are reinforced by the dominant culture of the institution. For instance, a White middle class female is more likely than her low-income Hispanic female classmate to be offered research opportunities because her embodied cultural capital closely resembles the

Figure 2.1 Habitus, Field, and Cultural Capital

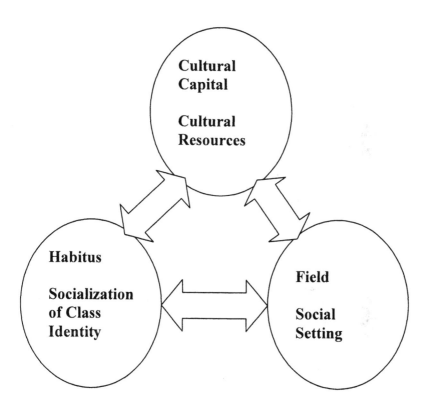

cultural background of the majority of her professors at a predominantly white middle class university. On the other hand, underrepresented students not only experience structural inequalities when they enter college but they continue to experience it until they drop out or graduate. Therefore, students who benefit from cultural favoritism have a greater chance to graduate than students who are perceived to have "cultural deficiencies."[24]

One of the greatest challenges that underrepresented students encounter in college is that they often experience alienation and marginalization because their embodied cultural capital does not provide them access to the institutional cultural capital and social capital they need to master the hidden curriculum. If students learn the hidden curriculum, they could feel more like an "insider" in the academy. The hidden curriculum is a set of implicit rules pertaining to the norms, values, and expectations that unofficially govern how people interact and evaluate one another.[25] Institutional cultural capital is connected to the hidden curriculum because individuals need institutional cultural capital to decode, interpret, and understand the hidden curriculum. The hidden curriculum is important because it indirectly influences an individual's ability and performance in the formal curriculum.[26] The formal curriculum is a set of written requirements, rules, policies, and practices that serve as official guidelines for how to engage with individuals and evaluate their quality of work in higher education.

Teachers have preconceived notions and stereotypes of their students' intellectual abilities based on students' family background characteristics even before teachers evaluate the formal academic work of the students.[27] One study found that students' grades were indirectly affected by non-academic factors such as the students' racial and socioeconomic status.[28] Although some underrepresented students obtained high scores on their academic tests, they were still labeled by teachers as having low academic abilities based on racial and social class stereotypes. On the other hand, low academic performing White middle class students were given the privilege of being perceived as possessing high intellectual capabilities because their embodied cultural capital and institutional cultural capital were validated by their teachers.[29]

Students are being evaluated on their embodied cultural capital, institutional cultural capital, and their knowledge of the hidden curriculum.[30] The hidden curriculum is important because teachers use it as an informal indicator of their students' ability and performance in the formal curriculum.[31] In order to succeed at both the hidden and formal curriculums students have to build strong relationships with people who have "insider" knowledge about how the school functions and what forms of cultural capital are validated and rewarded within the institution. Social relationships that generate social capital could benefit all social actors within the network and foster mutual obligations among people.[32]

Social capital is a social relations resource that represents the quantity and quality of information, resources, knowledge, and skills shared among individuals in relationships or social networks.[33] It is difficult for individuals to acquire institutional cultural capital without social relationships; thus, social capital provides access to institutional cultural capital. In other words, institutional cultural capital is created and assigned meaning and validity through social relationships.[34] Figure 2.2 describes the relationship among social capital, institutional cultural capital, the hidden curriculum, the formal curriculum, and the mentoring process.

The mentoring process is the social phenomenon that connects the concepts of cultural capital and social capital. Mentors are "inside agents" that possess the knowledge of how colleges operate and they know the process through which students are labeled as either "superstars" or "problematic." Mentors could help students learn how to express cultural behaviors befitting of "superstars" and

Figure 2.2 Mentoring Connections

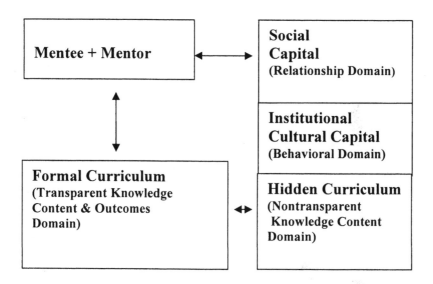

downplay behaviors that are associated with "problem" students. In other words, mentors could unveil the hidden curriculum to students, which could allow more teachers to perceive students as having the "right" institutional cultural capital needed to succeed in both the hidden curriculum and the formal curriculum. Numerous research studies support the idea that schools have a responsibility to help students acquire the institutional cultural capital and social capital critical to their overall academic success.[35]

Connecting the Concepts with a Mentoring Example

In an attempt to explain how the concepts intersect with one another in a mentoring relationship I offer the following example of a fictitious student mentee and her faculty mentor. The student is a Hmong female who comes from a low-income family and she is the first person to attend college in her family. Both her parents raised her in a traditional Hmong culture. For example, females are expected to respect elders, cook and clean, and show deference to males *(an example of habitus)*. She is an introvert and a conscientious student. She receives a "C-" on the first paper in her English class. She does not want to go see the White male English professor and this is the story she tells her American Indian female mentor.

> I do not want to appear stupid in front of the professor. I do not expect to do well in my English class because I am not a good writer. If the professor goes over the paper with me, I will only feel worst about my poor writing skills. Also, the professor is a little intimidating because I am not comfortable with talking with people in such high authority *(an example of embodied cultural capital)*. I will start my next writing assignment earlier and get a friend to read over it several times before I turn the second paper in. Therefore, I do not need to meet with the professor because I know what I need to do to improve my grade *(an example of institutional cultural capital)*.

After allowing her mentee to explain the situation, the mentor tries to encourage her mentee to rethink her decision of not going to see the English professor. The mentor reminds her mentee that she is no longer in high school but college *(an example of field)* and that in order to succeed in college you have to follow the rules of higher education and one of the rules is that you are expected to reach out and ask for help when you need it *(an example of the hidden curriculum)*.

The mentor points to her biochemistry book *(an example of objectified cultural capital)* and states:

> Just like you have mastered the information in this book because you love your major, you should find something you love about your English class and that passion will help you succeed in the course. You have to talk with your English professor because he will be able to tell you what he wants. You should not try to guess by trial and error what the professor wants; you should ask him directly how you could improve your overall writing. You do not know what you do not know, so ask for help *(an example of institutional cultural capital)*. If you get assistance now with your first paper, it will help you later on with your second paper; otherwise, you will probably make the same mistakes on future papers, which will negatively affect your grade in the course *(an example of the formal curriculum)*. Furthermore, you should meet with your professor about your paper because this is a good way to establish a relationship with him and it is also good to have strong relationships with faculty for letters of recommendations and job opportunities. Remember, faculty know and talk with other faculty members on and off campus *(an example of social capital)*. I know you want to go to graduate school so the earlier you learn this skill the better.

The above example highlights the value of mentoring relationships in helping students understand the connection between acquiring institutional cultural capital and social capital and their overall mastery of the hidden curriculum and formal curriculum. Although Bourdieu's concepts provide a useful theoretical framework for my study, the major limitation of the cultural capital theory is that it ignores how race and gender intersect with social class.[36] Regardless of Bourdieu's conceptual shortcomings, many scholars continue to apply his concepts to explain racial and social class inequalities in schools.[37]

Like previous researchers, I recognize the value of utilizing Bourdieu's concepts to examine social stratification in higher education. In fact, the major conceptual categories my study employs to understand mentoring are institutional cultural capital, social capital, and the hidden curriculum. These three conceptual frameworks foreground my research because each of them addresses at least one of the three essential features of the academic mentoring process: (1) understanding the major components of academic success (e.g., the hidden curriculum and formal curriculum), (2) demonstrating behaviors and skills that reflect an individual's understanding of the knowledge she/he needs to achieve academic success (e.g., institutional cultural capital), and (3) understanding the importance of academic social relationships and social networks (e.g., social capital).

The concept of the hidden curriculum reminds us that mastering the domain of the hidden curriculum is an important component for achieving academic success because it indirectly influences students' abilities and performance in the formal curriculum.[38] The institutional cultural capital concept provides the language to discuss the specific behaviors and skills necessary to navigate the hidden curriculum.[39] The social capital concept calls our attention to the fact that often times the hidden curriculum can be revealed to students via social relationships and networks with staff, faculty, and administrators (e.g., mentoring relationships).[40] Thus, these three conceptual categories serve as pillars for understanding the relationship between mentoring and academic success.

Academic Cultures in the United States

This section provides empirical evidence from my research to address the issue of academic culture.[41] Both mentors and mentees were asked to describe the academic culture of the University of Wisconsin-Madison. After employing an open coding technique in which I constructed themes based on the words and/or concepts evoked by the mentors and mentees, seven major themes emerged.[42] The two themes most expressed by both mentors and mentees were the ones that described the academic culture as extremely competitive rather than cooperative, and that it embodies and rewards certain types of behaviors, attitudes, norms, and expectations.

Jay, an African-American upper-middle class female, non-first-generation student, made the following statement about the academic culture of the university.

> Well, it's very competitive. It is the most competitive one that I know of be-
> tween my friends. And, when people don't know that, they don't take it very
> seriously, for like, if we get an "A" here it is a really big deal, but when it is,
> like, at UW-Spirits it's not that big of a deal. So, it is very competitive and so
> whenever you get your exams back, for example, everyone wants to know how
> well you did so that they could feel better about themselves. I think everyone
> generally has low self-esteem issues with their grades and everything like that.
> And, so it is very competitive. And, I think that is pretty unnecessary because
> it's a pretty stressful environment.

Jay's emphasis on the competitive aspect of the campus environment is echoed in Grace's description of the academic culture. Grace, a Hispanic female administrator who comes from a first-generation working class background, stated:

> Well, I feel that this is a very competitive place. I think that as an institution we
> promote that a lot in almost everything that we do. I think not only do we pro-
> mote competitiveness, because everybody has GPA requirements that you have
> to meet in order to get in and stay here in a college or school. I also think that it
> is driven with loans and your financial aid package; it is like you have to main-
> tain a certain GPA. And you have to be able to complete so many credit hours
> or then you don't become eligible for financial support. A lot of it is driven in
> that way, that you not only do well but you do it in a timely fashion (laughter).
> And, I think this is a world-class institution and I think that we have some
> wonderful, wonderful programs here and wonderful, wonderful professors here,
> but the bottom line is that we are very competitive.

These two excerpts represent typical responses made by many mentors and mentees who considered "competitiveness" to be at the core of the academic culture. Jay believes that the academic climate on campus encourages students to be too competitive, and as a result, it creates a very stressful environment. Similarly, Grace explicitly states that the university promotes competitiveness among its students in how the institution structures their admission and probation policies, and distributes financial aid packages. To succeed, students have to learn how to navigate the competitive academic culture of higher education. Further, students who enter college without knowing and possessing the "appropriate" institutional cultural capital and social capital to "compete" within the academic culture could greatly benefit from mentoring relationships. Finally, these two themes both operate within the domain of the hidden curriculum, which supports my thesis that understanding the hidden curriculum is important in achieving academic success (see Table 2.3).

Table 2.3 Themes about Academic Culture

1. Extremely competitive rather than cooperative,
   (Ex. emphasize grades more than learning process)
   (mentors=5 and mentees=8)# *[hidden curriculum]**

2. Demonstrate knowledge of appropriate behaviors, attitudes, norms, and expectations of academic culture (mentors=4 and mentees=3)#
   *[hidden curriculum]**

3. Diversity in terms of academic majors/courses that are offered (mentors=2 and mentees=2)# *[formal curriculum]**

4. Wonderful professors and healthy level of competition (mentors=1 and mentees=2)# *[formal curriculum]**

5. Need balance between academic and social life (mentors=1 and mentees=2)# *[formal curriculum and hidden curriculum]**

6. Faculty governed, class system (Ex. professors at the top and students at the bottom) (mentors=1 and mentees=0)# *[formal curriculum]**

7. Based on a Euro-Centric Model (mentors=1 and mentees=0)#
   *[formal curriculum and hidden curriculum]**

#The number of respondents who expressed the particular themes
*The connection between the themes and the formal curriculum and/or hidden curriculum

Knowledge and Skills Needed for Academic Success

The first research question examined the types of institutional cultural capital and social capital students need to achieve academic success. Mentors and mentees were asked what types of academic knowledge and skills do students need in order to succeed in college (see table 1.2). The top four themes that emerged were time management, academic strategies, creating networks, and interpersonal communication skills. The themes that I will explore more in-depth are time management and academic strategies.

For instance, Larenda, an Asian working class woman and a first-generation college student believed that time management was the most important academic social skill that students need in order to achieve academic success. She exclaimed:

> Well, just for example both of them are time management. You have to be able to stay on top of things and be able to balance everything. You can't just come here and just think that you are going to do all of your homework, and do all your school work because (laughter) that's not going to be a good thing. You can't just come here and think you are going to just be social, so you need to find the balance between both of those. And, most people never do (laughter), you are either one or the other and it's real hard. And, I find for myself that it's hard for me to do it too, because I work a lot and have a boyfriend and other things.

Larenda perceives balancing academics and social activities as a crucial academic and social skill for achieving academic success. Grace also shares this perspective:

> I think that to be really successful, students have to understand the culture of the university and each university is going to have a different culture. And, they have to learn how to use it to their advantage and to maneuver within it. I think that students have to learn the skills of really leading themselves, rather than having others lead them. And, that is a question of maturity and vision. They have to learn academic strategies, study skills, resources, planning preparations, all of that. They have to learn interpersonal and fiscal skills. Interpersonal, how to get along with people, how to manage their budgets, how to find the resources that would allow them to pay for their courses and get through and have a little time to play, which is also very important. We could go off on that subject too, because some students get so tied up in their academics that they lose that personal time that they really need. So, it's really kind of time management.

Grace discusses the intersection between academic culture and academic success. She argues it is critical for students to know how to maneuver within the academic culture of the university. She suggests that students have to possess academic (e.g., time-management), interpersonal, and fiscal skills in order to navigate the academic culture and achieve academic success. Some of the skills Grace recommended (e.g., knowing how to get along with people) belong in the domain of the hidden curriculum and are not readily transparent to many students. Thus, one could infer that if mentoring relationships explicitly taught some of the skills that Grace suggested, these relationships could benefit students who either do not know that a hidden curriculum exists or do not know how to effectively navigate it.

Most of the themes for this question are associated with the domain of the hidden curriculum exclusively or both the formal curriculum and hidden curriculum. However, the two themes regarding basic educational skills and knowledge about educational requirements and policies exclusively belonged to the domain of the formal curriculum, this would suggest that only knowing the formal curriculum is not enough to achieve academic success. The findings support my thesis that achieving academic success requires mastery in both the hidden curriculum and formal curriculum.

Transmission of Knowledge between Mentors and Mentees

The second question examined how mentors helped their mentees acquire institutional cultural capital and social capital. The mentors were asked what types of academic knowledge and skills are transmitted from mentors to mentees. The following statements made by the two mentoring pairs are a representative sample of the various responses to the question.

Henreitta is a very compassionate and outgoing administrator who tries to empower her mentee by encouraging her to take a proactive role in her education. She exclaimed:

> I encouraged her to ask questions and be assertive because students of color need a deeper knowledge base of the dynamics of this campus. I tell them that they might not be valued here as they would be in Milwaukee because of what they look like. I talk about competition here, it is cutthroat but doable. I tell them that you have a right to be here and treated equally. You have to have a take charge attitude. I share my experiences and give positive encouragement. I tell them it is not what you know, but who you know *(Black female, working class, first-generation)*.

The institutional cultural capital and social capital that Henreitta wanted to help her mentee acquire was associated with the following themes: understanding academic culture ("deeper knowledge base of the dynamics of this campus...not valued because of what they look like"); interpersonal communication skills ("ask questions and be assertive"); behaviors, attitudes, norms, and expectations ("you have to have a take charge attitude"); competition ("competition here, it is cutthroat"); self-confidence ("you have a right to be here and treated equally"); and networking ("it is not what you know, but who you know"). The themes represent a range of both higher degree (e.g., understanding academic culture) and lower degree (e.g., competition) knowledge and skills related to the domain of the hidden curriculum.

There is a hierarchical order of institutional cultural capital and social capital operating within the domain of the hidden curriculum. In other words, the more nebulous the particular academic process is, the more likely it could require higher degree institutional cultural capital and social capital to understand the nuances of the process and to navigate it. For example, it is an easier academic process and requires lower degree institutional cultural capital and social capital for a mentor to encourage a mentee who has received a "D" on an exam to schedule a meeting with the professor of the course. However, it is a more difficult academic process and requires higher degree institutional cultural capital and social capital to teach students the appropriate verbal and non-verbal behaviors that they should express during the meeting with their professors. For instance, students who focus on how they could improve their studying techniques for the next exam, rather than emphasizing the problems with the current exam questions, are more likely to have positive interactions with the professor, which could produce desirable outcomes (e.g., a better score on the next exam).

Henreitta's mentee, Luz, is a quiet and reflective student who did not know how to navigate the higher education system before she participated in the mentoring program. Luz discussed the lessons she learned from her mentor. She stated:

> She tried to get me to focus especially after I realized how I started was not working for me. She suggested possible classes and different majors I might want to try. She suggested that I go with what interested me not with what interested everybody else. She encouraged me to form study groups with classmates, work hard and do my best but don't compare myself to others. She encouraged me to talk to people when I am stressed about relationships and roommates issues. She said she would be available to talk with me. She shared personal experiences with me about how she studied in graduate school *(Hispanic female, lower-middle class, first-generation)*.

The institutional cultural capital and social capital Luz learned from her mentor was associated with the following themes: academic strategies ("she suggested possible classes and different majors I might want to try"); self-confidence ("work hard and do my best but don't compare myself to others"); interpersonal communication skills ("she encouraged me to talk to people when I am stressed about relationships and roommate issues"); and networking ("she encouraged me to form study groups with classmates").

The findings indicate that a hierarchy of knowledge and skills exists within the domain of the hidden curriculum, and that mentors have an easier time transmitting lower degree institutional cultural capital and social capital than higher degree institutional cultural capital and social capital to their mentees. For instance, transmitting institutional cultural capital and social capital in terms of behaviors, attitudes, norms, and expectations (e.g., higher degree) is more difficult than transmitting institutional cultural capital and social capital that relate to networking or academic strategies (e.g., lower degree). However, achieving academic success requires that mentees acquire both lower degree and higher degree institutional cultural capital and social capital.

Tom is a reserved and strategic administrator who believes that students can achieve academic success if they learn and follow the rules of the higher education system. Tom conveyed the following:

> It actually makes a big difference if you know you are going to miss class; let your TA know now. They will really appreciate the fact that you let them know in advance. Otherwise, if you tell them afterwards even if it is the best excuse in the world it looks like you couldn't plan especially when they know that you knew a long time ago that you weren't going to be there. It comes off as rude, a little common courtesy goes a long way and TAs and professors will bend over backwards for you. I have encouraged him to go to the office hours of his professors when he has problems or issues. I try to get my mentee to capitalize on the connections that he already has with people on campus. He knows a lot of people but doesn't use it to his advantage. I encourage him to always have a plan B *(White male, middle-middle class, non-first-generation)*.

The institutional cultural capital and social capital that Tom tried to help his mentee acquire was associated with the following themes: behaviors, attitudes, norms, and expectations ("a little common courtesy goes a long way and TAs and professors will bend over backwards for you"); academic strategies ("if you know you are going to miss class let your TA know now"); and networking ("I have encouraged him to go to the office hours of his professors when he has problems or issues").

Tom's mentee, Jovaun, is a very energetic student leader who often questions the racial and social class biases within the higher education system. Jovaun credits his mentor for giving him new perspective on school and life in general. He remarked:

> My mentor gave me good advice and opened up my mind to a lot of things. I wanted to do a major that makes money and that was my mentality for a while. However, my mentor told me don't you want to use your life experiences in anything that you want to do? He didn't choose my major but he helped me to choose a direction that I wanted to take that major. I think that is what he has imparted to me like, don't run away from what you were and what happened to you but make sure you try to help people so that they don't have to be in the same situation. He encouraged me to shoot for lofty goals but to be grounded *(Black male, lower class background, first-generation college student)*.

The institutional cultural capital and social capital that Jovaun learned from his mentor was associated with the following themes: be open to new cultures and new ideas ("opened up my mind to a lot of things"); academic strategies ("he didn't choose my major but he helped me to choose a direction that I wanted to take that major"); and self-confidence ("he encouraged me to shoot for lofty goals but to be grounded"). Once again, the mentor tried to transmit to his mentee the higher degree knowledge and skills associated with the hidden curriculum (e.g., behaviors, attitudes, norms, and expectations). However, his mentee recounted only learning lower degree (albeit important) knowledge and skills (e.g., be open to new cultures and new ideas, academic strategies).

In other words, Tom, like Henreitta, desired to transmit both higher degree and lower degree institutional cultural capital and social capital to their mentees but they both experienced more difficulties with transmitting the former (e.g., behaviors, attitudes, norms, and expectations of the academic culture). In addition, Tom's and Henreitta's mentees acquired different types of institutional cultural capital and social capital even though they were in the same mentoring program. Since a standard mentoring curriculum did not exist, the quantity and quality of institutional cultural capital and social capital mentors shared with their mentees placed some mentees at a greater disadvantage than their peers in navigating the hidden curriculum.

The Link between Social Capital and Institutional Cultural Capital

In order to understand why it is more challenging to transmit higher degree institutional cultural capital and social capital within mentoring relationships, we have to explore first the connection between social capital and institutional cultural capital. For instance, mentors who experience more problems with helping their mentees acquire higher degree institutional cultural capital and social capital are less likely to have strong mentoring relationships. If mentoring relationships are not strong they could generate less social capital and as a result, students could receive less institutional cultural capital within the social relationship. Therefore, this section addresses more deeply how social capital is operationalized in mentoring relationships and the four major components for building strong mentoring relationships which could produce higher degree institutional cultural capital and social capital.[43]

Social capital is an intangible form of capital that refers to having access to privileged channels of information and resources via social relationships (e.g., institutional cultural capital). It is presumed that social capital can only be acquired through social networks and not solely through material resources (i.e., economic capital) or personal educational investments (i.e., human capital).[44] For instance, a millionaire neurosurgeon could be denied membership to a private country club and the valuable information, privileges, and resources associated with it, if she does not have strong personal connections with current members at the club, even though she has acquired high levels of human capital and economic capital.

Several studies[45] utilize the term social capital to explain academic achievement without making distinctions between the major components, such as norms, sanctions, closure, and information channels.[46] Additionally, few studies provide an in-depth analysis of the "quality" of the relationship between mentors and mentees.[47] If we increase our knowledge about how social capital operates, we could also deepen our understanding of how institutional cultural capital is transmitted within mentor and mentee networks.[48]

One of the objectives of academic mentoring programs is that mentors will transfer some of their institutional cultural capital (i.e., cultural knowledge, behaviors, and skills that foster academic success) to students.[49] If the implicit mission of some mentoring programs is to close the gap between a student's home culture (i.e., embodied cultural capital) and the culture of the school (i.e., institutional cultural capital) mentors and menteees have to first understand the social capital process.[50] Although other scholars utilize the concept of social capital,[51] sociologist James Coleman's work provides a more comprehensive conceptual framework for understanding how social capital is generated and maintained within relationships.[52] Therefore, I examine the academic mentoring process through Coleman's social capital lens.

Many sociologists and education scholars who utilize social capital employ sociologist Coleman's conceptual framework.[53] Coleman states "social capital is defined by its function. It is not a single entity, but a variety of different entities having two characteristics in common: they all consist of some aspect of social structure, and they facilitate certain actions of individuals who are within the structure."[54] Coleman argues that some of the major entities of social capital include establishing norms, sanctions, closure, and information channels. His notion of social capital is that individuals can access one another's human capital (i.e., the embodiment of knowledge and skills) and other valuable resources (e.g., prestige, status, and money) through strong social networks. In other words, social capital is embedded within social relationships.

Social capital is created through the establishment of norms, which requires mutual trust and shared expectations between social actors in interpersonal relationships. Once norms are created they are reinforced through sanctions. Next, social capital is maintained through the closure (i.e., close bonds between people) of social networks. Social capital is also maintained and reproduced through the transmission of information channels (i.e., knowledge, skills, and resources) within social networks.[55] Institutional cultural capital is one example of information channels.

Coleman's four components of social capital are manifested within mentoring relationships. First, social capital is created when mentors and mentees establish norms (e.g., meet twice a month). Developing norms requires mutual trust and shared expectations between mentors and mentees. Second, social capital is reinforced when there are clear sanctions for violating the mentoring norms (e.g., students are not allowed to attend a bowling party if they do not have regular meetings with their mentors). Third, social capital is maintained through closure, which refers to close ties among the members within the social network.[56] For example, mentors should form relationships with other mentors and the director of the program to ensure that their mentees maximize their access to the cumulative knowledge, skills, and resources (i.e., information channels) available through the entire mentoring network.

Finally, information channels serve two functions: they create and maintain social capital. For instance, information channels contribute to the creation of social capital because mentors and mentees join mentoring programs to provide or acquire access to institutional cultural capital. On the other hand, information channels foster the maintenance and reproduction of social capital by regulating the quantity and quality of institutional cultural capital that are transmitted between mentors and mentees. For instance, if mentees perceive that they are not receiving significant or quality institutional cultural capital from their mentors, they are less likely to have a positive mentoring experience and maintain regular contact with their mentors.[57] Therefore, one of the major functions of academic mentoring programs should be to increase students' social capital, which could provide them with the higher degree institutional cultural capital they need to successfully navigate the hidden curriculum.

Empirical Support for the Four Components of Social Capital

In this section, I explore how social capital is created through norms, reinforced by sanctions, and maintained through closure and information channels. The first building block for creating social capital is establishing norms in mentoring relationships. Some of the norms mentors cited include: being accessible, maintaining regular contact, respecting confidentiality, and discussing academic issues. The norms the mentees emphasized were: maintaining open and honest communication, sharing personal background information, respecting confidentiality, and maintaining regular contact. If we want to better understand how norms are established, we should first examine how mentors and mentees describe the levels of trust between them and their expectations of one another.

Establishment of Norms—Trust and Expectations

During the one-hour mentoring orientation session for mentors and mentees, both mentoring program directors briefly discussed two general norms for establishing mentoring relationships. The directors emphasized the importance of (1) maintaining regular contact with their mentors/mentees and (2) respecting each other's confidentiality. However, the mentoring program directors did not develop or operate from a standard mentoring curriculum. As a result, the directors did not specify exactly how many times or how long mentors and mentees should meet with one another per semester. Although mentors and mentees could have theoretically established their own norms, it appears that the majority of them followed the two major norms (e.g., respecting confidentiality and maintaining regular contact) established during the orientation sessions.

Since an important principle for establishing norms in mentoring relationship is trust, I explored the level of trust between mentors and mentees in the study.[58] Many mentors commented that they had a low to moderate level of trust with their mentees. These mentors based their trust on minimal expectations, such as maintaining open communication channels and respecting one another's confidentiality. Tom commented:

> I think when we first met we were a little uncomfortable but fairly pleased with how things were going. It seemed like we were getting along okay. He did a really good job and I think we both did a good job of opening up to each other and saying this is me, and this is my background, maybe that will be useful. He told me some of his experiences both positive and negative with the university and things like that. I think over time, we have just gotten more comfortable with each other and we know more about each other and do things socially.

Mentors typically did not describe high levels of trust within their mentoring relationships. One plausible explanation for Tom's and his meentee's initial feelings of discomfort is that they come from different racial and socioeconomic backgrounds. Tom is a white male from a middle-middle class and non-first-generation background who serves as a mentor to Jovaun, a Black male from a lower class and first-generation background. However, the initial awkwardness that may have existed due to racial and class differences began to break down over several meetings, conversations, and activities. The finding supports previous studies that show inconclusive evidence that matching students with mentors of different racial or gender backgrounds results in a negative mentoring experience. Instead, research suggests friendship, nurturance, open-mindedness, and trustworthiness are key elements for fostering positive mentoring relationships.[59]

In contrast to the mentors, many mentees stated that they experienced moderate to high levels of trust within mentoring relationships. One plausible explanation for mentees' higher levels of trust could be attributed to generational differences. For instance, mentors (middle-aged adults) may not necessarily perceive a strong connection between sharing their personal information and building trust with their mentees (young adults). However, it is clear from the study that mentees interpreted their mentors' willingness to share aspects of their personal life with them as evidence of their mentors' trust in them. When I asked the mentees to describe the level of trust between them and their mentors, Jovaun stated:

> Tom is one of the few people outside of my girlfriend and my sister who I will tell things too. Tom knows a lot about my background history that I won't necessarily bring up unless I am asked. But, Tom didn't have to wait to ask, I just told him. "This is where I am from, and this is what I do." I am like, "Don't feel pity for me. I don't want anyone to feel pity for me. I felt you needed to know this in order to understand me better" and vice versa Tom broke down his story too. And, we are still different people, but we kind of went through some of the similar struggles especially academically. While we may be from two different worlds racially and economically and geographically. But academically we both f***ed up in our lives. But, to see him make it to where he is and eventually going to be a doctor, it kind of pushes me on. So, that is why I trust him, I trust his words that he is not trying to screw me over or hurt me like I feel a lot of people in my college have indirectly tried to do. I can forgive Tom for anything he does, but I can't forgive a lot of people. I believe in Tom and Tom believes in me.

Jovaun perceived his mentor as a role model regardless of their racial and social class differences. Instead of "feeling pity" for his mentee. Tom won the trust of Jovaun by sharing personal academic struggles and trials. Jovaun interpreted Tom's sharing of his personal story with him as a sign of open and raw honesty. Jovaun harbored some resentment toward other faculty members and administrators at the university because their words and actions have deeply hurt him. Now, he feels that he has at least one person at the university who he can trust and who believes in him. The finding is consistent with previous studies that state that the closeness of mentoring relationships is determined more by trustworthiness and friendship than racial and power differentials between students, faculty, and administrators.[60] One conclusion to draw from Jovaun's statement is that students who feel that their mentors share their personal lives with them are more likely to feel a "special bond" with their mentors, which is the first step in establishing trust within mentoring relationships.[61]

Mentors' and mentees' expectations influence how they perceive this special bond of trust. The common expectations expressed by mentors were that they would establish close relationships and provide academic information and resources. On the other hand, mentees indicated similar expectations, such as having adult friends at the university who could help them make a smooth transition to college life. I asked the mentors to describe their expectations. One mentor, Henreitta remarked:

> I would expect that once I develop a close relationship with my mentee she would be able to come to me if there is something going on. Number one, I

would expect her to come to me to ask questions and to get answers. Of course, I would expect her to graduate. But, I would expect her to see me as a refuge, you know, like if she is in trouble. I think it would be very disheartening to find out that one of my mentees dropped out and I did not know about it.

Henreitta expresses a great deal of concern for the overall well-being of her mentee. She wants her mentee to view her as a confidant who will be there for her and provide both academic and personal advice, however, Henreitta recognizes that she has to first reach out and show genuine care for her mentee. Henreitta comes from a working class and first-generation background, and she serves as a mentor to Luz, a Hispanic female from a lower-middle class and first-generation background. Throughout the interview, Henreitta stated that she has made a strong personal commitment to students of color and first-generation students to make sure they graduate.

Mentors have modest expectations of their mentees. They primarily want their mentees to feel comfortable enough with them to discuss academic topics. Henreitta believes that accessibility and maintaining open and honest conversations with mentees are the key components for establishing strong and positive mentoring relationships. Mentors seem to take a special interest in their mentees because they are young people of color and first-generation college students. Mentors are committed to assisting their mentees with overcoming racial and social class barriers in order to achieve academic success. They often replied that it was important for them to serve as "positive role models for students of color."

Likewise, mentees have modest expectations of their mentors. They expect their mentors to be role models and friends. When I asked the mentees what their expectations were, Larenda stated:

> I really wanted just a friend. I wanted a mentor to just hang out with, being a first-year student, just to know how this university is run, not to obtain information, but to see how it works, how it goes. For example, I don't want to just call her up and say, hey, can I have the number for this person or whatever. But when we talk, she is like, this is how it works, and she won't just say, hey, I will give you this information and this information and this is where you should go.

Larenda clearly indicates that she desires a friend who can help her understand how the university operates. Larenda values Grace, her mentor, because Grace goes beyond just providing important contact information; she actually explains the "inner workings" of the university. Larenda does not perceive her mentor as a "ready reference" resource person. Instead, Larenda considers Grace to be a friend who cares and takes additional time and effort to help her understand how the university works.

Mentees, like Larenda, need their mentors to help them adjust to college life. Many mentees stated that one of the major benefits of having a mentor is that they have a prominent person at the university who knows them better than anyone else and serves as their advocate.

Sanctions

Although mentors and mentees were quite vocal about their modest expectations of one another and the levels of trust between them, they did not elaborate on how sanctions operate within their mentoring relationships. Sanctions refer to how mentors and mentees enforce consequences for violations of norms within their relationship. I asked the mentors to describe the consequences for violating the norms of their relationships. Many of the mentors appeared confused by the question at first, and then simply stated that there are no real sanctions for violating the norms. Most mentors do not perceive violating the norms of their mentoring relationship to be a serious problem. For instance, Reggie, a Black male, middle-middle class, non-first-generation faculty expressed a typical sentiment held by many mentors:

> Again, the only norm would be to show up on time, and I think he only missed one meeting and I wasn't upset. I e-mailed hi, and I said, "What's up?" He said, "Oops," and I said, "Okay, let's try again." There were no other consequences.

Many mentees expressed similar responses as their mentors, namely that they do not think there are serious consequences for not adhering to the norms. The most common response by mentees is captured by Luz's remarks:

> I don't really think there are consequences, since our relationship turned into, like I said before, we are more like friends. We interact with each other's families. I don't think it would be a big deal breaker if one of us did something out of the ordinary.

Although both mentors and mentees spend a great deal of time discussing how trust and expectations establish norms, they minimize the importance of having consequences for violating these norms. Mentors and mentees do not think consequences are necessary because if norms are violated they are not considered deal breakers that will severely damage or end the relationship. They contend that the special bond they develop during their relationship will help reinforce the norms more than superimposed external sanctions. Therefore, the responses suggest that mentors and mentees are confident that their partners will not violate the norms because they respect and trust one another.

Closure

Lack of sanctions are not the only issues on which mentors and mentees seem to share the same opinion. They also agree that there is little closure within their mentoring relationships. Closure refers to mentors establishing close relationships and networks with other staff, faculty members, and administrators in order to help their mentees achieve academic success.[62] I asked the mentors to describe the interactions they had with their colleagues about their mentees' academic progress. The majority of the mentors provided brief responses to this question, which may indicate that they do not discuss their mentees' academic progress with other staff, faculty members, and administrators or the director of the mentoring program. A typical comment made by the mentors regarding this question is captured in Reggie's brief remark, "I don't have any interactions with them."

Mentees share the same perspectives regarding closure as their mentors. The mentees stated that they are not aware of any interactions between their mentors and other university officials with respect to their academic performance. Reggie's mentee, Robert, a Black male, upper-middle class, non-first-generation student made concise comments similar to Reggie's that are representative of the sentiments held by other mentees. In discussing his mentor's interaction with other staff, faculty members, administrators, and the mentoring program director, Robert said, "I don't think he meets with anyone to discuss my academic progress."

The mentors and mentees seemed uneasy when answering the question of closure. Some mentors stated that they did not know that was a component of the mentoring program. Other mentors cite confidentiality as the explanation for not discussing their mentees' academic progress with others at the university. On the other hand, mentees do not perceive their mentor's lack of contact with their colleagues as problematic. In fact, most mentees assert that their mentors should not discuss their academic progress with others without their consent. As discussed earlier, confidentiality is a norm that is important to both mentors and mentees. Therefore, one can understand why mentors choose not to discuss their mentees' academic performance with other staff, faculty members, and administrators, but it does not explain their lack of contact with the mentoring program directors. According to Coleman, sanctions and closure are important factors for sustaining social capital in relationships; however, the data suggest that the two components are underdeveloped and taken for granted within mentoring relationships.

Information Channels

The empirical evidence indicates that mentors and mentees create social capital in terms of building trust and establishing norms, but they fall short in maintaining the social capital because of a lack of sanctions and closure. Therefore, the next component of social capital that has to be explored is information channels, which refers to the knowledge, skills, and resources that mentors provide and mentees expect to receive during the mentoring relationship (e.g., institutional cultural capital). Information channels play a crucial role in the creation and maintenance of social capital. For instance, at the creation stage, mentees join mentoring programs because they desire to receive important information about how to succeed in college. In the maintenance stage, mentees are more likely to remain engaged in their mentoring relationship if they perceive they are receiving valuable knowledge, skills, and resources.

In order to increase our understanding of the significance of information channels in the creation and maintenance of social capital, I examined the specific knowledge, skills, and resources mentors believe they could offer and mentees think they could learn during the mentoring process. I asked the mentors to describe the types of knowledge, skills, and resources they could provide to their mentees. Most of the mentors suggested they could teach their mentees how to navigate the culture of the university by sharing their personal stories about how they were able to achieve academic success. For instance, Grace stated:

> I think one thing that has been really helpful, I hope is, that my professional training in student services and the fact that I think I have a lot of information in terms of resources that are available to her. If she is stuck on an issue it is easy for me to say to her, you might want to talk to so and so, because here are some services that are available for you as a student. So being on this campus for a long time and being familiar with how to navigate through this institution and the resources. And the fact that I am a woman of color, like she is and I have been there, and I have done that. And thinking about how could what I have gone through help her so she doesn't have to go through some of the obstacles that I have gone through. So, kind of sharing that stuff, I hope it is helpful to her.

Henreitta echoed similar comments in her statement:

> Familiarity with the university is number one, I think above all. And I will help her navigate the culture and break down cultural barriers. I am a success story. Also, I have a compassionate ear, and I offer her a place of refuge, I would say.

Both Grace and Henreitta articulate the idea that they have access to institutional knowledge, skills, and resources. They contended they understand the culture of the university and they want to transfer that knowledge (e.g., institutional cultural capital) to their mentees. Although the mentors imply that understanding how to navigate the culture of the university is crucial to academic success, they do not provide specific examples about how they will actually teach the academic culture to their mentees. However, the mentors emphasize that sharing personal information about how they were able to break down cultural barriers will motivate their mentees to believe that they can achieve academic success as well.

Moreover, the empirical evidence indicates that learning to navigate the culture of the university is indeed knowledge that mentees also hope to acquire from their mentors. The common themes mentioned by mentees with regard to the types of knowledge they think their mentors could offer them include teaching them about the academic culture, sharing with them how to overcome personal academic challenges, and providing access to campus resources. For example, Larenda replied:

> Since she was very familiar with the campus, she offered many, many opportunities on where to go and how to go about it. She didn't go with me, but she gave me advice and little pieces of information that might help me. All I can say is that she told me how it was like when she was younger and what she had gone through to make it. And I was happy to see that there are other ways of making it.

Luz echoed Larenda's comments:

> Well, I think the experience of having been there and making the same mistakes that you could relate to. It lets you know that there is nothing new about what you are going through and that was the most beneficial thing for me.

Robert briefly captured the attitudes of many mentees with respect to the type of information they seek from their mentors:

> I think the biggest thing that he can offer me is the fact that he has been in the university longer than I have. He has been in the university system and he can draw off of what has happened in past years, what he has found has worked or hasn't worked for his students or other people that he has worked with in the university. He has knowledge of the workings of the university.

Apparently, learning how the university works is important to the majority of the mentees; however, the mentees did not provide detailed examples of how their respective mentors assisted them in understanding the academic culture. Both mentors and mentees were at a loss for words when I inquired about specific examples of how the academic culture was taught or learned during the mentoring process. Mentors and mentees were uncomfortable and provided brief answers to follow-up questions related to navigating the university culture, which mirrors the same type of hesitation and brief comments they expressed when addressing questions related to the topics of sanctions and closure.

Summary

The research suggests that most mentors have a strong desire to share their knowledge about the culture of the university with their mentees.[63] However, it appears that mentors have difficulties in transmitting higher degree institutional cultural capital and social capital to their mentees because both mentors and mentees are unable to sustain high levels of social capital within their mentoring relationships. The data reveals that mentors and mentees establish norms by building trust and adhering to modest expectations, which is one of the key elements for creating social capital in mentoring relationships.[64] On the other hand, mentors and mentees fall short in the area of maintaining social capital throughout their relationships because they do not have real consequences for norm violations (i.e., sanctions), they do not foster strong networks (i.e., closure) with other academic stakeholders (e.g., staff, faculty, administrators, and directors of mentoring programs) and they are unable to successfully transfer higher degree institutional cultural capital (i.e., information channels) in their mentoring relationships.[65]

If mentors and mentees seek to provide or acquire institutional cultural capital and social capital they need to work more on sustaining the social capital that they generate through mutual trust and shared expectations by devoting more time to fortify the components of sanctions, closure, and information channels. The findings illuminate the gap between the institutional cultural capital and social capital that mentors want to transmit to their mentees and the capital that mentees actually acquire through their mentoring relationship. Once the gap is narrowed for "at-risk" students, they are less likely to feel marginalized in colleges. Since mentees have access to different institutional cultural capital and social capital depending on which mentor they are matched with and have a more difficult time receiving higher degrees of both capital, creating a new mentoring model is one approach to address these issues. In chapter three, I present a new mentoring cycle model that could help students acquire and sustain the higher degrees of institutional cultural capital and social capital they need to master the hidden curriculum.

Krista Connects with a Mentor

In chapter one, Krista joined the mentoring program. Two weeks after Krista completed her mentoring application forms she was assigned a mentor. Krista's mentor, Angela Fernandez, is a Latina English professor who comes from a middle-class, non-first-generation background. Mary sends an email message to both Krista and Angela and encourages them to connect with one another.

Krista reads her email from Mary with a smile on her face and exclaims with joy:

> Yes! I have a mentor and she is a woman of color! Sweet! I guess this mentoring thing is not going to be that bad after all. Hey, she is an English professor, cool this is going to be a great match because I am a communications major. Maybe, she can help me select my next English course that I have to take next year. I wonder if she can help me with my Spanish class, I am struggling in that course too. I am sure we will be able to bond over a lot of things because we are women of color. I bet we are going to . . . wait a minute, I need to slow it down a little bit.

> I have never met this professor. What if she is like my other professors, friendly, but keeps a certain distance from me. I cannot quite explain it but my teachers and I don't really click with one another. I am not trying to say they are prejudice but there is something. Well, I can't think about that now. I need to focus on how I can impress Dr. Fernandez. I really want this relationship to work. I wonder if I should email her or wait for her to email me. She is a busy professor I think I should wait until she emails me. Yeah, that sounds like a great idea. I will wait for her to contact me but in the meantime I am going to find out as much as I can about her. I will google her name, check out her facebook page and review online comments about her teaching from former students. I want to find out as much as I can about her.

Krista eagerly checked her email daily to see if Dr. Fernandez had sent her a message. On the third day when she did not receive an email, she began to feel that maybe her mentor did not really want to have a relationship with her. She thought about contacting Mary to share her concerns but then she decided that she would just wait. She waited for a week, and then she received an email from Mary to see if she had made contact with her mentor. Krista wrote Mary the following email:

> Dear Mary,

> I have not made contact with my mentor. I have waited for a week but she never emailed me. What should I do? Thanks, Krista.

Mary sent the following email back to Krista:

Krista,

In response to your question, I encourage you to send an email today to Dr. Fernandez. You should introduce yourself to her and let her know that you are excited about having her as your mentor and that you would like to meet with her at her earliest convenience. You should provide her with your class and work schedules and your phone number. You want to show Dr. Fernandez that you can be proactive. I am sure when you send her an email she will respond to it. If you do not hear from her by the end of the week please send me an email.

If you have any other questions please contact me.
Mary Washington,
Director of Achieving the Dream Academic Mentoring Program

Krista read Mary's email a couple of times and silently thought:

Oh, I didn't know I was suppose to contact her. I thought since she was the professor she would contact me. Now, I feel really stupid. Mary thinks I am stupid and Dr. Fernandez thinks I am stupid too. It is going to be awkward writing her now, what should I say, it has been over a week since the first email. Why do I have to make first contact? Why can't professors be proactive sometimes? Right, they are so busy, they can't take two minutes out of their day to send a student an email. Fine, I'll bite the bullet and send her an email right now. I guess this professor is going to be just like my other professors. I don't know why I thought she would be different. Oh yeah, I know why, I thought she would be different because she is Latina. Oh well, let me send this email before I am accused of being "non-proactive" again. I can be proactive I just didn't know what to do in this situation. I don't want them to think of me as a lazy student. I am an introvert, not a jerk, but why should they care. Clearly, they don't know me, or even want to get to know me.

Krista sent an email to Dr. Fernandez apologizing for not taking the initiative to send her an email last week. She provided her mentor with her class and work schedules and her phone number. Within two days, Dr. Fernandez emails Krista with several dates and times she is available to meet with her. They both agree to meet the following Tuesday at 2 pm in Dr. Fernandez's office.

Krista tells herself that she is going to keep an open mind about her mentor and not hold it against her that she did not email her last week. Krista prepares for her meeting with Dr. Fernandez by reading over her notes that she has written about her mentor's research and teaching interests. It is Tuesday, 1:50 pm and she sits in a chair outside her mentor's door. Krista is trying to calm her nerves before entering the office. She breaths in deeply and exhales and asks God to give her the strength to not make a fool out of herself.

Krista knocks on the door.

"Come in," says Dr. Fernandez.

Krista enters the office with a smile and a lot of nervous energy. She extends her sweaty hand and remarks:

> Hello, Dr. Fernandez, it is a pleasure to finally meet you. Thank you so much for being willing to serve as my mentor. I know you are very busy with your research on women in literature in the twentieth century and teaching classes. Your poetry class is very popular and students love your classes. I am very lucky to have you as my mentor.

Dr. Fernandez humbly responds:

> Thank you, Krista, for your kind words, it appears you have done a lot of research about me. I am sorry but I am at a disadvantage, because I don't know a lot about you. So, could you please tell me a little about your academic and social interests.

Krista smiles and holds her head down low and says:

> Well, I love writing and public speaking even though I am an introvert and shy. I was the editor of my high school newspaper. I want to major in Communication Arts and eventually become a journalist and creative writer. I like to play video games with friends and watch good action movies. Is there anything else you would like to know about me.

Dr. Fernandez inserts:

> Yes, tell me what you want to get out of your mentoring experience.

Krista pauses for several seconds and finally mumbles:

> I don't really know, my advisor, Amanda, recommended that I join the mentoring program to improve my grades. I also think it would be nice to have a professor, like, friend, that I could talk to outside of the classroom.

Dr. Fernandez looks Krista in the eyes and smiles and in a calm tone states:

> Krista, I will do my best to help you get the resources you need to improve your grades and I hope you will feel comfortable with me over time so that you can talk about anything with me. I hope I can be a role model for you. I know that it is difficult for students of color on this campus but one of the reasons why I am still here is to mentor underrepresented students. I don't want you to feel alone on campus, if you need anything please reach out and contact me be-

cause I can put you in contact with the appropriate people on campus who will meet all your needs. I am here for you, okay.

Krista nods and says with deep gratitude:

Thank you so much, I really appreciate you saying that.

Dr. Fernandez immediately takes out her phone to schedule the next meeting and states:

Let's meet next time and have a meal, my treat, we can get to know each other better by breaking bread with one another. Would two weeks from now at 6pm work for you?

Krista nods and says with excitement:

Yes, that will work for me; I don't have to eat dorm food that day.

They both laugh and Dr. Fernandez reminds Krista:

You have earned your place to be here at the American Dream University and you cannot give up on your dreams.

Krista responds with enthusiasm:

Thank you for believing in me and I will not give up.

Dr. Fernandez stands up, warmly shakes Krista's hand and says:

I'm looking forward to our dinner in two weeks.

As Krista leaves the office, she thinks to herself:

I am so glad I kept an open-mind about Dr. Fernandez. I really like her, she seems so cool. I cannot wait to see her again and I get free food! I like this mentoring thing.

Definitions of Major Concepts

Habitus is one's cumulative cultural capital from childhood to adulthood that is primarily formed and shaped by one's family's social class background and schools. Habitus is a lifestyle that embodies one's social class identity, which influences how one perceives, appreciates, and interacts with people within and outside of one's social class background. For example, a student majors in biochemistry to prepare her for medical school because she has been socialized and encouraged to become a doctor by her family and teachers.

Field is a class based social setting that gives value and meaning to cultural capital. Individuals within the social setting compete to control and determine the worth of the cultural capital within it. Field is linked to habitus and cultural capital. Cultural capital cannot exist without fields. For example, the family, the education system, the criminal justice system, and the political system are all examples of social fields.

Cultural Capital is a cultural resource manifested through behaviors that mirror cultural dispositions, norms, knowledge, attitudes, preferences, tastes, mannerisms, abilities, competencies, and skills that individuals learn because of their habitus. For example, a student gives his professor a gift card to a bookstore along with a thank you card expressing how much he enjoyed the class. There are three types of cultural capital: embodied, objectified, and institutionalized/institutional.

Embodied Cultural Capital is cultural capital that becomes internalized and an integral part of an individual. For example, a senior sociology student has internalized academic knowledge about the major theories of the discipline.

Objectified Cultural Capital is cultural capital that takes on the physical form of a distinct object that symbolizes the embodied cultural capital of the individual who possesses the object. For example, a sociology theory book on a student's bookshelf is an indicator that the student has some embodied cultural capital of sociology.

Institutionalized/Institutional Cultural Capital is cultural capital that exists within an institution. Institutional cultural capital refers to the quantity and quality of information and knowledge individuals have about the culture of the institution, which is manifested in their behaviors and skills. For example, a student informs her professor that she will be absent for one class four weeks in advance and asks permission to turn in the homework assignment due that day early.

Social Capital is a social relations resource that represents the quantity and quality of information, resources, knowledge, and skills that are shared among individuals in relationships or social networks. For example, a student learns about several paid research opportunities because of her relationship with her professor.

Hidden Curriculum is a set of unwritten norms, values, and expectations that unofficially governs how individuals interact with and evaluate one another, this influences individuals' ability and performance in the formal curriculum. For example, a student is expected to be proactive and schedule an appointment with a professor if he earns a failing grade on an exam.

Formal Curriculum is a set of written requirements, rules, policies, and practices that serve as the official guidelines for how to engage with individuals and evaluate their quality of work. For example, a student who consistently receives failing grades on exams and papers will not pass the course.

Notes

1a. Henry Giroux, "The Politics of Postmodernism," *Journal of Urban and Cultural Studies* 1, no.1 (1990): 5-38.

1b. Henry Giroux, *Border Crossings: Cultural Workers and the Politics of Education* (New York: Routledge, 1992).

2a Giroux, "The Politics of Postmodernism," 1990.

2b. Giroux, *Border Crossings: Cultural Workers and the Politics of Education,* 1992.

3. Samuel Bowels and Herbert Gintis, *Schooling in Capitalist America: Educational Reform and the Contradictions of Economic Life* (New York: Basic Books, 1976).

4. Susan Aud, William Hussar, Grace Kena, Kevin Bianco, Lauren Frolich, Jana Kemp, and Kim Tahan, *The Condition of Education 2011* (NCES 2011-033), U.S. Department of Education, National Center for Education Statistics (Washington, DC: U.S. Government Printing Office, 2011), 68-69.

5. Paul Osterman, *College for All?: The Labor Market for College-Educated Workers* (Washington, DC: Center for American Progress, 2008).

6a. Randall Collins, "Functional and Conflict Theories of Educational Stratification," *American Sociological Review* 36 (1971): 1002-1019.

6b. Richard Schaefer, *Racial and Ethnic Groups* (Upper Saddle River, NJ: Prentice Hall, 2011), 15.

7a. Collins, "Functional and Conflict Theories of Educational Stratification," 1971.

7b. Schaefer, *Racial and Ethnic Groups,* 2011, 16.

8a. Pierre Bourdieu, *Distinction: A Social Critique of the Judgment of Taste,* Richard Nice (Translation), (Cambridge, MA: Harvard University Press, 1984).

8b. Glenda Musoba and Benjamin Baez, "The Cultural Capital of Cultural and Social Capital: An Economy of Translations," in *Higher Education: Handbook of Theory and Research,* ed. John Smart (New York: Agathon, 2009), 24.

9a. Pierre Bourdieu, *Outline of a Theory of Practice,* Richard Nice (Translation), (Cambridge, UK: Cambridge University Press, 1977).

9b. Bourdieu, *Distinction: A Social Critique of the Judgment of Taste,* 1984.

9c. Pierre Bourdieu, "The Forms of Capital," in *Handbook of Theory and Research for the Sociology of Education,* ed. John G. Richardson (New York: Greenwood, 1986), 241-258.

10. Bourdieu, *Distinction: A Social Critique of the Judgment of Taste,* 1984.

11a. Bourdieu, *Distinction: A Social Critique of the Judgment of Taste,* 1984.

11b. Musoba and Baez, "The Cultural Capital of Cultural and Social Capital: An Economy of Translations," 2009, 24.

12. Pierre Bourdieu and Jean-Claude Passeron, *Reproduction in Education, Society and Culture* (Beverly-Hill, CA: Sage, 1990), 210.

13. For an in-depth literature review of cultural capital see Rachelle Winkle-Wagner's monograph. Rachelle Winkle-Wagner, "Cultural Capital: The Promises and Pitfalls in Educational Research," *ASHE Higher Education Report*, 36, no. 1 (2010).

14a. Bourdieu, *Distinction: A Social Critique of the Judgment of Taste*, 1984, 172, 437.

14b. Bourdieu, *Outline of a Theory of Practice*, 1977, 82-83.

15a. Bourdieu, *Distinction: A Social Critique of the Judgment of Taste*, 1984.

15b. Pierre Bourdieu and Loïc J.D. Wacquant, *An Invitation to Reflexive Sociology* (Chicago: University of Chicago Press, 1992), 17.

15c. Erin Horvat, "Understanding Equity and Access in Higher Education: The Potential Contribution of Pierre Bourdieu," in *Higher Education: Handbook of Theory and Research*, ed. John Smart (New York: Agathon, 2001), 207.

16a. Amaury Nora, "The Role of Habitus and Cultural Capital in Choosing a College, Transitioning from High School to Higher Education, and Persisting in College among Minority and Non-Minority Students," *Journal of Hispanic Higher Education* 2, no. 3 (2004): 180-208.

16b. Annette Lareau, *Unequal Childhoods: Class, Race, and Family Life* (Los Angeles: University of California Press, 2003).

16c. Kathleen Grove, *Building Bridges: The Use of Looping and the Development of Cultural Capital in an Urban Elementary School* (Dubuque, Iowa: Kendall/Hunt Publishing Company, 2005).

16d. MaryBeth Walpole, "Socioeconomic Status and College: How SES affects College Experiences and Outcomes," *Review of Higher Education* 1, no. 27 (2003): 45-73.

16e. Paul DiMaggio, "Cultural Capital and School Success: The Impact of Status Culture Participation on the Grades of U.S. High School Students," *American Sociological Review* 47, no. 2 (1982): 189-201.

16f. Vincent Roscigno and James Ainsworth-Darnell, "Race, Cultural Capital and Educational Resources: Persistent Inequalities and Achievement Returns," *Sociology of Education* 72, no. 3 (1999): 158-178.

17a. William Tierney, "Models of Minority College-Going and Retention: Cultural Integrity versus Cultural Suicide," *Journal of Negro Education* 68 (1999): 80-91.

17b. Lala Steelman and Brian Powell, "Acquiring Capital for College: The Constraints of Family Configuration," *American Sociological Reviews* 54, no. 5 (1989) 844-855.

17c. Alberto Cabrera and Steven La Nasa, "On the Path to College: Three Critical Tasks Facing America's Disadvantaged," *Research in Higher Education* 42, no. 2 (2001): 119-149.

17d. Erin Horvat, "Understanding Equity and Access in Higher Education: The Potential Contribution of Pierre Bourdieu," in *Higher Education: Handbook of Theory and Research*, ed. John Smart (New York: Agathon, 2001).

17e. Ernest Pascarella, Christopher Pierson, Gregory Wolniak, and Patrick Terenzini, "First-Generation College Students: Additional Evidence on College Experiences and Outcomes," *Journal of Higher Education* 75, no. 3 (2004): 249-284.

17f. Patricia M. McDonough, *Choosing Colleges: How Social Class and Schools Structure Opportunity* (Albany: State University of New York Press, 1997).

17g. Paul DiMaggio and John Mohr, "Cultural Capital, Educational Attainment and Marital Selection," *American Journal of Sociology* 90, no. 6 (1985): 1231-1985.

18. Bourdieu, "The Forms of Capital," 1986, 241-258.

19a. Bourdieu, *Distinction: A Social Critique of the Judgment of Taste*, 1984.

19b. Bourdieu, "The Forms of Capital," 1986, 241-258.

20a. Bourdieu, *Distinction: A Social Critique of the Judgment of Taste*, 1984.

20b. Bourdieu, "The Forms of Capital," 1986, 241-258.

21a. Bourdieu, *Distinction: A Social Critique of the Judgment of Taste*, 1984.

21b. Bourdieu, "The Forms of Capital," 1986, 241-258.

22a. Bourdieu, *Distinction: A Social Critique of the Judgment of Taste*, 1984.

22b. Bourdieu, "The Forms of Capital," 1986, 241-258.

23a. Bourdieu, *Distinction: A Social Critique of the Judgment of Taste*, 1984.

23b. Bourdieu, "The Forms of Capital," 1986, 241-258.

24a. Pierre Bourdieu, "Cultural Reproduction and Social Reproduction," in *Knowledge, Education, and Cultural Change: Papers in the Sociology of Education*, ed. Richard Brown (London: Taylor & Francis, 1973), 71-112.

24b. Bourdieu and Passeron, *Reproduction in Education, Society and Culture*, 1990.

25a. Philip Jackson, *Life in Classrooms* (New York: Holt, Rinehart, and Winston, 1968).

25b. Michael Apple, *Education and Power* (New York: Routledge, 1982).

25c. Michael Apple, *Ideology and Curriculum*, 2nd ed. (New York: Routledge, 1990).

25d. Bowels and Gintis, *Schooling in Capitalist America*, 1976.

25e. Eric Margolis, Michael Soldatenko, Sandra Acker, and Marina Gair, "Peekaboo: Hiding and Outing the Curriculum," in *The Hidden Curriculum in Higher Education,* ed. Eric Margolis (New York: Routledge, 2001), 1-19.

26a. George Farkas, "Cognitive Skills and Noncognitive Traits and Behaviors in Stratification Processes," *Annual Review of Sociology* 29, no. 1 (2003): 541-562.

26b. George Farkas, Robert Grobe, Daniel Sheehan, and Yuan Shaun, "Cultural Resources and School Success: Gender, Ethnicity and Poverty Groups within an Urban School District," *American Sociological Review* 55, no. 1 (1990): 127-142.

27a. Farkas, "Cognitive Skills and Noncognitive Traits and Behaviors in Stratification Processes," 2003, 541-562.

27b. Farkas, Grobe, Sheehan, and Yuan Shaun, "Cultural Resources and School Success: Gender, Ethnicity and Poverty Groups within an Urban School District," 1990, 127-142.

28. Farkas, Grobe, Sheehan, and Shaun, "Cultural Resources and School Success: Gender, Ethnicity and Poverty Groups within an Urban School District," 1990, 127-142.

29. Jeannie Oakes, Amy Wells, Makeba Jones, and Amanda Datnow, "Detracking: The Social Construction of Ability, Cultural Politics and Resistance to Reform," *Teachers College Record* 98, no. 2 (1997): 482-510.

30. Oakes, Wells, Jones, and Datnow, "Detracking: The Social Construction of Ability, Cultural Politics and Resistance to Reform," 1997, 482-510.

31a. Farkas, Grobe, Sheehan, and Shaun, "Cultural Resources and School Success: Gender, Ethnicity and Poverty Groups within an Urban School District," 1990, 127-142.

31b. Oakes, Wells, Jones, and Datnow, "Detracking: The Social Construction of Ability, Cultural Politics and Resistance to Reform," 1997, 482-510.

32. Bourdieu, *Distinction: A Social Critique of the Judgment of Taste*, 1984, 122.

33a Bourdieu, "The Forms of Capital," 1986, 241-258.

33b. James Coleman, "Social Capital in the Creation of Human Capital," *American Journal of Sociology* (Issue Supplement) 94 (1988): S95-120.

33c. James Coleman, *Foundations of Social Theory* (Cambridge, MA: Belknap Press, 1990).

34. Bourdieu, *Distinction: A Social Critique of the Judgment of Taste*, 1984.

35a. Ricardo Stanton-Salazar, "A Social Capital Framework for Understanding the Socialization of Racial Minority Children and Youths," *Harvard Educational Review* 67 (1997): 1-40.

35b. Ricardo Stanton-Salazar and Sanford Dornbusch, "Social Capital and the Reproduction of Inequality: Information Networks among Mexican-American High School Students," *Sociology of Education* 68 (1995): 116-135.

35c. Gilberto Arriaza, "Schools, Social Capital, and Children of Color," *Race, Ethnicity and Education* 6 (2003): 71-94.

35d. Tierney, "Models of Minority College-Going and Retention: Cultural Integrity versus Cultural Suicide," 1999, 80-91.

35e. Peter Collier and David Morgan, "'Is that Paper Really Due Today?' Differences in First-Generation and Traditional College Students' Understandings of Faculty Expectations," *Higher Education* 55 (2008): 425-446.

35f. Annette Lareau and Elliot Weininger, "Cultural Capital in Educational Research: A Critical Assessment," *Theory and Society* 32 (2003): 567-606.

35g. Mary Henningsen, Kathleen Valde, Gregory A. Russell and Gregory R. Russell, "Student-Faculty Interactions about Disappointing Grades: Application of the Goals-Plans-Actions Model and the Theory of Planned Behavior," *Communication Education* 60, no. 2 (2011): 174-190.

36a. Melvin Oliver and Thomas Shapiro, *Black Wealth/White Wealth: A New Perspective on Racial Inequality* (New York: Routledge, 1997).

36b. Thomas Shapiro, *The Hidden Cost of being African American: How Wealth Perpetuates Inequality* (New York: Oxford University Press, 2004).

37a. Erin Horvat, "The Interactive Effects of Race and Class in Educational Research: Theoretical Insights from the Work of Pierre Bourdieu," *Penn GSE Perspectives on Urban Education* 2, no. 1 (2003): 1-25.

37b. Laura Perna, "Differences in the Decision to Attend College among African Americans, Hispanics, and Whites," *Journal of Higher Education* 71, no. 2 (2000): 117-141.

37c. Matthijs Kalmijn and Gerbert Kraaykamp, "Race, Cultural Capital and Schooling: An Analysis of Trends in the United States," *Sociology of Education* 69, no. 1 (1996): 22-34.

38a. Farkas, "Cognitive Skills and Noncognitive Traits and Behaviors in Stratification Processes," 2003, 541-562.

38b. Farkas, Grobe, Sheehan, and Shaun, "Cultural Resources and School Success: Gender, Ethnicity and Poverty Groups within an Urban School District," 1990, 127-142.

39a. Bourdieu, *Distinction: A Social Critique of the Judgment of Taste*, 1984.

39b. Bourdieu, "The Forms of Capital," 1986, 241-258.

39c. Apple, *Education and Power*, 1982.

39d. Apple, *Ideology and Curriculum*, 1990.

40a. Coleman, "Social Capital in the Creation of Human Capital," 1988, S95-120.

40b. Tierney, "Models of Minority College-Going and Retention: Cultural Integrity versus Cultural Suicide," 1999, 80-91.

40c. Collier and Morgan, "'Is that Paper Really Due Today?' Differences in First-Generation and Traditional College Students' Understandings of Faculty Expectations," 2008, 425-446.

40d. Lareau and Weininger, "Cultural Capital in Educational Research: A Critical Assessment," 2003, 567-606.

40e. Henningsen, Valde, Russell and Russell, "Student-Faculty Interactions about Disappointing Grades: Application of the Goals-Plans-Actions Model and the Theory of Planned Behavior," 2011, 174-190.

41. The empirical findings in this chapter come from my unpublished dissertation. Buffy Smith, *Demystifying the Higher Education System: Rethinking Academic Cultural Capital, Social Capital, and the Academic Mentoring Process*, 2004.

42. Anselm Strauss and Juliet Corbin, *Basics of Qualitative Research: Grounded Theory Procedures and Techniques* (Newbury Park, CA: SAGE Publications, Inc., 1990).

43. The information and findings in this section was published in one of my earlier articles. Buffy Smith, "Accessing Social Capital through the Academic Mentoring Process," *Equity and Excellence in Education* 40, no. 1 (2007): 36-46.

44a. Alejandro Portes, "Social Capital: Its Origins and Applications in Modern Sociology," *Annual Review of Sociology* 24 (1998): 1-24.

44b. Stanton-Salazar, "A Social Capital Framework for Understanding the Socialization of Racial Minority Children and Youths," 1997, 1-40.

45a. Ronit Dinovitzer, John Hagan and Patricia Parker, "Choice and Circumstance: Social Capital and Planful Competence in the Attainment of Immigrant Youth," *Canadian Journal of Sociology* 28, no. 4 (2003), 463-488.

45b. Raquel Farmer-Hinton and Toshiba Adams, "Social Capital and College Preparation: Exploring the Role of Counselors in a College Prep School for Black Students," *The Negro Educational Review* 57 (2006): 101-116.

46a. Coleman, "Social Capital in the Creation of Human Capital," 1988, S95-120.

46b. Coleman, *Foundations of Social Theory,* 1990.

47. Smith, *Demystifying the Higher Education System: Rethinking Academic Cultural Capital, Social Capital, and the Academic Mentoring Process,* 2004.

48. Bourdieu, "The Forms of Capital," 1986, 241-258.

49a. Raquel Farmer-Hinton and Toshiba Adams, "Social Capital and College Preparation: Exploring the Role of Counselors in a College Prep School for Black Students," 2006, 101-116.

49b. Berta Laden, "Socializing and Mentoring College Students of Color. The Puente Project as an Exemplary Celebratory Socialization Model," *Peabody Journal of Education* 74 no. 2 (1999): 55-74.

49c. K. Philip and Leo Hendry, "Making Sense of Mentoring or Mentoring Making Sense? Reflections on the Mentoring Process by Adult Mentors with Young People," *Journal of Community & Applied Social Psychology* 10 (2000): 211-223.

49d. Eileen Shultz, George Colton and Cynthia Colton, "The Adventor Program: Advisement and Mentoring for Students of Color in Higher Education," *Journal of Humanistic Counseling, Education and Development* 40, no. 2 (2001): 208-218.

50. Bourdieu, "The Forms of Capital," 1986, 241-258.

51a. Bourdieu, "The Forms of Capital," 1986, 241-258.

51b. Robert Putnam, *Bowling Alone* (New York: Simon & Schuster, 2002).

52a. Coleman, "Social Capital in the Creation of Human Capital," 1988, S95-120.

52b. Coleman, *Foundations of Social Theory,* 1990.

53. Coleman, "Social Capital in the Creation of Human Capital," 1988, S95-120.

54. Coleman, *Foundations of Social Theory,* 1990, 303.

55a. Coleman, "Social Capital in the Creation of Human Capital," 1988, S95-120.

55b. Coleman, *Foundations of Social Theory,* 1990.

56a. Coleman, "Social Capital in the Creation of Human Capital," 1988, S95-120.

56b. Coleman, *Foundations of Social Theory,* 1990.

57. Smith, *Demystifying the Higher Education System: Rethinking Academic Cultural Capital, Social Capital, and the Academic Mentoring Process,* 2004.

58a. Coleman, "Social Capital in the Creation of Human Capital," 1988, S95-120.

58b. Coleman, *Foundations of Social Theory,* 1990.

59. Tsedal Beyene, Marjorie Anglin, William Sanchez, and Mary Ballou, "Mentoring and Relational Mutuality: Proteges' Perspectives," *Journal of Humanistic Counseling, Education and Development* 41, no. 1 (2002): 87-102.

60a. Beyene, Anglin, Sanchez, and Ballou, "Mentoring and Relational Mutuality: Proteges' Perspectives," 2002, 87-102.

60b. Marilyn Haring, "Networking Mentoring as a Preferred Model for Guiding Programs for Underrepresented Students," in *Diversity in Higher Education: Mentoring and Diversity in Higher Education,* ed. Henry T. Frierson (Greenwich, CT: JAI Press Inc., 1997), 63-76.

60c. Wynetta Lee, "Striving toward Effective Retention: The Effect of Race on Mentoring African American Students," *Peabody Journal of Education* 74, no. 2 (1999): 27-43.

61. Smith, *Demystifying the Higher Education System: Rethinking Academic Cultural Capital, Social Capital, and the Academic Mentoring Process,* 2004.

62a. Coleman, "Social Capital in the Creation of Human Capital," 1988, S95-120.

62b. Coleman, *Foundations of Social Theory,* 1990.

63a. Becky Packard, "Student Training Promotes Mentoring Awareness and Action," *Career Development Quarterly* 51, no. 4 (2003): 335-345.

63b. David Pulsford, Kath Boit and Sharon Owen, "Are Mentors Ready to Make a Difference? A Survey of Mentors' Attitudes towards Nurse Education," *Nurse Education Today* 22, no. 6 (2002): 439-446.

64a. Coleman, "Social Capital in the Creation of Human Capital," 1988, S95-120.

64b. Coleman, *Foundations of Social Theory,* 1990.

65a. Coleman, "Social Capital in the Creation of Human Capital," 1988, S95-120.

65b. Coleman, *Foundations of Social Theory,* 1990.

Chapter 3

Decoding the Hidden Curriculum

In a 2011 survey, senior college admission directors admitted to giving preferential treatment to wealthy students even if they had lower grades and test scores. Many of the officials argue that they are pressured to recruit students who can pay their full tuition without financial aid. As a result, low-income students who require more scholarships, grants, and other financial aid assistance are the lowest priority for some universities.[1] Since the majority of the wealthy students are White who attend predominantly white institutions, these schools implicitly reward middle class and upper class White students. The unwritten recruitment preference policy is another example of how cultural favoritism operates in higher education.[2]

One cannot ignore the real financial crisis some colleges and universities are experiencing with trying to increase student enrollment amid the growing concerns from families about the rising cost of tuition.[3] Although this is a critical time in our higher education system, we cannot afford to minimize the challenges that underserved students encounter in school because we need these students to succeed if we are going to be globally competitive in the twenty-first century. It is an unfair burden to ask "at-risk" students to continue to suffer until universities naturally evolve through demographic changes into more racially and socioeconomically diverse institutions; they need more opportunities to thrive in college, now. One way to provide underrepresented students with the skills they need to achieve academic success is to implement a mentoring model that explicitly teaches students how to decode the hidden curriculum.

The mentoring model I propose could be effective in assisting students with mastering the hidden curriculum. The mentoring model is comprised of three cycles: advising, advocacy, and apprenticeship. The cycles are influenced by four major theoretical perspectives of mentoring: involvement theory, academic and social integration theory, social support theory, and social and cognitive development theory.[4] In addition to the theories, the cycles are grounded in the conceptual frameworks of institutional cultural capital, social capital, and hidden curriculum.

Four Major Theoretical Perspectives of Mentoring

The first perspective (i.e., **involvement theory**) is often cited as providing the theoretical framework for understanding the relationship between student involvement and academic success. Alexander Astin argues that the more students take a proactive role in their learning process the more likely they are to achieve academic success and graduate from college.[5] For instance, students who conduct independent research projects with professors are more likely to experience greater academic satisfaction, which could contribute to their overall academic achievement. Mentoring programs that operate from this theoretical perspective encourage their mentors to provide research opportunities to their mentees in order to foster greater academic involvement and academic success among their mentees.[6]

A distinct, yet closely related approach to involvement theory is Vincent Tinto's **academic and social integration theoretical model**.[7] Tinto states that if students' family background and attitudes toward school reflect the norms and expectations of their college environment they are more likely to have a higher level of academic and social integration and, as a result, are less likely to drop out of college. Mentoring programs that adopt this theoretical approach encourage mentors to create positive academic and social experiences for their mentees as a means of helping them feel less alienated and isolated at school. For instance, mentors who provide their mentees with numerous opportunities to talk and socialize with other faculty, staff, and administrators give their mentees access to those academic networks, which could help students feel more connected to the university.

The **social support theory** is also associated with academic and social integration. This theory argues that stress can impede students' academic progress.[8] Therefore, it is imperative that students have supportive relationships that will help them effectively cope with stress and achieve academic success. The major classifications of social support are "(1) emotional support (esteem, affect, trust, concern, and listening), (2) appraisal support (affirmation, feedback, and social comparison), (3) informational support (advice, suggestion, directives, and information) and (4) instrumental support (aid-in-kind, money, labor, time, and modifying environment)."[9] Mentoring programs that incorporate this theoretical approach encourage mentors to meet with their mentees on a regular basis to discuss academic and nonacademic concerns. For example, if a student has financial-aid issues, her mentor might call a colleague in the Financial Aid office and make a personal request of the colleague to schedule a meeting with her mentee.

Finally, some scholars examine the relationship between developmental theories and mentoring. Researchers emphasize that mentors have to be aware of the **cognitive levels and developmental stages** of their mentees in order to effectively mentor them.[10] Other scholars focus on how mentors can foster mentees' intellectual development and competence through role modeling.[11] Mentoring programs that promote this theoretical perspective encourage mentors to serve as role models and mentees are encouraged to imitate the academic attitudes and behaviors of their mentors.

Although the four theoretical perspectives of mentoring have overlapping characteristics, each has different primary and secondary emphases. The involvement theory's primary emphasis is on behavior and its secondary emphases are attitudes, social support, and social and cognitive development. The academic and social integration theory's primary emphasis is on attitudes and its secondary emphases are behavior, social support, and social and cognitive development. The social support theory's primary emphasis is on social support, and its secondary emphases are attitudes, behavior, and social and cognitive development. Lastly, the social and cognitive development theory's primary emphasis is on social and cognitive development whereas its secondary emphases are attitudes, behavior, and social support.

The main goal of each of the four theoretical perspectives is to help students achieve academic success. My new mentoring conceptual framework includes all four theories because collectively, the involvement, integration, social support, and social and cognitive development theories offer unique insights into the academic and social factors that impede and/or foster students' academic success. However, each theory is limited when it is separated from the other theories, because each theory over-emphasizes its primary function at the expense of the other theories' primary functions. One approach to addressing this theoretical weakness is to have only one primary function that is common and the central focus of all four theories.

Since the implicit purpose of all four theories is to help students understand and successfully decode the hidden curriculum, I propose that explicitly teaching students how to acquire institutional cultural capital and social capital should be the primary function and focus of these theoretical frameworks. In order to understand how mentoring relationships can explicitly unveil the hidden curriculum, one has to understand first the interrelated and complex relationships among institutional cultural capital, social capital, and the hidden curriculum. Since the previous theories do not explicitly address how to reveal to students the hidden curriculum, I present a new conceptual framework for understanding the academic mentoring process by employing sociologists' and educational theorists' concepts of institutional cultural capital, social capital, and the resistance theorists' perspective on the hidden curriculum.

Conceptual Framework for New Mentoring Cycles

Institutional Cultural Capital

According to Bourdieu, "institutional cultural capital" is evident when the embodied cultural capital of the dominant group becomes normalized and embedded within an institution.[12] For instance, the dominant groups in most predominantly white colleges and universities come from White middle class and upper class backgrounds, and as a result, these institutions primarily operate and govern from a White middle class and upper class cultural perspective. Once the values of the governing groups become embedded within the curriculum and programs of colleges and universities, the students who receive the most validation and rewards are those who reflect and/or adhere to the values and norms of the institution. Thus, schools reinforce White middle-class and upper class culture through classroom norms such showing a preference for students who nod their heads as a form of acquiescence.

This chapter does not focus on the "deficiencies" of college students "home culture" or embodied cultural capital, such as the way students are socialized based on their family backgrounds to perceive and interact with teachers, nor on their objectified cultural capital, such as their tastes and preferences for certain teaching styles and methods.[13] Instead, it concentrates on how students access the institutional cultural capital of higher education. The aim of this chapter is to provide students with access to the hidden and embedded cultural capital of the institution (e.g., the most appropriate and effective way students should talk about grades with their professors), regardless of what type of embodied or objectified cultural capital they bring with them to school. Although schools could have a preference for and reward some students who possess certain embodied and objectified cultural capital attributes, schools should be mindful to not systematically exclude any student from having access to the embedded cultural capital of the institution.[14] Thus, the goal of this chapter is not to offer suggestions on how to modify or refine the embodied or objectified cultural capital that students bring with them to school. Rather, I present a new mentoring model for how colleges and universities could provide students, especially underrepresented students, equal access to the institutional cultural capital and social capital of their schools.

Social Capital

In general, Bourdieu's and Coleman's work focus on the valuable social resources and benefits that individuals and families accrue because of their social relationships and social networks.[15] More specifically, their scholarship on social capital indicates that children's educational achievement is affected by structural constraints of their schools, which provides students unequal access to institutional resources based on their social class and racial backgrounds.[16]

Bourdieu's and Coleman's notion of social capital offers a comprehensive conceptual framework for understanding how colleges and universities can systematically constrain students' access to the cultural capital of the institution by operating and governing from a curriculum that is nontransparent, hidden, and inaccessible to many students of color and socioeconomically disadvantaged students. My research examines how universities provide students with unequal access to institutional cultural capital and social capital due to hidden and embedded racial and class biases. Therefore, I employ concepts of institutional cultural capital and social capital to conceptually ground this study and explore how undergraduate mentees access institutional cultural capital and social capital through their formal academic mentoring networks with staff, faculty, and administrators.

Hidden Curriculum

The hidden curriculum is the manifestation of the biased institutionalized cultural capital of higher education. According to Philip Jackson, the hidden curriculum refers to "the values, dispositions, social and behavioral expectations that brought rewards in school for students . . . these features of school life and requirements for conformity to institutional expectations had little to do with educational goals, but were essential for satisfactory progression through school."[17] The hidden curriculum is embedded within the academic culture of colleges and universities, which unofficially governs the behaviors and interactions among faculty, staff, administrators, and students.

The fact that many colleges and universities have an academic culture that is based on a White middle class and upper class value system is problematic to some degree. However, it becomes an issue of inequality when students from different racial groups and socioeconomically disadvantaged backgrounds are penalized for not having access to the knowledge of how to interpret and successfully navigate the hidden curriculum of higher education. The concept of the hidden curriculum originated in the early works of sociologist Emile Durkheim.[18] Durkheim argued from a functionalist perspective that schools played an important role in society because they helped socialize children to become functional citizens by teaching them a set of common values held by members of the larger society. This common set of values would include attending class on time and on a regular basis with the "appropriate bearing and attitude," completing and doing "reasonably well" on homework assignments, and refraining from disruptive behaviors in the classroom.[19] Subsequently, Jackson advanced Durkheim's notion of the hidden curriculum by providing examples of specific behaviors that are rewarded in public grade school classrooms. These behaviors included "learning to wait quietly, exercising restraint, cooperating, keeping busy, showing allegiance to both teachers and peers, being neat and punctual, and conducting oneself courteously."[20] Functionalists perceived schools to be positive social agents that assisted parents in preparing their children to develop into mature, responsible, and productive citizens; they did not perceive schools as serving the sinister needs of capitalists.

In contrast to functionalists, conflict scholars like Samuel Bowles and Herbert Gintis argue that there is a strong relationship between the norms of the school culture and the maintenance of the capitalist system.[21] They suggest that the hidden curriculum of schools reproduce the hierarchical divisions of labor in a capitalist society. Bourdieu concurs with the conflict's perspective that the hidden curriculum in schools serves the needs of the dominant groups in society. Thus, Bourdieu states that middle class students are more advantaged than low-income students because they possess the economic, cultural, and social capital that is valued and rewarded in schools.[22]

Critical resistance theorists have criticized both the functionalist and Conflict perspectives on the hidden curriculum for over-emphasizing structure at the expense of agency.[23] Resistance theorists agree with conflict theorists that the education system is an instrument of capitalism that reproduces an unequal and stratified society based on class, race, and gender. However, resistance scholars do not perceive teachers, staff, administrators, and students as passive social actors whose life chances are predetermined and controlled by the structure of educational institutions. Rather, they believe that teachers, administrators, and students are active social agents who can radically transform schools into more equitable and just institutions by negotiating, contesting, resisting, and exerting control over how they are socialized by the educational system.[24]

Since the critical resistance perspective acknowledges and emphasizes the importance of agency, I build my academic mentoring model based on this perspective of the hidden curriculum. The objective of this chapter is not to criticize colleges and universities for reproducing racialized, gendered, and classed hierarchies. Rather, the focus is on how faculty, staff, and administrators could be empowered and active social agents of change who question, challenge, and transform the status quo of higher education by creating academic mentoring relationships that reveal explicitly and systematically the hidden curriculum to students. Moreover, incorporating the resistance theorists' perspective on the hidden curriculum with the concepts of institutional cultural capital and social capital provides a solid comprehensive three-pronged conceptual foundation for building my three-cycle academic mentoring model: advising, advocacy, and apprenticeship.

A New Three-Cycle Mentoring Model

Bourdieu refers to the term academic apprenticeship as the vehicle for reproducing the socialization process that begins within the family.[25] In other words, individuals acquire certain social class and racial based mannerisms, taste, preferences, dispositions, knowledge, and skills through families and these cultural attributes are reinforced through academic apprenticeships in school.[26]

For instance, a student who grows up in a White middle class background is likely to feel comfortable with talking and asking questions to college educated professionals (e.g., teachers, corporate managers, and lawyers). The student learns to engage with professionals as equals from a young age. The student interacts with professionals through casual conversations at family dinner parties, musical recitals, and theatre events. Once the student begins college it is not difficult for her to initiate a conversation with a White middle class professor and build a relationship with the professor outside of the classroom.[27] On the other hand, a low-income, first-generation, and/or student of color is more likely to feel fearful and awkward in approaching a professor outside of the classroom because of his limited interaction with professionals during his earlier family socialization process. In other words, "at-risk" college students have a more difficult time developing academic apprenticeships with professors because of their habitus prior to college.[28]

Some students and faculty are able to create academic apprenticeships that appear to occur "naturally" but the reality is that these types of social relationships are often based on the shared habitus of students and faculty.[29] The negative side of academic apprenticeships are that they do not form naturally when there is a habitus mix-match between students and faculty. One strategy for resolving the cultural favoritism issue is to incorporate academic apprenticeships in all mentoring relationships.

In the new mentoring model, advising is the minimum, advocacy the medium, and apprenticeship the maximum cycle for transmitting institutional cultural capital and social capital. Within each cycle, mentors and mentees engage in varying degrees of mentoring. Cycles are used to describe the mentoring process that produces continuous growth over a period of time when certain actions are consistently repeated within the mentoring relationship. They represent a fluid and constant circular flow of institutional cultural capital and social capital among mentors and mentees. The cycles are symbolic of dynamic, open-ended, interconnected mentoring relationships in which one can advise, advocate, and engage in apprenticeship type behaviors within each mentoring session (see figure 3.1).

Mentors and mentees acquire and teach more institutional cultural capital and social capital as they progress from one cycle to the next because they bring the knowledge, skills, and experiences from the previous cycle(s) to the next cycle(s). It is highly unlikely for someone to start at the advising cycle and jump to the apprenticeship cycle without demonstrating some attributes of the advocacy cycle. Although mentors and mentees could become fixed and remain in one cycle and never move to the next cycle(s) if there is a weak social connection between them, the ultimate goal is to reach the apprenticeship cycle in order to transmit and acquire the highest quantity and quality of institutional cultural capital and social capital within mentoring relationships. The apprenticeship cycle is essential because it provides mentees the opportunity to acquire the maximum capital they need to master the hidden curriculum.

Figure 3.1 Three-Cycle Mentoring Model
Degrees of Institutional Cultural Capital and Social Capital

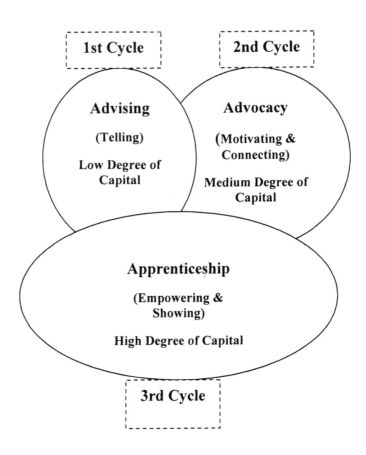

The Value of the Mentoring Cycles

The advising, advocacy, and apprenticeship cycles are conduits for the transmission of low to high degrees of institutional cultural capital and social capital during the mentoring process. The mentoring process encompasses three major actions: (1) advising—telling students what they should do (i.e., transmission of low degrees of capital) (2) advocacy—motivating and connecting students with key people on campus (i.e., transmission of medium degrees of capital), and (3) apprenticeship—empowering and showing students how to acquire the highest degree of institutional cultural capital and social capital from their academic mentoring relationships. The point at which the advising, advocacy, and apprenticeship cycles intersect represent the highest degree of institutional cultural capital and social capital that is transmitted within mentoring relationships. The significance of the new mentoring model is that it provides an intentional and intensive mentoring approach for unveiling the hidden curriculum.

Degrees of Advising

During the advising cycle, mentors and mentees engage in varying degrees of advising. For instance, a mentor advises a mentee to meet with her English professor because she earned a "D" on the paper but the mentor does not follow-up with the mentee regarding her meeting with the professor (e.g., low-degree of advising).

A mentor who provides the mentee with detailed knowledge on how to schedule a meeting with a professor in the most effective way is an example of advising at a high-degree. For example, the mentor could encourage the mentee to email the professor and schedule a meeting with her even if it is during official office hours. In the email, the mentee could briefly describe some of the issues she wants to discuss with the professor. The mentor not only advises the mentee on what to say but she explains why it is important to schedule immediately a meeting with the professor. The mentor tells the mentee that based on her actions she will be perceived as a proactive and conscientious student. As the mentor ends the mentoring session, she informs the mentee that she wants an update about the meeting with the professor within a week and the mentor immediately schedules a follow-up meeting with the mentee.

Degrees of Advocacy

Motivating students to build strong social connections with key academic stakeholders on campus, especially professors, is the primary focus of the advocacy cycle. The mentor provides the mentee with guidance on what she should and should not say to her professor in order to create and sustain a positive relationship with her professor. For example, the mentor encourages her mentee to go beyond her comfort zone and replace her fears of approaching a professor by taking the initiative to form a trusting relationship with the professor. The mentee could display her openness and willingness to trust her professor by allowing herself to be vulnerable and admit to the professor that she did not understand the instructions for writing the paper and that she would like the professor to explain the instructions again. The professor would most likely respect the student's honesty and her ability to be proactive in her learning process, which could set the stage for a positive mentoring relationship (e.g., low-degree of advocacy).

On the other hand, a mentor who provides a similar level of advocacy as in the previous example and connects with the mentee's professor to check on the mentee's academic progress is an example of a high degree of advocacy. The mentor could build social capital with the professors who teach her mentee in order to establish closure among the key academic decision makers who are closely connected to the mentee's academic success. The closure within the social network of the mentee could make it easier to enforce sanctions. For instance, if a mentee did not meet with her professor that could be considered as a violation of a norm in their mentoring relationship and as a sanction she could be placed on probation in the mentoring program.

Degrees of Apprenticeship

The mission of the apprenticeship cycle is to empower mentees to transform into powerful social agents who determine their academic destiny. As part of the empowering process, mentors have to show students through role-playing exercises, step-by-step, how to engage in appropriate conversations that could help them build stronger academic social relationships. In other words, mentors have to equip mentees with the institutional cultural capital and social capital they need to feel comfortable and effective in their ability to master the hidden curriculum.

For example, a mentor coaches her mentee on the attitudes and behaviors she could express before, during, and after her meeting with the professor. The mentor could write a detailed script for how the mentee could portray herself as a "superstar" student (e.g., a friendly, mature, responsible, proactive, intellectually curious, and overall respectful person). Before the meeting, the mentee could rewrite two pages of the paper based on the professor's feedback and email it to the professor at least two days before the meeting. During the meeting, the mentee brings both the original and revised papers. She responds to the professor's comments on the original paper and requests feedback on the revised paper. As the professor is giving advice on how she could improve the papers, the mentee listens attentively by nodding her head several times and gives verbal cues that she understands the professor's remarks. The mentee writes detailed notes during the meeting and requests specific recommendations for writing the next paper and improving her overall writing skills.

At the end of the meeting, the mentee firmly shakes the professor's hand and thanks the professor for taking time to meet with her and provide invaluable feedback. She concludes the conversation by requesting if the professor will meet with her again three weeks before the next assignment is due to read a draft of the paper. Finally, the day after the meeting, the mentee sends a thank you email expressing her appreciation again to the professor (e.g., low-degree of apprenticeship). In contrast, a mentor and mentee would not only do everything in the previous example but they would also practice the script repeatedly before the mentee meets with the professor. As a coach, the mentor engages in different role-playing scenarios of what could happen during the meeting. Then, the mentor and mentee perform the most common scenarios several times until the mentee's behaviors, attitudes, and mannerisms appear "natural." After the role-playing, the mentor reads the revised two-page paper, offers suggestions, and has the mentee rewrite it again. Now the mentee is ready to meet with the professor.

After the mentor has confirmed that the mentee has met with the professor, the mentor schedules a follow-up meeting with the mentee to discuss what went well during the meeting and what areas need to be improved before her next meeting with the professor. The mentor also schedules a meeting with the mentee's professor (after obtaining written permission from the mentee) to get an update from her perspective on the mentee's attitude and behaviors during the meeting. Once the mentor receives feedback from both the professor and mentee, the mentor creates a new script for how to have a more effective meeting with the professor. The mentor and mentee will practice the new script until it becomes a "natural process" for the mentee. They will repeat the process of practicing the script, performing the script, and getting feedback on the meetings until the mentee and her professor no longer experience challenges in their relationship and they are comfortable with one another (e.g., high-degree of apprenticeship).

Evidence Supporting Mentoring Model

In this section, I present a new three-cycle academic mentoring model that incorporates the major functions of the four theoretical perspectives of mentoring namely, integration, social support, involvement, and social and cognitive development. In addition, the three-cycle model is supported by empirical evidence and grounded in the three-pronged conceptual framework of institutional cultural capital, social capital, and the resistance theorists' perspective on the hidden curriculum.[30] Although all the cycles build upon one another and are grounded in the three-pronged conceptual framework and the four theoretical perspectives, each cycle emphasizes different theoretical and conceptual functions.

During the advising cycle, the primary emphases are on institutional cultural capital and integration. The advocacy cycle's primary emphases are on social capital and social support. The apprenticeship cycle's primary emphases are on the resistance theorists' notion of the hidden curriculum and involvement. The mentoring relationships within the cycles are not static; rather, they represent the full vitality of social relationships. Mentors and mentees can move forward or backwards between cycles or just remain at one cycle throughout the entire mentoring process. However, mentors and mentees can only advance to the next cycle if they increase the amount of institutional cultural capital and social capital they transmit and acquire within their relationship. In order to understand fully the academic mentoring process we have to examine each cycle separately.

First Cycle: Advising (Low Degree of Mentoring)

The first cycle of the mentoring model is the advising cycle. The attributes of the advising cycle include the combination of the integration theory's objectives of how to assist students in becoming integrated academically and socially within their schools and of how to teach students to decode and navigate the hidden curriculum. The advising cycle represents a low degree of transmission of institutional cultural capital and social capital from mentors to mentees. For example, mentors provide their mentees with general information about how to succeed in specific courses.

According to the twenty interviews in my study, three mentors and four mentees indicated that they did not provide/receive academic advising during their mentoring relationship. Four mentors and five mentees stated that they provided/received general academic advising (e.g., discussing what types of classes mentees were taking and how well they were doing in the courses). In addition, only one mentor and three mentees stated that they provided/received additional "inside" information about various academic options, such as course selections and professors' expectations. Although few mentors and mentees discussed "inside" information during their mentoring relationship, this type of knowledge is important because it represents part of the hidden curriculum of the university. The data presented in this section reveals the type of academic advising that was transmitted and acquired within mentoring relationships.

The following excerpts offer typical responses made by mentors and mentees who discussed various academic options and professors' general expectations of students during their mentoring relationship. The mentors and mentees responded to two advising questions: (1) describe the academic advising sessions you have with your mentee/mentor and (2) describe the best advice you gave/received from your mentee/mentor. Ronald, an administrator mentor, who is a Black and Middle-Eastern male from a middle-middle class background and whose mentee is an Asian-American woman, stated:

> Well, we go from one extreme to the next, (laughter) which is my speaking style (laughter). But, generally, we just start off slowly and if she would mention a particular situation, I would always preface everything I said by saying, well this is just my opinion but you may want to consider this, or you may want to consider going this route, but of course the final decision is left up to you. Not that I am telling you, that this is the best way, but this is the way that I have experienced it and it has worked well for me, so you need to take this info to see if it works well for you. And, most importantly, not just telling her you should do this and do that, but pointing her to other people whom could also supply her with information. And telling her that this person looks at life slightly different than I do, and that's why I am directing you to that individual be-

cause they can give a completely different perspective than I could ever give you, and that's what you need in order to make the right decision.

Another administrator mentor, Damon, who is an African-American male from a working class background and whose mentee is an African-American male, stated that the best academic advice he gave his mentee was:

> To use all his skills that he has learned both inside the university and outside the university for good, for positive good to make it ennoble and to really understand that character is what we have. And to know that he is a father and that he is in a marriage and to respect always what he wanted people to do for him, and that was to respect him, hear him, understand him, not always agree with him; but legitimatize his thoughts and ideas as an African-American man, as a student, and beyond.

We can see that both mentors perceive academic advising as an invaluable aspect of the mentoring process and we will discuss this further once we look at the responses made by the mentees regarding the advising they received.

Jovaun described his advising session with his mentor Tom as the following:

> It used to be, that Tom would tell me what classes that I can avoid and what are the science classes that I can kind of get out of. What are the classes that would be interesting to me and challenging, but won't be like seminars at the graduate school level, just get me out of boring classes and that's all I used to do. What kind of science classes can I get away from and how can I avoid psychology until senior year that's what it used to be like. But, now the closer I am to graduate the lesser flexibility that I have. But really, I rely on him more if I do have the options of taking this and I don't like it. How can I make myself like it and succeed and get an A or B or C, C's get degrees, but not much else. I think I rely on him to kind of ground me, to still say this class sucks, it kind of looks shitty on paper. And he will dig up information and drop his two cents and call somebody and try to get the 411 on things, I think that's what it is like now.

In terms of receiving the best academic advice from her mentor, Debra, an African-American and White female from a middle-middle class background and first-generation college student whose mentor is a White female, remarked:

> I think the best thing that she ever told me but I don't know if I always follow, this is to talk to professors. Don't just go to class and take the test and not ever have a conversation with the professor or go to office hours, I think that was it. Go to office hours even if sometimes you don't have a question and you just want to pop in to make sure you are on the right track, or just to say, "hi," that was probably the most important thing, but it is one of the hardest things to follow.

According to the interviews, mentees and mentors consider academic advising as an integral component of the mentoring process. The evidence provided also indicates that some mentors (albeit too few) try to provide their students with not only information about graduation requirements but they are also very concerned with giving their mentees several academic options regarding selecting courses and majors. The mentees value mentors who present them with various academic options and respect their ability to select the best choices for themselves, rather than just telling them what courses they should and should not take. In addition, some mentors give their mentees "inside" information about the pros and cons of taking particular courses with certain professors and emphasize general expectations of professors (e.g., students should take the initiative to get to know their professors by going to their office hours before a crisis arises).

It is important to note that this type of "inside" information is most likely accessible to students who are connected with at least one person who is an active member of the administrator, staff, and faculty network. If mentors use the social capital that they have with other members of the institution for the benefit of their mentees, it could provide their mentees greater access to the institutional cultural capital and social capital they need to achieve academic success. Providing such invaluable capital helps students become academically and socially integrated within the school.

Moreover, as Damon's comments indicate, some mentors encourage their mentees to integrate their embodied cultural capital or "home culture" with the institutionalized cultural capital or "university culture." These mentors do not suggest that their mentees modify or refine their home culture; rather, they encourage students to build upon it by adding to it the knowledge and skills they need to understand the university culture. This blending of the home culture with university culture is just another approach that mentors use to help students with their academic and social integration process. In short, although many mentoring programs, including the two in this study, do not require that their mentors provide general academic advising, it is clear that students certainly appreciated and benefited from the academic insights about courses and general expectations of professors that their mentors provided them. In sum, low degrees of institutional cultural capital and social capital are transmitted and acquired during the advising cycle of the mentoring process.

Second Cycle: Advocacy (Medium Degree of Mentoring)

The second cycle of the mentoring model is the advocacy cycle. The attributes of this cycle include the combination of the social support theory and social capital theory. Both theories focus on creating social support networks to help students achieve academic success and navigate the higher education system. The advocacy cycle also incorporates the attributes of the advising cycle and represents a medium degree of transmission and acquisition of institutional cultural capital and social capital during the mentoring process.

During the interviews, I asked mentors whether they interacted on a regular basis with other administrators, staff, and faculty on behalf of their mentees. The following are their responses: (1) two mentors stated that they did not interact with other administrators, staff, or faculty; (2) one mentor indicated that she interacted with only one other administrator, staff member, or faculty member; and (3) four mentors said that they interacted with at least two other administrators, staff members, or faculty members. The number of administrators, staff, and faculty that mentors have a relationship with is important because it is an indicator of the mentors' social capital. The more social capital mentors accumulate, the greater academic opportunities and support networks they are able to transfer to their mentees. For instance, if a mentor has considerable social capital with other administrators, staff members, and faculty members she could call some of her colleagues at the Writing Center, explain her mentees' needs, and find out which writing instructor would be the best person to work with her mentee.

In addition to finding information about whether mentors interacted with other administrators, staff, and faculty on behalf of their mentees, I also asked mentors how they helped their mentees network at the university. Although one mentor indicated that he did not help his mentee network, the other seven mentors had two different approaches to assisting their mentees with networking. The first approach refers to mentors who introduced their mentees to their colleagues only if their paths crossed at the office or at a restaurant. However, they did provide their mentees with the key names and phone numbers of the people who could help them with their particular issue. In fact, five mentors provided this type of networking to their mentees. The following response made by Tom is a typical example of this form of networking:

> I do sometime [help my mentee by networking] mostly it is if I know of a particular person, in a particular office, I will give him the name or the connection, or say, you should go talk to so and so about blah, blah. So, he will get the name and go talk to them generally.

This example represents the low degree of networking a mentor could offer their mentee. It does not require mentors to spend a lot of their social capital when referring students, in this manner, to other administrators, staff, or faculty.

Medium Level of Networking

In contrast, the second form of networking that two mentors employed on behalf of their mentees requires mentors to tap into their social capital reservoir. Cora, a Hispanic female, from a lower-middle class background whose mentee was an African-American female, stated:

> Okay, my mentee was one of the few students who got into the Department of Chemistry, and as you know there are very few African-Americans that ever

get that degree. So, I also was the one, who set up the faculty minority liaisons, so I could talk to the person in the Department of Chemistry about it. So, she was also working on a journalistic project like, she was the editor of *Skinner Enterprise*. So, I facilitated communication with the Dean to bring money into the *Skinner Enterprise,* so she and other students would not have to spend their time chasing around advertising funds. So, they could focus in on the task at hand and producing a good publication, the only publication by and about students of color on campus. I also talked to another person, faculty person, who was involved with *Skinner Enterprise* to help them out with that. As for administrators, I would advise her to see particular advising deans to deal with some of her issues. I remember one time, her assigned advisor and her relationship was not working and I counseled her about that, and other people who might be useful to her in making that decision. Again, I see academic advising and mentoring as complementary but distinctively different. And, I don't like to blur them.

Damon also elaborated on how he generously used his social capital for his mentee's benefit. He exclaimed:

> Introductions to colleagues, always, always when I was interrupted in a good way. I might add, I would have other people know who this person was and sometime it went as far as people asking me if he was a family member of mine. Or saying, hey, I know you, your name is Ari Brown, or something like that. And he of course laughing and smiling knowing that they had recognized him, knowing that he had been recognized in a positive way that had to make him feel good. Also, by nominating him for certain things not just doing it arbitrarily, but letting him know, I think you would be good for this, I am going to nominate you. I think you would be a good peer counselor and so pushing him out where it gives him responsibilities and confidence. And at the same time, not looking over his shoulders and have him work for other people. I think that really gave an added boost to him and also recommending him for a job on Callahan Street at Mitchell Sports, where he quickly became the assistant manager and was asked to stay on until the very end until they sold their franchise. I think these things helped him. I think him deejaying on the local radio all those things that he did from V98.3 to Mitchell Sports made him believe in himself. And the mentor's true goal is to lead their mentee to not just believing in the university, and having faith in the university, and having faith in people around them, but having faith and belief in themselves, which I think, lead to very good results.

The responses by these two mentors indicate that they went beyond just conducting "random courtesy introductions" between their mentees and colleagues. Damon and Cora also did not just give names and phone numbers to their mentees but they actually initiated contact with the key people who could increase their mentees' academic, social, and professional networks. Damon and Cora motivated their mentees to become integrated within the school by expanding their mentees support networks inside and outside the university (e.g., getting involved in the school newspaper and finding fun and interesting jobs near campus).

Mentees' Perception of Networking Benefits

The mentees' perception of the type of mentoring they received is quite different from the mentors. When I asked the mentees to describe how their mentors helped them network, two of them stated that their mentors did not introduce them to other administrators, staff, or faculty, and ten of them stated that their mentors were very good at referring them to different people and services on campus. Most of the mentees inferred that their mentors were helping them network if they referred them to someone else on campus that could address their academic needs. The following excerpts offer typical responses made by mentees who described how their mentors helped them network at the university. Basema, a sophomore Asian-American female from a lower-middle class background whose mentor was Carolyn, a White female staff member, remarked:

> I love that part of having a mentor, (laughter) she knows who to go to all the time. When I was going to do the study aboard thing. I was, like, whom should I talk to and she was like, Armando Hill, and she gave me his number and all that stuff. She always seems to know who to go to and I love that part about the mentoring thing. And, after studying that week in D.C. too, I really learned that you get places by who you know, not what you know, it's who you know. So, I was really excited when I learned that the program had mentoring with people like Carolyn who hold pretty high positions on campus.

Although Basema appreciated the referrals she received from her mentor, Basema did not recognize the significance of "random courtesy introductions" that her mentor performed at different mentoring events. She jokingly remarked:

> Yeah, I don't remember all of them (chuckle) but when, like, for the Everlean Mentoring Program, when we all get together, for the fall picnic, the one we just had, she introduced me to a whole bunch of people. You know, this is this person, and they do this (laughter). I don't remember too many of them. And at the spring reception, the same thing happened, this is this person, hi, this is my mentee. And I just say, hi, and shake their hands and I don't remember any of them. But it is good to know, she knows all these people.

Another mentee, Larenda stated:

> If I ask and I particularly want a phone number she will find it, you know. If I am walking down the street and she sees somebody, she will introduce me, if we are eating lunch or anything or any possible contact.

As the data indicate, the mentees considered their mentors to be "well-connected" at the university and felt that their mentors helped them network by providing them with names and phone numbers of other faculty and administrators and by introducing them to their colleagues during casual encounters. However, since many mentees stated that they did not recall the names or job positions of most of the people that were introduced to them by their mentors, one might question the effectiveness of these "random courtesy introductions." Therefore, I argue that effective networking requires more than just supplying students with the names and phone numbers of key people on campus and facilitating "random courtesy introductions" between students and campus administrators, staff, and faculty. The primary role of a mentor is not providing "campus directory assistance" and "random courtesy introductions"; rather, it is to develop and foster supportive and effective social networks between their mentees and colleagues.

As a result, mentors have to be more careful about not introducing their mentees to too many administrators, staff, and faculty; otherwise, it could become overwhelming for mentees and they will not remember their names and positions, which defeats the purpose of networking. To minimize this problem, mentors could introduce their mentees to primarily administrators, staff, and faculty who have the most direct influence on their mentees' overall academic career and success. In addition, mentors could follow-up with their mentees and colleagues to ensure that they are developing a positive professional relationship (e.g., the mentor could facilitate the first meeting between the mentee and faculty). In sum, one of the objectives of mentoring relationships is to create a supportive academic and social network for students. In order to develop this network, mentors and mentees have to transmit and acquire a medium degree of institutional cultural capital and social capital during the advocacy cycle of the mentoring process.

Third Cycle: Apprenticeship (High Degree of Mentoring)

The third cycle of the mentoring model is the apprenticeship cycle (the highest degree). The attributes of this cycle include the combination of the involvement theory and the resistance theorists' perspective on the hidden curriculum. Both theories focus on behavior. The involvement theory focuses on the behaviors of mentees whereas the resistance theorists' perspective on the hidden curriculum looks at the behaviors of mentors and mentees. One of the central premises of the involvement theory is that students are more likely to achieve academic success if they are actively involved and engaged in academic endeavors related to teaching and research.[31] On the other hand, resistance theorists could argue that mentors are empowered social agents capable of revealing the hidden curriculum of higher education to students if they become actively involved and engaged in helping their mentees acquire institutional cultural capital and social capital.[32] The apprenticeship cycle represents a high degree of transmission and acquisition of institutional cultural capital and social capital within mentoring relationships. For example, through role-playing exercises, mentors could teach their mentees various strategies for approaching professors about working with them on research projects.

During the apprenticeship cycle, mentors assist their mentees with practical and, at times, hands-on-experiences with specific issues related to the hidden curriculum. My research explored the following four academic topics: (1) receiving feedback on written assignments; (2) learning how to discuss grades with professors; (3) learning how to participate in classroom discussions; and (4) learning how to conduct an independent research project. The four topics were chosen because in order to achieve academic success as an undergraduate at the University of Wisconsin-Madison one has to demonstrate competency in both verbal and written communication skills. In addition, many students have to write research papers.

Feedback on Written Assignments

When mentors were asked if they ever read a paper or essay exam written by their mentees, five replied "no" and three replied "yes." The mentors who did not read their mentees' work indicated that they did not do so because their mentees never asked for help and/or they thought they were already good writers. However, these statements are troubling because if mentors were not familiar with the written work of their mentees it would be very difficult for them to know whether their mentees were good writers or not. In addition, one could argue that the role of a mentor is to anticipate the common and predictable academic hurdles that mentees will encounter and provide advice and guidance about how to navigate around those hurdles, especially since many students are unable to recognize the hurdles for themselves. Therefore, if mentors elect not to read their mentees' papers they inadvertently place mentees at a disadvantage because their mentees are unable to reap the benefits from their mentors' expertise and experience with writing academic papers.

The three mentors who read their mentees' papers made similar comments as Tom made in the following excerpt:

> Usually, when I have commented at all it has been, like, maybe put this, this way, this part is unclear. I wouldn't even call it necessarily the fundamentals of good writing; a lot of it is just, you know, he is quite good with grammar actually. So, usually it is a matter of minor improvements; I mean, I don't have to do much or I don't suggest much. Although every once in awhile I do catch, like, actual errors; usually they're refinements or something that is technically correct, but maybe slightly off tone-wise.

Tom stated that he did not have to assist his mentee with the grammar of his papers, which would indicate that his mentee, Jovaun, has good writing skills, which demonstrates a level of competency in the formal curriculum. However, Jovaun does have a problem with finding the appropriate "tone" for his papers, which indicates he needs some guidance with navigating the domain of the hidden curriculum. Academic writing requires one to pay close attention to the grammar and tone of the paper. For instance, if Jovaun wrote a paper that was without grammatical flaws but the tone of the paper was perceived to be "inappropriate" (e.g., offensive language or a lack of formality), he could most likely receive an average grade on the paper. Therefore, if Tom provided Jovaun with critical feedback regarding the tone of his writing assignments, Jovaun could have a greater understanding of how to write "acceptable" academic papers. Although this type of institutional cultural capital is often not taught in typical college classes, it could be taught explicitly in mentoring relationships.

It is important to note that the eleven mentees who stated their mentors did not read their work did not feel their mentors were neglecting to teach them a crucial academic skill. In fact, many mentees did not see reading papers as part of the mentoring process. This speaks to the knowledge gap between mentees not knowing what they do not know, and mentors not helping their mentees become proficient academic writers, which is a major skill, associated with the hidden curriculum and formal curriculum. In addition, some mentees stated they did not think their mentors were experts in the mentees' fields of study and thus would not be able to give appropriate feedback. However, as mentioned earlier, mentors do not necessarily have to be experts in their mentees' major in order to teach them the basic rules for writing good academic papers. On the other hand, only one mentee responded that his mentor read his papers. Jovaun indicated that Tom provided him general advice on how he must continue to grow as a writer. According to Jovaun, Tom told him:

> If you grow and your writing doesn't grow, people are going to make statements and judgments about you. And you want those statements and judgments to be positive rather than negative. So, really use this for every class that you write in, but especially use this when you are trying to submit things for resumes, and job applications, and for graduate school. What you put down on paper reflects you, whether you want it to or not, it is reflecting you, it reflects how much commitment you are putting into the work.

Tom reveals to Jovaun that in life in general and specifically in the academy, he will be judged by his writing skills and therefore he must continue to develop as a writer in order to be successful in graduate school and beyond. The two quotes serve as examples of how both the mentor and mentee made a conscious effort to be involved in the teaching/learning of institutional cultural capital and social capital.

Discussion of Grades with Professors

In addition to becoming competent writers, students must learn the appropriate ways for discussing grades with professors in order to achieve academic success at colleges and universities. Mentors were asked if they had conversations with their mentees about how to discuss "low" grades with their professors; four replied "no" and four replied "yes." The mentors that said "no" gave answers ranging from, "the topic was never brought up by the mentees" to "my mentees are good students and they don't earn low grades." These responses suggest that mentors expect mentees to inform them of every academic problem that they are having in school. The responses also imply that mentors assume if their mentees have not indicated they are having academic problems, then they are probably not having academic issues. Unfortunately, some mentees do not always recognize that they need help until it becomes a crisis. Therefore, mentors should take the initiative to reflect on the knowledge and skills students need to navigate the academic culture of the higher education system, and take a proactive approach to reveal explicitly to them the hidden curriculum.

Four mentors did recognize the importance of sharing with their mentees various strategies for how to talk with professors about their grades without being disrespectful in the process. Sherry's response to this question best describes the sentiments of the other three mentors:

> So, my advice has always been whenever possible do a face-to-face interaction. I also encourage that it not be done in front of other people, in other words, right after class where there are a lot of students standing around, but to make an appointment and to talk to them face-to-face. I am a strong believer that personal interaction is critical and oftentimes makes a difference in terms of what a TA or professor is going to do. It is harder to say, no, in person than it is even if you call them on the phone or e-mail them. Now, however, that is not always the case, that's the best way of doing it if all the circumstances allow for it. But, if it is something that is really urgent, then what I also do is recommend that they try by e-mail, the good thing about that is then you have written documentation that you made an attempt to do it. But, even trying by e-mail to set up a time to meet in person, that's not always appropriate because of the time constraints. But the way you phrase things is really important and sorting that out *(White female, middle-middle class, non-first-generation administrator)*.

Sherry emphasizes the importance of mentees taking the initiative to schedule one-on-one meetings with professors.

Jovaun supports the statements made by Sherry with his remarks on how his mentor helped him to see the value of having "respectful engagements" with professors:

> Don't say, well, why are you doing this to me (chuckle)? I think a lot of times when I have done bad, part of it is the professor and part of it is me. So, I think he has been trying to get me to go and see, what is it that the professor and TA

doesn't like, and don't go and say what you don't like, because you can only change you. Because the professor, most of the times, can't really change you and really you have to modify yourself to deal with the certain different demands of people whether you like them or not. I think you kind of need to put on a mask not to really hide things from people. But put on a different mask to appease the people that you really need to get the most help from. If you piss them off or you say something or show disinterest then they are not going to be willing to put their neck out for you. That has helped me in some of my classes. I would be, like, yeah, I studied but I didn't study this, I didn't think it would be on the exam. I am just going to be blunt, what can I do? Should I keep doing what I do, should I study everything, should I change my method, what do I need to do to make you happy, and sometimes I say it in a condescending tone and sometimes not. But, really, granted you want me to learn and remember this, but ultimately, I have to do what you want to get a grade, that is, just as honest as this game is. You have to kiss ass, be it to their face or on tests and papers to make them happy and make them smile and do whatever. Sometimes, that is just the price you pay for a higher education.

Jovaun's comments are typical of the ones made by the five other mentees who described the conversations they had with their mentors about how to talk about grades with professors. Jovaun's remarks about "masking" sheds light on the frustration that many mentees feel when they talk about having to "play the game" in order to succeed in college.

Although many mentees felt they were being evaluated on some other criteria in addition to their knowledge of the formal curriculum, (e.g., competency in the course materials), they were unable to articulate or even understand the connection between the hidden curriculum and formal curriculum. Mentees are officially evaluated on their understanding of the formal curriculum. However, mentees' knowledge or lack of knowledge about the hidden curriculum influences their academic ability and performance in the formal curriculum.[33]

Therefore, it is crucial that mentors discuss the intersection between the hidden curriculum and the formal curriculum with their mentees. For instance, according to the data, both mentors and mentees agreed that achieving academic success requires having an understanding of what the unwritten and unspoken expectations of each professor are and fulfilling those expectations with a "smile." Since these "rules" or expectations are not written down in the student handbook or on professors' syllabi, mentees have to discover their professors' expectations through experience (trial and error) or through mentoring relationships. Thus, if mentees feel they have to put on a "mask" in order to achieve academic success, then mentors could teach mentees explicitly and systematically the institutional cultural capital and social capital that are required for effectively "masking" in higher education.

Participation in Classroom Discussions

Another component of the hidden curriculum is learning the appropriate ways to engage in classroom discussions. One pedagogic strategy employed by some professors and TAs for encouraging students to become involved and engaged within the academic process is to facilitate topical discussions among students in the classroom. Although learning the rules of how to participate in classroom discussion is part of the knowledge and skills related to the hidden curriculum, six mentors elected not to teach these skills to their mentees. The two mentors who did have conversations with their mentees about how to engage in classroom discussions made similar general comments. For instance, Henreitta's response to the question was the following:

> Yeah, yeah, we have had that conversation, if she has something to say, to say it. You know, get the professor's permission if there is a conversation that is going on and she feels that she has something to shed some insights into, then she should say it. You know, to speak with authority, um. Yeah, you know it is important that she feels that she is a part of the classroom, no different, you know, no greater, no less than anyone else in that class.

Henreitta provides her mentee with good advice and it could certainly help build up her mentee's self-esteem. However, if the objective is to reveal explicitly the hidden curriculum to mentees, mentors need more detailed conversations with their mentees about specific strategies for engaging in effective classroom discussions, such as explicitly stating the "appropriate" verbal and nonverbal behaviors mentees could express in the classroom. Although the two mentors gave very general advice, what is most troubling is that six mentors did not provide their mentees with even general advice.

This disturbing trend continued with the mentees; only three mentees reported that their mentors had conversations with them about how to engage in classroom discussions. Robert stated:

> He just said to make sure that I am active in the discussion, not only because you end up getting a better grade, because the TA likes the fact that you are being active in their discussion. But by discussing how you feel or how you think you are interpreting a subject area; your opinions about it, better develops your sense of understanding of the subject area that you are talking about.

Once again, this quote is evidence of the general advice that mentors provided their mentees. Overall, mentors could do a much better job of providing their mentees with more specific advice that could help them learn the "rules of the game" with respect to participating in classroom discussions. For instance, mentors could use role-playing techniques to demonstrate to their mentees how they could present counter-arguments with evidence in the classroom without being disrespectful or confrontational to professors or other students.

Conducting Independent Research Projects

The final question related to the apprenticeship cycle focuses on conversations mentors had with their mentees regarding how to conduct independent research projects. Although UW-Madison is a premier research institution, all twelve mentees and six of the eight mentors stated that they did not have a conversation about how to conduct independent research projects during their mentoring relationship. The two mentors who talked with their mentees about starting independent research projects provided similar advice. For instance, Reggie said he told his mentee to:

> Turn your work in on time, follow all the instructions that you are given just like every other student, do not make any special request unless there are extenuating circumstances. Keep the person who is the supervisor informed at all times on the progress of your research project, learn about plagiarism, and footnoting, and noting credit where credit is due, understand what a complete thought is, and what is your own thought as opposed to drawing from or paraphrasing other people's thoughts. Knowing how to cite people and learning how to use that in your own argumentation. But, really learning how the writing process including research works, how to research using research techniques using bibliographies and footnoting, but also understanding that writing does not appear like magic the night before.

Reggie's colleague Sherry gave her mentee the following advice:

> Well, first you have to think about a topic or an area that you are interested in researching. So my advice is to do some background homework on what it is and then you find a professor that you feel good about and then you approach him with your ideas. But, I think you need to be prepared beforehand and, if I were a professor, if I put myself into a professor's shoes, there would be some information that I would want to know ahead of time, before I would agree to work independently with a student. Also, some of the things I would discuss are the pros and cons to it. For example when you do independent research that means that there is not a person that is going to be watching over you, it really is an unstructured learning opportunity. And, you need to keep in mind of that and find ways in which you are going to have your deadlines met, and how you are going to do it. And, I think as a professor that would be one of the questions that I would have, for example.

Both Reggie's and Sherry's statements complement one another. Reggie's advice to his mentee about how to conduct research was a little more specific than the advice that Sherry gave her mentee regarding the same topic. Moreover, the two excerpts also highlight a problem that many students encounter in mentoring programs and that is not receiving similar quantity or quality of institutional cultural capital and social capital from their mentors. The quotes demonstrate that there is a need for an academic mentoring curriculum, which could help all mentees within the same program have similar access to high quantity and quality academic mentoring (see Chapter 4 for discussion of academic mentoring curriculum). In sum, the apprenticeship cycle could allow the highest degree of institutional cultural capital and social capital to be transmitted and acquired within mentoring relationships.

Summary

According to the data, most mentors provided their mentees with very general information about how to navigate the hidden curriculum in the advising, advocacy, and apprenticeship cycles. The general advice some mentors gave their mentees can be categorized as transmitting low to medium degrees of institutional cultural capital and social capital. Unfortunately, most mentees did not receive detailed information related to navigating the hidden curriculum or high degrees of institutional cultural capital and social capital during their mentoring sessions. For instance, some mentees were told to schedule appointments with their professors when they received a low grade on an exam. However, few mentors actually discussed with their mentees "what they should say" and "how they should say it" once they were in their professors' office. It is important for students to know the "appropriate" verbal and nonverbal approaches for communicating with professors about grades without appearing to be disrespectful, because if students are perceived to be "rude" they are less likely to receive the help they need in order to improve their grade on the next exam. Therefore, if students are not provided with equal access to higher degrees of institutional cultural capital and social capital during all three cycles of the mentoring process, they are less likely to maximize their academic ability and performance in the formal curriculum, which influences their overall academic success.

One of the most significant reasons for mentors failing to transmit higher degrees of institutional cultural capital and social capital to their mentees in the various cycles was because they primarily responded to topics that were proposed by their mentees. Although one can certainly understand and justify why mentors adopt this modus operandi, it does not produce effective mentoring relationships. In other words, it is unrealistic and unfair to expect students to seek help with the "hidden curriculum" issues when many of them "do not know" that they "do not know" what they "need to know" in order to succeed in school. The advantage of having a mentor is that she will assist mentees in avoiding academic minefields by anticipating their needs and addressing them before mentees become academically maimed. Thus, mentors have to be more proactive in teaching their mentees the institutional cultural capital and social capital they need to navigate the academic culture of higher education.

Therefore, the apprenticeship cycle in the mentoring process is critically important. It is during this cycle that mentors and mentees are able to transmit and acquire the highest degrees of institutional cultural capital and social capital. Resistance theorists could argue that the apprenticeship cycle is the cycle in which mentors could have the most influence in questioning, challenging, and changing the status quo of higher education by explicitly and systematically unveiling the hidden curriculum to students. In addition, if mentors incorporate the three-cycle mentoring model within their mentoring relationships, they could empower their mentees to advocate for themselves greater educational opportunities and resources.

Krista Opens Up Her Heart to Her Mentor

Krista is getting ready to meet Dr. Fernandez at a pizza restaurant near campus for dinner. Krista is a little nervous about meeting her mentor for dinner. She is hoping she is able to demonstrate proper dinner etiquette and not talk with her mouth full. She is glad that it is at a pizza place and not a fancy restaurant. She feels confident that she will not embarrass herself that much if she takes small bites when she eats her pizza. She jokes that at least she does not have to figure out which fork and spoon to use when eating her meal. However, she is concerned that she will not have anything interesting to say to Dr. Fernandez. She feels that she is going to bore her mentor and her mentor will not want to hang out with her anymore. She decides she will start the conversation with asking questions about her mentor's research, which should at least give her enough time to think of something else to talk about during the dinner.

Krista reaches the restaurant and looks for her mentor. Dr. Fernandez is sitting at a rear booth and waves at Krista. Krista is pleased that her mentor is happy to see her and she walks swiftly toward the booth.

Dr. Fernandez stands up and warmly shakes Krista's hand and states:

Hello, Krista, it is so good to see you again! I hope you like this place.

Krista sits down and quickly responds:

Absolutely, I love pizza and this is a cool place to eat!

Dr. Fernandez smiles and remarks:

Great! How have you been since our last meeting?

Krista pauses and reflects on how she should answer this question. Should she talk about school issues only or should she also talk about her social life and family issues? She decides to focus only on school related issues.

Krista softly responds:

It has been a tough semester, including the last two weeks, but the semester is almost over, so I am just trying to survive until the end of it and start all over next semester. I am hoping things will be better next semester; surely, it cannot be as bad as my first semester.

Dr. Fernandez detects the sadness in Krista's voice and facial expression. She tells Krista that it is okay to express her true emotions with her and whatever she tells her is confidential and she will not judge her.

Krista stares at Dr. Fernandez with amazement because she cannot believe she is interested in how she really feels. Krista hopes she can truly trust her mentor because she is ready to talk about her struggles on campus but does not know if her mentor is ready to hear all of it. However, she is so tired of suffering and feeling alone that she decides to tell her mentor everything and hope for the best.

Krista takes a deep breath and expresses the following:

> Dr. Fernandez, I have had a difficult time with my transition to this university. What I am telling you now is something that I have not revealed to anyone else on this campus because I do not know who I can trust here. I have shared my concerns with family and neighborhood friends but they don't really get what I am going through because none of them have ever attended college. They think I am living the "good life" on campus and compared to them, I guess I am. So, you see, I just continue to suffer in silence because my family and friends can't help me and the people at this university either ignore me or look upon me with disdain. I do not know where I can go for support but I need someone who will listen to me and tell me that I am not crazy for feeling the way I feel.

Dr. Fernandez affirms Krista by saying:

> As a faculty of color, I have experienced similar things so I definitely do not think you are crazy; please continue to share your story.

Krista thanks her mentor for the reassurance and continues her story.

> First, let me talk about my general feelings about this university. I grew up in a diverse neighborhood with poor Blacks, Mexicans, Africans, and Hmong and I went to a neighborhood school so it was quite diverse as well. Now that I am here at the American Dream University, it is a cultural shock for me because I walk around campus and I just see a crowd of White people, very few people of color. I am usually the only person of color in my class. I told myself that it would be okay and I could adjust to this new environment but the White students are not friendly; they are really fake. At the beginning of the semester, I would smile and say hello to them when I walked passed them on campus but most of them did not respond to my greetings. Some of them would give me this smirk but never say hello. What is up with that phony smile (laughter)? I no longer smile or say hello to White people now when I walk around campus. In fact, I try to avoid eye contact with them as much as possible; I learned this technique from them and now I do it too.

In the classroom, when we have to get into small groups, I am always the last one to be picked for a group. Then, when I am in the group, they completely ignore my perspective on the issue unless it is an issue about people of color; then they expect me to represent the opinions of all minorities. I usually leave the class on these days very frustrated and angry. Outside of class, I tried to form a study group with some of my classmates to prepare for an exam but the two students I approached rejected my requests. They gave me similar responses, like, they don't like study groups and they prefer to study on their own. Once again, I think these White students are fake because I saw those same two students with a group of other students in the library in one of those private study group rooms. I don't try to be friendly to those students anymore.

The professors are not much better than the students but they are more subtle with their dismissal of my comments. For instance, when I participate in class discussions, the teacher smiles and thanks me for my comments. She then calls on another student and that student shares a perspective that is similar to my original comment; however, the teacher gives the White student more praise for giving insightful remarks. I get a smile and a courteous, thank you, while the other student is celebrated for his keen intellect even though we said practically the same thing. I don't think that's fair. This has happened to me on several occasions in the classroom and as a result, I just stopped participating in the class. Then the professor has the nerve to say to me she noticed that I do not participate in class anymore, and is everything okay. I tell her that everything is okay but I think to myself, why should I participate when you minimize everything I say. I can't win and it is clear that they don't want me to win, either. Oh, Dr. Fernandez, can I tell you about another incident with a professor?

Dr. Fernandez nods reassuringly and says:

Yes, of course, I am listening.

Krista, thanks her mentor and continues.

Well, I had one professor who did not correct a student when he made a stereotypical comment in class. The student was a White male and he stated that American Indians are poor because they are all alcoholics. I could not believe what I was hearing but I just knew the professor would correct him but the professor, a White male, did not respond to the student's statement at all which gave the impression that the comment is factual. I know I should have said something but I don't know all the statistics on each group and I didn't want to argue with him without knowing the facts. But I thought the professor would know the statistics and correct the student or at least say that it is a stereotype. I lost respect for not only the student who said that comment but I also no longer trust or respect the professor. I think that if the professor did not stand up for American Indians he will not stand up for my group either. And the professor is always telling us that his door is open and we should visit him during office hours but I don't feel comfortable going to his office hours. I can't connect with him when I don't think he respects people of color. I know I should go see him because I did not perform well on the last exam but it is so hard to look at that teacher now. I know I need his help but I just don't feel like he cares about me as a student, a person, or African American.

Dr. Fernandez interrupts and says:

> Krista, you have shared some deeply moving stories that many students of color encounter at predominantly white universities; are there other issues you want to talk about this evening?

Krista remarks:

> Yes, I also experience negative reactions from students because of my class background. When I walk around campus I notice that the majority of students wear designer brand clothes and shoes, drive nice cars, own the latest computers and smart phones, and they seem to always have money to eat off campus a couple of nights during the week. I constantly hear them talk about their family's vacations, what they did and what they bought. I always feel ashamed when students talk about vacations because my family is too poor to travel. Moreover, I guess I am a little envious that these students can fully take advantage of their college experience by joining numerous student organizations. However, I have to work twenty plus hours a week to help pay for my tuition even with my scholarship. I hate it when White students make sarcastic remarks about students of color getting "full-rides" when they know nothing about my struggle.

> Overall, I feel like I am climbing a mountain without a rope and I am one step from falling down. I keep thinking why did I come here and why did they recruit me, if they really don't want me here. I am sorry, Dr. Fernandez, I have been talking the entire time and our pizza is cold now. I will shut up.

Dr. Fernandez laughs and says:

> Don't worry about it; we can always take the pizza home and warm it up in the microwave. Seriously, I am honored that you trust me enough to share your story with me. I will keep the details in confidence. However, I want you to know that the university has made significant process in recruiting diverse students but it has a lot of room for improvement when it comes to creating a welcoming campus climate that affirms and validates the experiences of underrepresented students.

> I wish you had never had your negative experiences but I want to make sure you are aware of the support services here on campus that can help you find your niche at the university. I have several recommendations for you. First, you should contact the Multi-Ethnic Resource Support Center. Second, you should attend a couple of meetings and events sponsored by the student of color organizations. I will also make some contacts with my faculty friends, some of whom are White, but trust me, they understand their racial and class privileges and their positions of power. I want you to meet them because I do not want you to believe that all White professors are like the ones you had this semester. I do

not want you to give up on being friendly and approachable, so please try to keep an open-mind about your White peers and professors because not all of them are fake. I still want you to try to reach out to your professors and build relationships with them. It will make a difference in your overall academic success. Krista, are you willing to follow through on my recommendations?

Krista says quietly, with a hint of resignation in her voice:

Yes, Dr. Fernandez, I will follow your recommendations.

Dr. Fernandez responds with a passionate voice:

I will do my best to surround you with a strong support team but I need you to work with me on creating and sustaining your support team. Are you willing to work with me?

Krista exclaims:

Yes, ma'am, I am willing to work with you. Thank you!

Dr. Fernandez smiles and promises:

Tomorrow morning, I will send you an email with the phone number and the name of the contact person for the Multi-Ethnic Resource Support Center and by next Friday, I will introduce you to some of my White colleagues/friends so you can learn to become more comfortable talking with professors. Now, I want you to promise that by next Friday, you will schedule office visits with all four of your professors, and then connect with one of the student of color organizations. Do you promise to do the things I suggested?

Krista nods and says:

Yes, I promise!

Dr. Fernandez responds:

Krista, if you follow my recommendations I can be the rope that you need to climb your mountain and I will not let you fall, okay? Well, it is getting late so let's put our pizza in a box and go home. I will send you an email tomorrow. It is not too late to end this semester in good standing. You can do it! I believe in you!

Dr. Fernandez stands up extends her hand, and gives Krista a friendly, firm handshake and leaves the restaurant. Krista packs up her pizza, walks back to the dorm, and ponders the following thought:

School ends in four weeks. Can I really turn it around? Well, if Dr. Fernandez believes in me, I am going to do my best. What do I have to lose? As my grandmother would say, God did not bring me this far to leave me. Okay, God, I am going to need your help to excel in these last four weeks.

Notes

1. *Clashes of Money and Values: A Survey of Admission Directors,* Inside Higher Ed, 2011, www.insidehighered.com (accessed September 22, 2011).

2a. Pierre Bourdieu, *Distinction: A Social Critique of the Judgment of Taste,* Richard Nice (Translation), (Cambridge, MA: Harvard University Press, 1984).

2b. Glenda Musoba and Benjamin Baez, "The Cultural Capital of Cultural and Social Capital: An Economy of Translations," in *Higher Education: Handbook of Theory and Research,* ed. John Smart (New York: Agathon, 2009), 24.

2c. Pierre Bourdieu, "Cultural Reproduction and Social Reproduction," in *Knowledge, Education, and Cultural Change: Papers in the Sociology of Education,* ed. Richard Brown (London: Taylor & Francis, 1973), 71-112.

2d. Pierre Bourdieu and Jean-Claude Passeron, *Reproduction in Education, Society and Culture* (Beverly-Hill, CA: Sage, 1990).

3. *Clashes of Money and Values: A Survey of Admission Directors,* Inside Higher Ed, 2011, www.insidehighered.com (accessed September 22, 2011).

4. Maryann Jacobi, "Mentoring and Undergraduate Academic Success: A Literature Review," *Review of Educational Research* 61, no. 4 (1991): 505-532.

5a. Alexander Astin, *Four Critical Years: Effects of College on Beliefs, Attitudes and Knowledge* (San Francisco, CA: Jossey-Bass, 1977).

5b. Alexander Astin, "Student Involvement: A Developmental Theory for Higher Education," *Journal of College Student Personnel* 25, (1984): 287-300.

6. Ernest Pascarella, "Student-Faculty Informal Contact and College Outcomes," *Review of Educational Research* 50, no. 4 (1980): 545-595.

7a. Vincent Tinto, "Dropout from Higher Education: A Theoretical Synthesis of Recent Research," *Review of Educational Research* 45, (1975): 89-125.

7b. Vincent Tinto, *Leaving College: Rethinking the Causes and Cures of Student Attrition* 2nd ed. (Chicago: University of Chicago Press, 1993).

8. Richard Pearson, *Counseling and Social Support: Perspectives and Practice,* (Newbury Park, CA: Sage, 1990).

9. James House, *Work Stress and Social Support* (Reading, MA: Addison-Wesley, 1981), 23.

10. Russell Thomas, Patricia Murrell, and Arthur Chickering, "Theoretical Bases and Feasibility Issues for Mentoring and Developmental Transcripts," in *Mentoring-Transcript Systems for Promoting Student Growth,* ed. Robert Brown and David DeCoster (San Francisco: Jossey-Bass, 1982), 49-65.

11. Arthur Chickering, *Education and Identity* (San Francisco, CA: Jossey-Bass, 1969).

12. Pierre Bourdieu, "The Forms of Capital," in *Handbook of Theory and Research for the Sociology of Education,* ed. John G. Richardson (New York: Greenwood, 1986), 241-258.

13. Bourdieu, "The Forms of Capital," 1986, 241-258.

14. Bourdieu, "Cultural Reproduction and Social Reproduction," 1973, 71-112.

15a. Bourdieu, "The Forms of Capital," 1986, 241-258.

15b. James Coleman, "Social Capital in the Creation of Human Capital," *American Journal of Sociology* (Issue Supplement) 94 (1988): S95-120.

15c. James Coleman, *Foundations of Social Theory* (Cambridge, MA: Belknap Press, 1990).

16. Annette Lareau, "Linking Bourdieu's Concept of Capital to the Broader Field: The Case of Family-School Relationships," in *Social Class, Poverty and Education: Policy and Practice*, ed. Bruce Biddle (New York: Routledge Falmer, 2001), 77-100.

17a. Philip Jackson, *Life in Classrooms* (New York: Holt, Reinhart and Winston, 1968).

17b. Eric Margolis, Michael Soldatenko, Sandra Acker, and Marina Gair, "Peekaboo: Hiding and Outing the Curriculum," in *The Hidden Curriculum in Higher Education*, ed. Eric Margolis (New York: Routledge, 2001), 4-5.

18. Emile Durkheim, *Moral Education* (New York: The Free Press, 1961).

19. Margolis, Soldatenko, Acker, and Gair, "Peekaboo: Hiding and Outing the Curriculum," 2001, 6.

20. Margolis, Soldatenko, Acker, and Gair, "Peekaboo: Hiding and Outing the Curriculum," 2001, 5.

21. Samuel Bowels and Herbert Gintis, *Schooling in Capitalist America: Educational Reform and the Contradictions of Economic Life* (New York: Basic Books, 1976).

22. Bourdieu, "Cultural Reproduction and Social Reproduction," 1973, 71-112.

23a. Michael Apple, *Education and Power* (New York: Routledge, 1982).

23b. Michael Apple, *Ideology and Curriculum*, 2nd ed. (New York: Routledge, 1990).

23c. Paulo Freire, *Education for Critical Consciousness* (New York: Continuum, 1982).

23d. Paulo Freire, *Pedagogy of Hope* (New York: Continuum Publishing Company, 1994).

23e. Henry Giroux, *Theory and Resistance in Education: A Pedagogy for the Opposition* (New York: Bergin and Garvey, 1983).

24a. Apple, *Education and Power*, 1982.

24b. Apple, *Ideology and Curriculum*, 2nd, 1990.

24c. Freire, *Education for Critical Consciousness*, 1982.

24d. Freire, *Pedagogy of Hope*, 1994.

24e. Giroux, *Theory and Resistance in Education: A Pedagogy for the Opposition*, 1983.

25. Bourdieu, "Cultural Reproduction and Social Reproduction," 1973, 71-112.

26a. Bourdieu, "Cultural Reproduction and Social Reproduction," 1973, 71-112.

26b. Bourdieu, *Distinction: A Social Critique of the Judgment of Taste*, 1984.

26c. Bourdieu, "The Forms of Capital," 1986, 241-258.

27a. Bourdieu, *Distinction: A Social Critique of the Judgment of Taste*, 1984.

27b. Bourdieu, "The Forms of Capital," 1986, 241-258.

28a. Ricardo Stanton-Salazar, "A Social Capital Framework for Understanding the Socialization of Racial Minority Children and Youths," *Harvard Educational Review* 67 (1997): 1-40.

28b. Ricardo Stanton-Salazar and Sanford Dornbusch, "Social Capital and the Reproduction of Inequality: Information Networks among Mexican-American High School Students," *Sociology of Education* 68 (1995): 116-135.

28c. Gilberto Arriaza, "Schools, Social Capital, and Children of Color," *Race, Ethnicity and Education* 6 (2003): 71-94.

28d. William Tierney, "Models of Minority College-Going and Retention: Cultural Integrity versus Cultural Suicide," 1999, 80-91.

28e. Peter Collier and David Morgan, "'Is that Paper Really Due Today?' Differences in First-Generation and Traditional College Students' Understandings of Faculty Expectations," *Higher Education* 55 (2008): 425-446.

28f. Mary Henningsen, Kathleen Valde, Gregory A. Russell and Gregory R. Russell, "Student-Faculty Interactions about Disappointing Grades: Application of the Goals-Plans-Actions Model and the Theory of Planned Behavior," *Communication Education* 60, no. 2 (2011): 174-190.

28g. Annette Lareau and Elliot Weininger, "Cultural Capital in Educational Research: A Critical Assessment," *Theory and Society* 32 (2003): 567-606.

29a. Bourdieu, "Cultural Reproduction and Social Reproduction," 1973, 71-112.

29b. Bourdieu, *Distinction: A Social Critique of the Judgment of Taste*, 1984.

29c. Bourdieu, "The Forms of Capital," 1986, 241-258.

30. The empirical findings in this chapter come from my unpublished dissertation. Buffy Smith, *Demystifying the Higher Education System: Rethinking Academic Cultural Capital, Social Capital, and the Academic Mentoring Process*, 2004.

31a. Alexander Astin, *Four Critical Years: Effects of College on Beliefs, Attitudes and Knowledge*, 1977.

31b. Alexander Astin, "Student Involvement: A Developmental Theory for Higher Education," 1984, 287-300.

32a. Apple, *Education and Power*, 1982.

32b. Giroux, *Theory and Resistance in Education: A Pedagogy for the Opposition*, 1983.

33a. Bourdieu, *Distinction: A Social Critique of the Judgment of Taste*, 1984.

33b. Bourdieu, "The Forms of Capital," 1986, 241-258.

33c. George Farkas, Robert Grobe, Daniel Sheehan, and Yuan Shaun, "Cultural Resources and School Success: Gender, Ethnicity and Poverty Groups within an Urban School District," 1990, 127-142.

33d. Jeannie Oakes, Amy Wells, Makeba Jones, and Amanda Datnow, "Detracking: The Social Construction of Ability, Cultural Politics and Resistance to Reform," 1997, 482-510.

Chapter 4

Transforming Mentoring Programs

Since many low-income and first-generation students are at the highest risk of dropping out of college within the first four semesters, many universities have created mentoring programs to improve underrepresented students' retention and graduation rates.[1] According to research, mentoring programs that are effective in increasing the retention rates of "at-risk" students are also successful at helping the general student population persist in college.[2] Many higher education institutions develop mentoring programs as a way to demonstrate their commitment to diversity.[3]

Therefore, the purpose of this chapter is to provide a synthesis of best practices for designing mentoring programs that reveal the hidden curriculum of higher education to students. Based on my literature review of numerous mentoring programs, research, and experience, I offer the following recommendations for restructuring mentoring programs to help "at-risk" students understand and navigate the hidden curriculum.[4] The ideal mentoring program could specify its target student population (e.g., low-income and first-generation freshmen and sophomores). The program could be based on a four-tiered mentoring network. For instance, the students could be paired with four mentors: (1) administrator/staff/faculty mentors, (2) student peer mentors (junior and senior students), (3) family member mentors, and (4) community advocate mentors.

Although the main objective is to assist the freshmen and sophomores to succeed in college, all the mentors and mentees receive benefits because they collectively provide information, resources, encouragement, and support to one another within the mentoring network. For example, mentees benefit because they learn the unwritten rules of higher education and mentors receive internal gratification for serving as role models to the next generation. In addition, mentors could learn new knowledge and information from their mentees.

Selecting a Definition of Mentoring

Before we discuss how to restructure the recruiting, matching, training, and evaluation processes, we have to select a mentoring definition and review the literature on the different mentoring models. As stated in Chapter 1, there is no consensus among scholars regarding a universal definition of mentoring.[5] A mentor is often thought of as a sponsor, advisor, role model, supervisor, tutor, and/or motivator.[6] Friedman argues for a very narrow definition of mentoring: a person is considered a mentor only if she combines the roles of advisor, sponsor, research supervisor, supporter, and role model and participates in a one-on-one mentoring relationship.[7] Galbraith and Cohen have a broader definition of mentoring.[8] In their review of the mentoring literature, they found several common themes in the various definitions of mentoring, including the following:

> Mentoring is a process within a contextual setting; involves a relationship of a more knowledgeable individual with a less experienced individual; provides professional networking, counseling, guiding, instructing, modeling, and sponsoring; is a developmental mechanism (personal, professional, and psychological); is a socialization and reciprocal relationship; and provides an identity transformation for both mentor and mentee.[9]

But Zelditch believes the definition of mentoring could encompass and acknowledge different forms of mentoring in higher education, and the notion of mentoring should not be constrained to just one-on-one mentoring relationships.[10] Zelditch suggests that we could simply consider "mentoring as an intensive kind of teaching;"[11] this definition is probably the most appropriate one to use for designing a mentoring program that explicitly reveals the hidden curriculum of higher education to students.

The Phases and Functions of Mentoring

Although the definition of mentoring is debatable, there is more agreement on the four major phases and functions of mentoring. Many scholars cite Kram's seminal work about mentoring relationships within the corporate sector.[12] Kram delineates four major phases of the mentoring relationship: initiation, cultivation, separation, and redefinition.[13] During the initiation phase, the mentor serves primarily as a role model to the protégé. In the cultivation phase, the mentor and protégé relationship grows stronger as the mentor becomes the protégé's coach, counselor, and sponsor, and provides exposure and visibility (networking) within the institution. The separation phase is a time marked by ambivalence as both the mentor and protégé prepare for separation. Finally, the redefinition phase is a transition in which the mentor and protégé relationship is replaced with a friend/peer relationship. Kram's work is significant because it illuminates how mentors and mentees negotiate with one another in order to achieve psychosocial and vocational goals.

According to Schockett and Haring-Hidore, the two primary functions of mentoring relationships are psychosocial and vocational.[14] Psychosocial mentoring provides support to protégés through "role modeling, encouraging, counseling, and colleagueship."[15] Vocational mentoring supports the protégés through "education, coaching, consulting, sponsoring, and providing visibility, exposure, and protecting."[16] Psychosocial and vocational functions are incorporated in most models of mentoring, including one-on-one and networking.

Academic Mentoring: Positive and Negative Outcomes

Conversations about academic mentoring often emphasize individual benefits and not institutional goals. Recently, scholars have begun to take a new approach to studying mentoring by looking at both the individual and institutional benefits of academic mentoring.[17] These scholars argue that mentoring programs are able to assist mentors and mentees with their personal and academic development in a supportive environment, which in turn could foster a sense of duty and loyalty to the advancement, continuity, and stability of the institution. For instance, many faculty mentors satisfy their generative needs (i.e., their desire to leave a legacy for the next generation) by helping student mentees achieve academic success and feel more connected to the university. As a result, colleges and universities are better able to accomplish their recruitment and retention goals within a supportive community.

Although the majority of the research on academic mentoring emphasizes the positive outcomes of mentoring, it cannot be ignored that negative mentoring exists, occurs on a regular basis, and has real consequences. In fact, Wilson outlines three effects negative mentoring can have on minority students: (1) lowering academic expectations; (2) encouraging students to consider "easy" majors; and (3) reinforcing students' low self-esteeem by not academically challenging them to do better.[18] According to Collins,[19] negative mentoring experiences often influence some people to make charges that, "traditional mentoring promotes and maintains the status quo by socializing protégés into the 'rules of the game' and many of the 'rules' one must learn in order to be in the 'inner circle' are discriminatory against women and minorities."[20] Although the previous evidence highlights primarily how negative mentoring affects mentees, one could also infer negative mentoring could impede mentors from successfully meeting their emotional and psychological needs to "give back" to the next generation, and that schools could encounter more obstacles in achieving their diversity and retention goals.

On the other hand, scholars remind us that we should always be aware that "mentors who are positive need not be of the same sex or race of the protégé."[21] In fact, according to Knox and McGovern[22] there are six important characteristics of a mentor: "a willingness to share knowledge, honesty, competency, a willingness to allow growth, a willingness to give positive and critical feedback, and a directness in dealings with the protégés."[23] If mentors embody these characteristics, they could create a positive mentoring experience for their mentees, regardless of their mentees' sex or race.

Grooming Mentoring Model

Many colleges and universities try to foster positive individual and institutional achievement, development, and growth by designing mentoring programs based on either a one-on-one or networking mentoring model. One-on-one mentoring is also known as the "grooming model."[24] The major attributes of the grooming model of mentoring are a one-on-one relationship, matching primarily based on racial and gender characteristics, and benefits that flow from mentor to protégé.[25]

According to Haring, however, the three attributes of the grooming model are problematic because they are based on assumptions supported by inconclusive evidence.[26] Haring offers counterarguments for each assumption:

●Mentoring relationships do not have to be one-on-one to be effective and rewarding.

●There is inconclusive evidence on whether using racial and gender characteristics to match mentors and protégés produce the most effective mentoring relationships.

●The unidirectional and hierarchical approach implies that protégés are not perceived to be and thus are not treated as valued contributors to the mentoring relationship.[27]

Overall, the grooming model, whether designed with the original or modified attributions outlined above, could lead to two major problems. First, it could provide justification for why mentoring relationships fail when the mentors and mentees do not belong to the same gender or racial group. As a result, the mentors and mentees are not required to reflect on the structure of the mentoring program or how their individual approaches to mentoring could have contributed to their negative mentoring experiences. Instead, they find solace in the presumed fact that their relationship was ineffective due to racial and gender differences. Second, the grooming model could cause mentors to unconsciously and without malicious intent mold their protégés to be like them (the cloning effect). Moreover, some scholars are very concerned that many good-hearted White mentors will encourage underrepresented protégés to replace their home culture with the majority culture in order to succeed in higher education.[28]

Network Mentoring Model

Haring suggests that in order to avoid some of the problems associated with the "grooming" model we could use the "networking" model of mentoring which is more inclusive (administrators, staff, faculty, and students) and is coordinated by an appointed facilitator.[29] The networking model also purports to be more inclusive of different cultural values, experiences and perspectives. Haring describes the two primary components of the networking model in this way:

- The mentoring program is structured in a way that fosters group interaction among administrators, faculty, and students so that everyone in the group can exchange both psychosocial and vocational benefits with one another (one-on-one mentoring is not the emphasis).
- There is a de-emphasis on hierarchy and power within the network model. For example, an individual could serve as a mentor to someone in the network on one occasion because she has expertise in an area. At another time, she could become a protégé seeking advice from another expert in the network. Protégés are perceived to be and treated as valued contributors to the mentoring relationship, unlike many one-on-one mentoring relationships.[30]

There are a number of advantages for using the networking model of mentoring:

- There is no need to find a "perfect" match (less emphasis on racial and gender characteristics).
- Protégés are less likely to be cloned by a particular mentor.
- More students can be included in the network (thus reducing the pressure to assimilate).
- "Natural chemistry" between mentor and protégé is not a crucial issue because relationships are less intense.
- Students learn more about the institutional culture from various perspectives (e.g., staff, faculty, administrators, and other students).
- Students in the network have more power because they belong to a group. Success of all the protégés in the group is the main focus, not success for just a selected few.[31]

On the other hand, Haring also acknowledges the challenges of the networking model:

- Difficult to organize and maintain the energy necessary to sustain an effective mentoring program.
- The effectiveness of the mentoring program is greatly influenced by the skills of the facilitator/director. A skilled facilitator/director will bring key people and resources within the institution to the program. However, an unskilled facilitator/director will either dominate the network with her agenda or create a poorly organized network.
- Each participant has to make a serious commitment to give and receive benefits from the network at various times.
- Networks need to include "senior" individuals in the institutions (e.g., individuals who have been part of the institution for a significant number of years). Senior members are very important because they can offer greater insights into the politics and culture of the institution.[32]

Since there are several challenges with the grooming and networking models, mentoring programs could incorporate both one-on-one connections and relational networks that intentionally teach students how to increase their institutional cultural capital and social capital in order to thrive in college.

Create Mission Statement for Mentoring Programs

Once mentoring program directors decide on the structure of their programs, their next task is to create a mission statement. The major stakeholders of the university have to believe in the mentoring program's mission statement, which should reflect the core values of the university. The directors could organize advisory boards for the mentoring programs, which could include administrators, staff, faculty, student leaders, family members of student leaders, and community advocates. The advisory board is responsible for helping the directors write the mission statement, support the mentors and mentees, and evaluate the program.

An example of a mission statement is the following:

The mission of the Aim High Mentoring Program is to assist low-income and first-generation freshmen and sophomores with acquiring the institutional cultural capital and social capital students need in order to thrive at the Right On University. Mentors and mentees share and benefit from the resources, support, and encouragement that are generated because of their mentoring network. Mentoring networks provide students with a deeper understanding of how to navigate the hidden curriculum of higher education. The mentoring program will help the Right On University increase its retention and graduation rates of low-income and first-generation students.

As stated in the previous example, the targeted student population and the objectives of the mentoring program should be clearly defined in the mission statement. Ideally, mentoring programs could have measurable goals that address components of the university's strategic plan (e.g., diversity and academic success issues). Since, mentoring programs could produce positive institutional benefits, the top executives of the university could reward the intense service commitments of the administrator/staff/faculty mentors. For instance, these mentors could be given university recognition for their significant service and provided some financial compensation.

Recruiting Process

After mentoring program directors have collaborated with their advisory boards to construct their mission statements they are ready to begin the recruitment process. The mission statement serves as one of the most effective recruitment tools for providing mentors and mentees with a collective identity and purpose. The program directors could select mentors (e.g., administrators/staff/faculty, student peers, family members, and community advocates) and mentees who embody the characteristics that reflect the mission of the program. Directors could conduct in-depth interviews with each mentor and mentee to assess their skills, social awareness, and academic and non-academic interests.

Ideal Traits for Mentors and Mentees

Mentors should demonstrate some of these characteristics:[33]

- Culturally Competent—demonstrates awareness and knowledge of, respect for, and sensitivity to mentees' multiple social identities
- Skilled at Interpersonal Relations—caring for, sharing information, and empathizing with mentees
- Effective Communicator—attentive listener to mentee's needs
- Promoters of Self-Esteem—build up mentees' self-confidence
- Celebrators of Assertiveness—encourage mentees to be risk-takers
- Flexible—encourage mentees to view people and situations from multiple perspectives
- Problem Solvers—encourage mentees to seek creative solutions to problems

Mentees should also embody several of these attributes:

- Attentive Listeners—receptive to mentors' advice and counsel
- Open-Minded—open to trying new ideas suggested by mentors
- Committed—dedicated to work hard and follow the rules of the mentoring program
- Self-Motivated—be proactive in the learning and mentoring process
- Positive Attitude—take a positive approach to working with mentors
- Goal-Oriented—work with mentors in achieving academic goals

Benefits for Mentors and Mentees

In addition to selecting mentors and mentees based on the above criteria, program directors should discuss with the candidates the multiple benefits that mentors and mentees receive by participating in the program. The benefits for the mentors include the following:[34]

- Take pride in helping students thrive in college by teaching them how to understand and navigate the hidden curriculum of higher education
- Learn new ideas from mentees
- Contribute to the overall growth of mentees in their academic and social development

On the other hand, mentees receive the following benefits:

- Establish meaningful academic and social relationships with mentors
- Acquire institutional cultural capital and social capital
- Increase level of self-motivation and self-discipline
- Learn how to successfully set and achieve academic goals

Finally, for institutions to receive benefits such as increasing the retention and graduation rates of underrepresented students the mentoring program must be fully staffed, funded, and recognized as providing an essential and valuable service for the university.

The Matching Process

Once the most qualified mentors and mentees have been selected based on the attributes listed in the previous section the next task is to match mentors with mentees based on their profiles. In order to foster successful mentoring relationships, program directors should not assign more than two mentees to a mentor.

Some directors intentionally create same-race mentoring matches because they believe these relationships are more effective than cross-race matches. Although many mentees initially want to be paired with mentors who share their racial identity in order to minimize cultural misunderstandings, the race of the mentor is not the major factor that influences the success of the relationship.[35] In fact, most mentees indicate that their mentor's ability to be culturally sensitive and provide constructive feedback in an encouraging way is more important than sharing the same racial background as the mentor.[36]

Several studies have indicated that teachers who are not culturally competent in addressing the needs of underrepresented students have a negative impact on the students' academic achievement.[37] If teachers' project low expectations and behave in culturally insensitive ways toward their underserved students, they are less likely to develop a positive teacher and student relationship, which could lead to negative student outcomes.[38] It is therefore recommended that teachers maintain high academic standards and provide students with the skills and resources they need to reach those goals.[39] Since mentoring is similar to teaching, mentors are also responsible for helping their mentees achieve high academic standards. In order for "at-risk" students to achieve academic success, they need mentors and teachers who understand their home culture and is able to teach them the culture of higher education.

In addition to having mentors who are culturally competent and sensitive, mentees often desire to be matched with mentors who have similar personality traits and interests.[40] If directors do a good job of screening and selecting mentors and mentees during the recruiting process it could make the matching process easier and more efficient. Research findings indicate that there is no conclusive evidence that same race mentoring relationships are more successful than cross-race mentoring relationships.[41] Therefore, mentoring directors could focus less on finding the "perfect match," and more on helping mentees acquire the institutional cultural capital and social capital they need to thrive in college.

The Training/Orientation Process

Although the matching process is an important task, the overall success of the mentoring program is greatly influenced by the quality of the training/orientation sessions that is offered to the mentees and mentors. Directors have to make the training/orientation sessions mandatory, without exception, for all mentors and mentees. The in-depth training/orientation process could cover the purpose, the required components, roles and responsibilities, and the mentoring curriculum. At the beginning of the training/orientation session directors have to inspire mentors and mentees to make commitments to one another to have successful mentoring relationships. In order to motivate mentors and mentees, directors could explain why the mentoring program is based on a particular definition, mission statement, and network model. When mentors and mentees have a shared understanding of the purpose and goals of the program they are more likely to identify themselves as a collaborative team working together on unveiling the hidden curriculum of higher education.

Directors have to be cheerleaders for mentors and mentees but they also have to enforce requirements of the program. I recommend that there could be four core requirements of the program: (1) individual meetings, (2) networking workshops, (3) reflection papers, and (4) community service. In addition to the required components, program directors could have opening and closing receptions for all participants every year. The closing reception of the second year could include an award ceremony for mentors and a graduation celebration for mentees.

Both mentors and mentees could sign a contract indicating that they agree to commit two years of service in the program. The contract could also include the four major requirements of the program and the sanctions associated with violating those expectations. For instance, students who do not meet with their mentors each month could receive one demerit and given a warning. If a mentee receives two demerits within the same semester, that student could be placed on probation status in the mentoring program. If the student commits another violation, her or his contract could be terminated and they could be asked to leave the program. It is important to note that mentors are expected to adhere to the same requirements and if they violate them, they could also be released from the program.

Mentors' Roles and Responsibilities

Administrator/staff/faculty mentors are volunteers who are required to meet one-on-one with their freshmen and sophomores once a month (total of three meetings per semester) for at least one hour at each meeting to discuss a hidden curriculum topic. The administrator/staff/faculty mentors are encouraged to email their mentees weekly for a virtual check-in meeting. In addition to mentoring their mentees, mentors are expected to advise and support student peer mentors in the program. The administrator/staff/faculty mentors could give their mentees homework assignments directly related to the hidden curriculum. For example, mentors could have their mentees create a study plan for each of their courses.

In addition to individual meetings, all mentors in the network have to attend two mandatory in-depth networking workshops per semester that reemphasize the hidden curriculum topics covered in the one-on-one mentoring meetings. One phase of the workshop could focus on mentors sharing with other mentors effective strategies for unveiling the hidden curriculum to students. The second phase of the workshop allows mentors time to professionally network with all participants in the program (a major benefit for participating in the mentoring network). After each individual meeting and networking workshop, all mentors could write a one to two page reflection paper that specifies the three strategies they used to help their mentees learn the hidden curriculum topic and give their overall impression of the mentoring session. The reflection papers could be submitted to the program directors within one week after the mentoring meetings/workshops.

Unlike administrator/staff/faculty mentors, student peer mentors (junior and seniors) receive a small stipend per semester for books and school supplies. The peer mentors have the same responsibilities as the administrator/staff/faculty mentors. The main difference between student peer mentors and administrator/staff/faculty mentors is that student peer mentors could address hidden curriculum issues from a student perspective. Student peer mentors could also benefit by receiving academic and career advice from administrator/staff/faculty mentors and community advocate mentors within the network.

Community advocate mentors are volunteers who provide opportunities for mentees to give back to the community. It is important for mentees' overall personal development and self-esteem that they be able to receive support but also help others in need. Community advocate mentors work with the mentees for at least ten hours per semester on a project. Community advocates are required to discuss the same hidden curriculum topics as the administrator/staff/faculty mentors and student peer mentors each month and write a reflection paper about their mentoring experience. The community advocate mentors benefit from the mentoring network because they could establish positive relationships with key players in the university and have students work with them on community service projects.

Family mentors are important to the overall success of mentoring networks. They could be parents, grandparents, older siblings, aunts, uncles, cousins, or close family friends of the freshmen and sophomores. The main responsibility of family mentors is to reinforce the hidden curriculum topics covered by the other mentors each month. If family mentors are unable to meet with the mentees one-on-one each month or attend the two mandatory workshops, they could have at least two in-depth phone calls per month with their mentees regarding hidden curriculum issues. Family mentors who strongly encourage their mentees to not work more than twenty hours a week or become overwhelmed with family related issues could give their mentees the peace of mind they need to succeed in college. The mentoring program directors could contact the family mentors (and all other mentors) once a month to assess the mentoring relationships. Family mentors have the option to either write reflection papers (like the other mentors) or provide feedback via the telephone to the program directors. Research findings indicate that parents of "at-risk" students have high educational aspirations for their children but they do not have the knowledge or resources to prepare them for academic success.[42] However, if parents could participate in a mentoring network they could have access to the information and resources they need to help their children thrive in college.

Mentees' Roles & Responsibilities

The freshmen and sophomore mentees are required to meet one-on-one once a month for at least an hour with each of their four mentors (the only exception are family mentors) to discuss hidden curriculum issues. Mentees are responsible for completing homework assignments assigned by their mentors. In addition, they could write one to two page reflection papers that describe three things they learned about the hidden curriculum topics after every individual meeting and workshop. The papers could be submitted to the program directors within a week of their mentoring sessions. Every week, the mentees could email their mentors to give them an update on their college experience. The mentees are expected to attend two in-depth workshops per semester. During the first phase of the workshop, they could share with other mentees the advice they received from their mentors regarding the hidden curriculum. The second phase of the workshop provides a forum for all the mentees and mentors to network with one another.

The mentees could sign a mentoring contract indicating that they agree to participate in individual meetings, workshops, and ten hours of community service, and write and submit reflection papers. The contract could address the sanctions for violating the requirements. Mentees could also sign a confidentiality waiver, which could allow their administrator/staff/faculty mentors permission to contact other administrators, staff, and faculty about their academic performance only on a need-to-know basis (the waiver does not grant the other mentors this right). In addition to increasing mentees' institutional cultural capital and social capital, mentees who successfully complete the two-year mentoring program could be eligible to serve as student peer mentors when they are juniors and seniors.

Acculturation versus Assimilation

The training/orientation session could include a discussion about the distinction between acculturation and assimilation. According to the American Heritage College Dictionary, acculturation is defined as, "the modification of the culture of a group or an individual as a result of contact with a different culture."[43] On the other hand, Richard Schaefer offers the following definition for assimilation: "the process by which a subordinate individual or group takes on the characteristics of the dominant group."[44] This definition presents assimilation as a process in which individuals replace cultural traits of their group with another group or adopt cultural traits of another group. However, the acculturation definition describes a process in which people adapt or modify their group culture when interacting with a different group.

Mentoring program directors have to strongly articulate to mentors and mentees that assimilation is not the goal of the mentoring program. Directors could remind mentors that they are not expected to groom their mentees into "thinking and acting" like White middle class and upper class students. Mentors are expected to help their mentees learn the hidden rules of higher education but not make them feel ashamed of their racial identities and/or social class backgrounds during the process. Likewise, mentees are not required to reject their home culture in order to acquire the institutional cultural capital and social capital they need to thrive in college. Mentees are encouraged to learn and adapt to the cultural norms, values, and expectations of higher education but they do not have to disavow their racial and social class identities during the mentoring process. In other words, mentees could simultaneously achieve academic success and be authentic to their home culture.

Academic Mentoring Curriculum

One way to discourage the practice of assimilation in mentoring programs is to have all mentors adhere to the same academic mentoring curriculum. The program directors in consultation with their advisory board members could create a handbook based on the mentoring curriculum. They could develop a handbook unique to their university that reflects the norms, values, expectations and the rules of the game at their university (no single handbook could fit all institutions). The handbook could include sections on the purpose of the program, the mission statement, the definition of mentoring, the mentor and mentee roles and responsibilies, the mentor and mentee commitment contract forms, the mentee confidentiality waiver, the community service volunteer forms, instructions on how to write reflection papers, frequently asked questions for mentors and mentees, contact information for campus resources and support groups, and finally contact information for program directors, staff, and the mentoring advisory board members. Although these sections are all important, this handbook is unique because it also provides definitions of key concepts such as institutional cultural capital, social capital, the hidden curriculum, and the three cycles of mentoring.

The academic mentoring handbook could provide a detailed mentoring schedule for the hidden curriculum topics mentors could cover at different times in the semester. The handbook could provide mentors with sample scripts of how to approach navigating the culture of higher education. It is important to emphasize that mentors are required to teach the same hidden curriculum topics at their individual meetings but mentors, like teachers, are not expected to have the same mentoring pedagogy. In other words, the mentoring content is standardized but the mentoring methods would reflect the various creative teaching styles of the mentors. Although mentors and mentees are free to discuss other relevant and timely issues, they have to address at least two hidden curriculum topics per meeting. Some of the topics that could be included in the mentoring handbook are the following: faculty/student relationships, classroom conduct/etiquette, strategies for forming peer study groups, time management, note-taking/study skills and racial and social class climate issues.

A typical mentoring schedule for the mentees' first semester is covering two hidden curriculum topics such as time-management and note-taking/study skills. All mentors could discuss these two issues with their mentees at every individual meeting for the first semester. Both topics could also be covered in the two mandatory workshops. Although the mentoring handbook includes sample scripts for each mentoring session, mentors have the freedom to create and use their own script. An example of a script that addresses how mentors could cover the two topics during the first semester is described below.

> As your mentor, I would like to discuss with you two challenges that you could face in your transition from high school to college. Developing effective time management and study habits are crucial skills you need to master in order to achieve academic success. In terms of time management, you are now responsible for setting your own priorities, you cannot expect your parents or professors to make you study and do your homework. You are a young adult and you will be treated like one by staff, administrators, and professors here at this university. If you have an exam on Friday morning and you go out to party on Thursday night, you and only you will be held accountable for your grade in the course. If you do not take detailed notes on the readings from your textbooks, you will probably not perform well on your exams. Therefore, I would strongly encourage you to purchase an academic planner and block out time for classes and at least 20 hours for studying and homework each week. Next, you should block out time for your work schedule (no more than 15 hours a week), and finally your social life (student organizations, parties, family, church, community, etc.).

> My recommendations for establishing effective study habits are to read your syllabus carefully and write all the due dates for your assignments in your academic planner. In terms of writing papers, I suggest you divide the paper into smaller components. For example if a five-page paper is due on Oct. 26th then you should write a draft two-page paper by Oct. 1st and give it to your professor so she can review it and give you feedback on it to make sure you are meeting her expectations. On the other hand, if you want to perform well on exams you should review your notes for each class every week and meet with the professors to show them your notes to make sure you are studying the information that they think is important. If you develop good time management and study skills, you could have an enjoyable and successful college experience.

Incorporating the Three Mentoring Cycles

In addition to constructing sample scripts, program directors could provide suggestions for incorporating the three mentoring cycles for teaching topics that relate to the hidden curriculum. For instance, the first individual mentoring meeting could occur by the third week of classes. The focus of the meeting could be to provide general advising (the advising cycle—transmission and acquisition of low degrees of institutional cultural capital and social capital) to mentees on time management and note-taking/study skills. For example, all the mentors (administrators/staff/faculty, peers, family members, and community advocates) could provide mentees strategies for balancing their academic and social commitments and give general advice for succeeding in school. Mentors could share with their mentees the same strategies and recommendations that are presented in the mentoring handbook, however, mentors could provide additional advice that is not in the academic mentoring handbook. As a result, mentees could hear the same information about the hidden curriculum from multiple perspectives. At the end of this meeting, a typical homework assignment could be to write an academic study plan that includes at least twenty hours devoted to studying each week.

The next mentoring meeting could occur around the seventh week of classes. Mentors could go over the academic study plan homework assignment with the mentees and talk about the grades students have received on papers and exams. At this meeting, mentors could go beyond just providing general advice they could advocate for their mentees (advocacy cycle—transmission and acquisition of medium degrees of institutional cultural capital and social capital). For instance, administrator/staff/faculty mentors could contact their colleagues in the academic support services to share with them the challenges their mentees are having with study skills (permission granted by mentees' confidentiality waiver form). The homework assignment could be to talk with a staff member of academic support services about time management and note-taking/study skills and they could obtain the signature of the staff member to verify their meeting.

The final individual meeting of the semester could take place by the eleventh week of the semester. At this meeting, mentors could review what the mentees learned from the staff members at the academic support services. The mentors now take an even more hands-on approach (apprenticeship cycle—transmission and acquisition of high degrees of institutional cultural capital and social capital) to helping their mentees. Mentors could conduct role-playing exercises with the mentees in which the mentors play the role of the students and the mentees play the role of the teachers as they practice the hidden curriculum scripts outlined in the mentoring handbook. The mentors could request that mentees show them, not just tell them, how they develop a realistic and effective study plan that balances the demands of their academic and social lives. In addition, mentees could also show their mentors the best methods for taking notes and studying for different types of exams. When mentees are able to practice the information that they learned, the information becomes their internalized knowledge about the culture of the university. As a result, they could become more confident and empowered students.

The above examples represent how all mentors throughout the first semester could cover two hidden curriculum related topics; the following examples are topics that could be covered during the next three semesters. For instance, the second semester could cover topics such as establishing meaningful relationships with faculty and positive relationships with classmates. The third semester could include conversations that explore majors, careers, and research and internship opportunities. The final semester could be more flexible and allow mentees to identify their concerns and fears about barriers that could prevent them from graduating from college. The fourth semester could also address the transition process of moving from formal mentoring to informal mentoring and graduating from the formal mentoring program.

The Evaluation Process

The academic mentoring handbook could be revised every two years based on feedback from mentors, mentees, and advisory board members. The evaluation process is critical to having an effective mentoring program that fulfills its mission statement and accomplishes the goals of increasing retention and graduation rates among underrepresented students. The evaluation process could include reflection papers by mentors and mentees, an end of the semester questionnaire that consist of quantitative and qualitative questions/items, a pre-assessment and post-assessment of students' knowledge about hidden curriculum topics, and a focus group comprised of mentors and mentees discussing best practices for teaching and learning institutional cultural capital and social capital.

Program directors could receive reflection papers (one to two pages) from all mentors and mentees after the individual mentoring meetings and two networking workshops every semester. The reflection papers explicitly address issues concerning topics related to the domain of the hidden curriculum. Mentors could submit a total of five reflection papers and mentees could submit a total of fourteen reflection papers each semester. The mentees write more papers because they meet with four different mentors once a month. In addition, at the end of each semester all mentors and mentees could be asked to complete a brief survey. The following represent possible sample survey items:

1. How would you rate the networking workshops? Scale: excellent, very good, good, satisfactory, poor
2. How was the quality of your experience as a participant in the mentoring program? Scale: excellent, very good, good, satisfactory, poor

3. The mentoring program director was accessible and easy to talk to and seek advice from when necessary. Scale: always, most of the time, somewhat, very little, not at all
4. How was your relationship with your mentor/mentee? Scale: excellent, very good, good, satisfactory, poor
5. Do you think the amount of time you spent with your mentee/mentor was sufficient? Scale: always, most of the time, somewhat, very little, not at all
6. What was most satisfying about participating in the mentoring program?
7. What was least satisfying about participating in the mentoring program?
8. What would you suggest to improve the mentoring program?

One of the key features of the evaluation process is that the mentoring directors could implement a pre-assessment and post-assessment that could allow directors to compare mentees' level of institutional cultural capital and social capital at the beginning of the mentoring program and at the end of the program. The pre-assessment could be given to students at the start of the first semester. Mentees could complete the post-assessment during the fourth semester. Examples of pre-assessment and post-assessment items are the following:

1. Describe three strategies for developing good time management skills. (institutional cultural capital)
2. Describe three strategies for developing effective study habits. (institutional cultural capital)
3. Describe three approaches for developing meaningful relationships with faculty. (social capital)
4. Describe three approaches for developing meaningful relationships with classmates. (social capital)
5. Describe three strategies for how to get a research internship with a professor. (institutional cultural capital and social capital)

Finally, mentors and mentees could participate in a focus group during the last networking workshop of the fourth semester. Mentors could be divided into smaller groups, such as all the community advocate mentors meeting together and all the student peer mentors meeting together. Mentees could be separated based on their grade levels (freshmen and sophomores). The main objective of the focus groups is to discuss what worked and did not work with helping students understand and navigate the hidden curriculum. Once the assessment data is analyzed, the directors and advisory board members could use the information to revise the academic mentoring handbook.

Krista Discovers New Hope

Krista ended her first semester with a 2.15 GPA but by the end of her sophomore year, she had increased her overall GPA to 2.65. However, she has not yet declared her major and is avoiding taking her required math and science courses. She continues to work with Dr. Fernandez but she only met with the professors Dr. Fernandez recommended once and she did not form a relationship with them. Krista is more active on campus. For instance, she is the secretary for the Black Pride student organization and she is an active member in two other student organizations. Krista lost her academic scholarship, and now works 10 hours a week at the campus library, 20 hours at a local retail store, and is studying approximately 12 hours a week. Krista's overall attitude has improved. She is no longer thinking about dropping out of school and credits her mentor and connections with other students of color with giving her new hope that she can finish college.

Dr. Fernandez is pleased with Krista's improvement in her academic performance and her overall positive disposition toward her college experience. However, Dr. Fernandez is a little disappointed that Krista did not make more of an effort to build relationships with her colleagues. She feels that Krista does not understand how important it is to have strong relationships with multiple professors. Dr. Fernandez has suggested that Krista reduce her involvement in student organizations and spend more time studying for her courses. She hopes that Krista will continue to develop and mature over the next two years but worries at times because Krista still struggles with understanding what she needs to do to succeed in the culture of higher education.

Notes

1a. Paul B. Thayer, "Retention of Students from First Generation and Low Income Backgrounds," (ERIC ED446633), *Opportunity Outlook* (May 2000): 2-8.

1b. Anat Gofen, "Family Capital: How First-Generation Higher Education Students Break the Intergenerational Cycle," *Family Relations* 58, no.1 (February 2009): 104-120.

2a. Thayer, "Retention of Students from First Generation and Low Income Backgrounds," 2000, 2-8.

2b. Gofen, "Family Capital: How First-Generation Higher Education Students Break the Intergenerational Cycle," 2009, 104-120.

3a. Thayer, "Retention of Students from First Generation and Low Income Backgrounds," 2000, 2-8.

3b. Gofen, "Family Capital: How First-Generation Higher Education Students Break the Intergenerational Cycle," 2009, 104-120.

4a. Buffy Smith, *Demystifying the Higher Education System: Rethinking Academic Cultural Capital, Social Capital, and the Academic Mentoring Process*, 2004.

4b. David P. James, "Developing and Designing a Mentoring Program in Higher Education." Workshop, annual meeting of the International Mentoring Association, Washington, DC, March 2001.

4c. Dawn Lewis and David James, "Using Faculty Members to Ensure Academic Success for Community College Students through Mentoring Best Practices: Benefits of the Faculty-Student Mentoring Program." Workshop, annual meeting of the International Mentoring Association, Orlando, Florida, March 2012.

4d. Connie Vance, *Fast Facts for Career Success in Nursing* (New York: Springer Publishing Company, 2011).

4e. Richard W. Riley, Marshall S. Smith, Terry K. Peterson, Adriana de Kanter, Diana Phillips, and Judy Wurtzel, *Yes, You Can: Establishing Mentoring Programs to Prepare Youth for College* (Washington, DC: U.S. Department of Education, 1998).

4f. Connie R. Tingson and Jennifer McGowan, *University Mentorship Program Guidebook,* Office of New Student Programs (University of Michigan, 2000).

4g. Jeanne Nakamura, David Shernoff and Charles Hooker, *Good Mentoring: Fostering Excellent Practice in Higher Education* (San Francisco, CA: Jossey-Bass, 2009).

5. The information and findings in this section was published in one of my earlier articles. Buffy Smith, "The Great Hope of Academic Mentoring Programs: The Unfulfilled Promise," *African American Research Perspectives* 11, no. 1 (Summer 2005): 169-181.

6a. Sharon Merriam, "Mentors and Protégés: A Critical Review of the Literature," *Adult Education Quarterly* 33 (1983): 161-173.

6b. Charles C. Healy, "An Operational Definition of Mentoring," in *Diversity in Higher Education: Mentoring and Diversity in Higher Education,* ed. Henry Frierson (Greenwich, CT: JAI Press Inc., 1997), 9-22.

7. Nathalie Friedman, *Mentors and Supervisors: A Report Prepared for the Institute of International Education* (New York: Columbia University, 1987).

8. Michael Galbraith and Norman Cohen, *Mentoring: New Strategies and Challenges* (San Francisco: Jossey-Bass, 1995).

9. Reginald Wilson, "Negative Mentoring: An Examination of the Phenomenon as it Affects Minority Students," in *Diversity in Higher Education: Mentoring and Diversity in Higher Education,* ed. Henry Frierson (Greenwich, CT: JAI Press Inc., 1997), 177-185, 178.

10. Morris Zelditch, "Mentor Roles in Graduate Studies," in *Diversity in Higher Education: Mentoring and Diversity in Higher Education,* ed. Henry Frierson (Greenwich, CT: JAI Press Inc, 1997), 23-37.

11. Zelditch, "Mentor Roles in Graduate Studies," 34.

12. Kathy Kram, *Mentoring at Work: Developmental Relationships in Organizational Life* (Glenview, IL: Scott, Foresman & Co., 1985).

13. Kram, *Mentoring at Work: Developmental Relationships in Organizational Life.*

14. Melanie Schockett and Marilyn Haring-Hidore, "Factor Analytic Support for Psychosocial and Vocational Mentoring Functions, *Psychological Reports* 57 (1985): 627-630.

15. Marilyn Haring, "Networking Mentoring as a Preferred Model for Guiding Programs for Underrepresented Students," in *Diversity in Higher Education: Mentoring and Diversity in Higher Education,* ed. Henry Frierson (Greenwich, CT: JAI Press Inc, 1997), 63-76, 64.

16. Haring, "Networking Mentoring as a Preferred Model for Guiding Programs for Underrepresented Students," 63-76, 64.

17a. William Bergquist, *The Four Cultures of the Academy: Insights and Strategies for Improving Leadership in Collegiate Organizations* (San Francisco: Jossey-Bass, 1992).

17b. Marie Wunsch, "New Directions for Mentoring: An Organizational Development Perspective," *New Directions for Teaching and Learning* 57 (1994): 9-13.

18. Wilson, "Negative Mentoring: An Examination of the Phenomenon as it Affects Minority Students," 177-185, 178.

19. Nancy Collins, *Professional Women and Their Mentors: A Practical Guide to Mentoring for the Woman Who Wants to Get Ahead* (Englewood Cliffs, NJ: Prentice Hall, Inc., 1983).

20. Theresa McCormick, "An Analysis of Five Pitfalls of Traditional Mentoring for People on the Margins in Higher Education," in *Diversity in Higher Education: Mentoring and Diversity in Higher Education,* ed. Henry Frierson (Greenwich, CT: JAI Press, Inc., 1997), 187-202, 191.

21. Wilson, "Negative Mentoring: An Examination of the Phenomenon as it Affects Minority Students," 177-185, 184.

22. Pamela Knox and Thomas McGovern, "Mentoring Women in Academia," *Teaching of Psychology* 15, no. 1 (1988): 39-41.

23. Mary Otto. "Mentoring: An Adult Developmental Perspective," *New Directions for Teaching and Learning* 57 (1994): 15-24.

24. Haring, "Networking Mentoring as a Preferred Model for Guiding Programs for Underrepresented Students," 63-76.

25. Haring, "Networking Mentoring as a Preferred Model for Guiding Programs for Underrepresented Students," 64.

26. Haring, "Networking Mentoring as a Preferred Model for Guiding Programs for Underrepresented Students," 63-76.

27. Haring, "Networking Mentoring as a Preferred Model for Guiding Programs for Underrepresented Students," 64-67.

28. Yvonne Gonzales-Rodriguez, "Mentoring to Diversity: A Multicultural Approach," *New Directions for Adult and Continuing Education* 66 (1995): 69-77.

29. Haring, "Networking Mentoring as a Preferred Model for Guiding Programs for Underrepresented Students," 63-76.

30. Haring, "Networking Mentoring as a Preferred Model for Guiding Programs for Underrepresented Students," 68.

31. Haring, "Networking Mentoring as a Preferred Model for Guiding Programs for Underrepresented Students," 68-69.

32. Haring, "Networking Mentoring as a Preferred Model for Guiding Programs for Underrepresented Students," 69-70.

33a. David P. James, "Developing and Designing a Mentoring Program in Higher Education."

33b. Richard W. Riley, Marshall S. Smith, Terry K. Peterson, Adriana de Kanter, Diana Phillips, and Judy Wurtzel, *Yes, You Can: Establishing Mentoring Programs to Prepare Youth for College.*

33c. Dawn Lewis and David James, "Using Faculty Members to Ensure Academic Success for Community College Students through Mentoring Best Practices: Benefits of the Faculty-Student Mentoring Program."

33d. Connie Vance, *Fast Facts for Career Success in Nursing.*

33e. Nakamura, Shernoff and Hooker, *Good Mentoring: Fostering Excellent Practice in Higher Education*.

34a. James, "Developing and Designing a Mentoring Program in Higher Education."

34b. Lewis and James, "Using Faculty Members to Ensure Academic Success for Community College Students through Mentoring Best Practices: Benefits of the Faculty-Student Mentoring Program."

34c. Connie Vance, *Fast Facts for Career Success in Nursing*.

34d. Nakamura, Shernoff and Hooker, *Good Mentoring: Fostering Excellent Practice in Higher Education*.

34e. Buffy Smith, *Demystifying the Higher Education System: Rethinking Academic Cultural Capital, Social Capital, and the Academic Mentoring Process*, 2004.

35. Belle Liang and Jennifer West, "Youth Mentoring: Do Race and Ethnicity Really Matter?" *Research in Action* 9, 3-22 (Alexandria, VA: Mentor/National Mentoring Partnership, 2007).

36. Liang and West, "Youth Mentoring: Do Race and Ethnicity Really Matter?"

37a. Lisa Delpit, *Other People's Children: Cultural Conflict in the Classroom* (New York: The New Press, 1995).

37b. Gloria Ladson-Billings, "Toward a Theory of Culturally Relevant Pedagogy," *American Educational Research Journal* 32, no. 3 (1995): 465-591.

37c. Claude Steele, "Stereotype Threat and Black College Student," *About Campus* (May/June 1999): 2-4.

37d. Louis Gallien and Marshalita Peterson, *Instructing and Mentoring the African American College Student* (Boston, MA: Pearson Education, Inc., 2005).

38a. Delpit, *Other People's Children: Cultural Conflict in the Classroom*.

38b. Ladson-Billings, "Toward a Theory of Culturally Relevant Pedagogy," 465-591.

38c. Steele, "Stereotype Threat and Black College Student," 2-4.

38d. Gallien and Peterson, *Instructing and Mentoring the African American College Student*.

39a. Delpit, *Other People's Children: Cultural Conflict in the Classroom*.

39b. Ladson-Billings, "Toward a Theory of Culturally Relevant Pedagogy," 465-591.

39c. Steele, "Stereotype Threat and Black College Student," 2-4.

39d. Gallien and Peterson, *Instructing and Mentoring the African American College Student*.

40. Liang and West, "Youth Mentoring: Do Race and Ethnicity Really Matter?"

41a. Maryann Jacobi, "Mentoring and Undergraduate Academic Success: A Literature Review," *Review of Educational Research* 61, no. 4 (1991): 505-532.

41b. Liang and West, "Youth Mentoring: Do Race and Ethnicity Really Matter?"

42. Gofen, "Family Capital: How First-Generation Higher Education Students Break the Intergenerational Cycle."

43. *The American Heritage College Dictionary*, 3rd edition (Boston, MA: Houghton Mifflin Company, 2000), 9.

44. Richard Schaefer, *Racial and Ethnic Groups* (Boston, MA: Pearson, 2011), 423.

Chapter 5

Play to Win: Learn the Rules

The purpose of this chapter is to offer strategies to underserved students on how to thrive in college. The format is structured as an advice column to Dr. Mentor who dispenses wisdom based on her mentoring experience and the experiences of her former students and mentees. [1]

Expert on American Indians Affairs

Dear Dr. Mentor,

I am the only American Indian (Cherokee) in the class and my classmates keep asking me questions about Indian culture. I am getting really tired of being the resident expert on American Indian issues. What could I do to let them know that they are making me feel uncomfortable?

Expert on American Indian Affairs

Dear Expert on American Indian Affairs,

I am surprised you do not know everything about American Indian culture. As an African American woman, I know everything there is to know about African-American women. In fact, I carry the pocketsize Black Women Reference Book and when people ask a Black women factoid I can quickly give them a response. When I do not know the answer to a question, I call the 24 hours Black Women Facts Hotline, 1-800-BW-FACTS. I feel comfortable citing from my reference book because it is updated every year at the Annual What is New in Black Culture Conference. You might want to investigate whether American Indians hold an annual conference, publish a reference book, or provide a facts hotline; it could help you tremendously; it has helped me.

Seriously, you have a right to feel frustrated with how your classmates are treating you. I know it is tempting to yell at them, "It is not my responsibility to educate all of you people about my culture. I had to learn your culture without your help so, why can't you learn my culture without my help?" It might feel good to say that but the reality is they will label you as an overly sensitive and angry American Indian. I would recommend a few things: (1) always tell people that your ethnicity is just as complex and diverse as their ethnic groups, (2) your opinion is just that: your opinion, and it does not represent all the perspectives within your ethnic group, (3) encourage them to read one of your favorite books written by an American Indian, (4) engage with them in a conversation about their ethnic group, and (5) let them know you are open to establishing a friendship with them but you do not want to be treated or interviewed as an "ethnic subject."

It is important to make sure that you respond at all times in a respectful yet direct way to let people know you appreciate their interest in your culture but you are not a spokesperson for your ethnic group. You want the relationship to be based more on your other wonderful characteristics (e.g., kindness and sense of humor) than your ethnic identity. I believe you can have a friendly, open, and honest conversation with your classmates about why certain questions make you uncomfortable. Once students have a heart-to-heart conversation about an issue, behaviors usually change, which provides the ideal conditions for forming genuine friendships.

I encourage you not to give up on your classmates because they need you and you need them to develop more fully as human beings.

Too Sensitive

Dear Dr. Mentor,

I am a sophomore Latina female student and I have a sociology professor who makes awkward comments in class about racial groups. For example, she said Mexican women are more likely to drop out of school because they want to raise families and that is more important to them than school. As a proud Latina who loves her family and plans to graduate from college, I was offended by her comments. I talked to my other Latina friends about the teacher's comments and they said that she was a racist. My friends think I should just ignore the comments if I want to pass the class with a good grade. I want to talk to her about the comments but she does not seem very friendly. Maybe, I am too sensitive and I should just ignore her comments. Dr. Mentor, what should I do?

Too Sensitive

Dear Too Sensitive,

I wish I could tell you that I cannot believe your professor made those remarks. However, I know from personal experience that some professors are not culturally competent. There is not one right way to respond to these types of comments. You could ask yourself if these are comments you could ignore and still maintain a positive relationship with your professor, or do you feel that these comments are deal breakers and you can no longer remain silent and be engaged in class discussions? If you decide they are deal breakers that jeopardize your ability to pursue a positive relationship with your professor, then I would recommend you discuss the issue with the professor.

Although you might feel a righteous outrage toward the professor because of her culturally insensitive comments, you want to be careful how you start the conversation. First, you want to make sure you schedule an appointment to meet with the professor during her office hours. Next, you cannot demonstrate anger during your meeting; it is important to keep a respectful and calm tone. As you talk about the comments make sure you ask clarifying questions and do not make accusatory statements. For instance, you could say the following:

> Dr. Washington, I appreciate you taking the time to talk with me this afternoon. I am enjoying your class. I am here today because I misunderstood part of your lecture last Wednesday. I believe I could have written inaccurate notes; I have in my notebook that, "Mexicans are more likely to drop out of school because they would rather raise families and that is more important than school." As a Latina, I was a little confused by the statement because it does not reflect my experience or the experiences of my Mexican friends. I probably misinterpreted the lecture, therefore, could you please explain to me what I should have written in my notes about that issue?

Hopefully, the professor will recognize she made a generalization and then modify her statement with qualifiers and state that she did not mean to imply that the statement was true for all Mexican women, nor did she want to suggest Mexican families do not value education. Usually, if you show respect, humility, and ask clarifying types of questions, you are less likely to offend professors. Remember, professors misspeak and make mistakes like everyone else. When you make inaccurate statements, you would want your professors to allow you to clarify your statements; therefore, you should extend the same courtesy to them. I would encourage you to spend less time on labeling professors racists or nonracists; rather, focus more attention on what you could do to foster a positive relationship with your professors.

Wanna Be Research Assistant

Dear Dr. Mentor,

I am a psychology major and I want to attend graduate school when I complete my undergraduate degree. Ultimately, I want to earn my Ph.D. in clinical psychology. One of my professors is a renowned professor in the field and I want to work with him on one of his research projects. He has a reputation of being a "hard-nose" when it comes to his research assistants but I do not care; I still want to work with him. I know working with him will help me get into top graduate programs. However, it does not appear that he hires students of color or women as research assistants. I do not know what I should do to let him know that I desperately want to work with him. Please help me, Dr. Mentor.

Wanna Be Research Assistant

Dear Wanna Be Research Assistant,

You could rearrange your class schedule around his classes and offer to serve as his personal assistant. You could carry his briefcase and books to class. You could help him update his lectures with multimedia interactive features. You could clean his office, make copies, file folders, return books to the library, and buy his lunch and hope that he recognizes your potential as a promising young scholar.

All jokes aside, you could maintain some integrity and simply ask the professor if he is hiring new research assistants. If he says, yes, you should let him know you have a strong interest in serving as his research assistant. You should be prepared to explain what specific research project you want to work on with him. You should give him your résumé and a one-page essay describing the skills you would bring to his research team.

However, if your professor clearly states that he does not have plans to hire additional research assistants, you should politely thank him for his time, and contact other professors who might have research opportunities for you. You should not assume that the reason he does not want to work with you is due to your race or gender. If he is a famous professor, I am sure he has said "no" to White male students who also wanted to work with him. Many students make the mistake of only wanting to work with the most popular professors. As a result, students miss the opportunity to gain valuable research experience with other wonderful professors.

Remember, you could still be accepted to a top tier graduate program even if you do not work with a famous professor. Your goal should be to establish strong positive relationships with at least four professors in your college career (you usually need three recommendation letters). You could ask former professors if you could work with them on a research project. It is important to build social capital with multiple professors so please do not focus on networking with just one professor. You should learn to validate yourself and recognize your inner greatness. You do not need to work with a renowned professor in order to be a successful clinical psychologist. You determine your destiny; do not give that power to anyone else.

Proud Chemistry Major

Dear Dr. Mentor,

I just declared chemistry as my major. I think this is the most important day of my undergraduate career. I am now taking classes I love and I never have to take another English literature course again. I plan to go to medical school at an Ivy League.

However, I am having problems working with my assigned research lab partner. My partner is a White male who believes he is always right, even when he is clearly wrong. Another thing I do not like about my partner is that he presents himself to our White male professor as the one who is doing most of the work, which is clearly not the case.

The professor seems to have a better relationship with my partner than me. I often think that they have a special relationship because they are both White males and I am a Hmong female. I need advice on what I could do to stop my partner from taking credit for my hard work. Please, Dr. Mentor, help me find my voice.

Proud Chemistry Major

Dear Proud Chemistry Major,

I want to share with you some strategies for helping you develop into a strong confident woman who is not afraid of the spotlight. I recommend that you keep a separate report from your partner on the hours you work and the tasks you complete. You could request a one-on-one meeting with your professor at least once a month. During each meeting you could present your report and give an update on the research project.

You have to demonstrate to your professor you are passionate about his research project and that there is no task too small or big that you cannot successfully complete. In addition, you could express interest in publishing with him and offer to help with the literature review. I would not spend a lot of time trying to get your partner to respect you. Your energy needs to be devoted to performing excellent work in the lab and being more vocal about your accomplishments.

Even if you are an introvert or shy, you have to be confident and share your achievements with your research supervisor/professor. The more confidence you display, the more confidence your professor will have in you. You should not develop a negative attitude toward your partner. Do not play by his rules. People who think they have to demean and belittle others to advance in life will never achieve inner joy, peace, and contentment. Remember, if you strive for excellence and respectfully promote your achievements, you will thrive in college and life.

I am Not a "D" Student

Dear Dr. Mentor,

My teacher gave me a "D" on my first economics exam. I have never received anything lower than a "C" in my previous courses. I did not study as much as I should have but I do not think I deserve a "D." I know I should go talk with the professor but she is intimidating.

I am not a "D" student but I am afraid that when she goes over the exam with me I am going to feel stupid. Should I get help now and feel dumb, or should I wait until the next exam to meet with the professor? I am sure I will do better on the second exam. What do you think I should do?

I am Not a "D" Student

Dear I am Not a "D" Student,

First, you should not be demoralized by your exam grade. I think you should immediately schedule an appointment with your economics professor to discuss the exam. I hope you will not allow your fear to prevent you from establishing a good relationship with her.

Many students feel intimidated by their professors at first but once students get to know their professors they become more comfortable around them. Your professors want to help you but you must first reach out to them. Throughout the meeting, you should remain respectful, calm, and take full responsibility for your exam score. You should admit to the professor you did not effectively study for the exam and you would like her to give you tips on how to study better for the next exam.

Remember, your professor did not give you the grade; you earned the grade. You should not make excuses for your low grade; rather you should make a commitment to improve your grade on the next exam. You should not try to negotiate additional points for the exam but it is okay to ask the professor if she has an extra credit policy.

The main reason you do not want to wait until the next exam before you meet with the professor is that you could likely make the same types of mistakes you made on the first exam. Most professors are willing to spend the time and energy that is necessary to help students be successful in their classes. As a student you must ask for assistance early and often and you will receive the resources and help you seek. Finally, you should never equate your performance in a class with your overall self-worth as a human; grades do not define a person's humanity.

Mentoring Mismatch

Dear Dr. Mentor,

Recently, I joined a research mentoring program. I was assigned a mentor two months ago and I do not believe we are a good match for one another. Every time we meet, my mentor reminds me of how lucky I am to have her as my mentor. She never asks me about my academic and social interests. She only talks about herself and her research.

I have asked the professor if I can assist her with one of her research projects but she said that I did not have the advanced research skills to help her. Instead, she said I could help type her lecture notes and create labels for office folders. I do not see any benefit of having her as a mentor. I am thinking about quitting the program if I cannot change mentors. What advice could you offer me?

Mentoring Mismatch

Dear Mentoring Mismatch,

I do not see the problem with listening attentively and hanging on every word your mentor utters. After all, we mentors have impeccable wisdom to share with young people. If you could only stop thinking about your need to be heard and acknowledged, you would have an enjoyable mentoring experience.

Well, of course mentoring programs are supposed to be student-centered. Your mentor should have learned that in her mentoring training sessions. You were assigned to be your professor's mentee, not her personal office assistant. I wish I could give you strategies on how to get your mentor to minimize how much she talks about her life, but I also suffer from that same condition. It is a well-known hazard of the profession.

However, what concerns me the most is that you are not gaining research experience. Even if you have not taken a research methods class, you can do more than type lecture notes and create labels for folders. You should contact the mentoring program director and update her/him on your mentoring experience. The director has the authority to remind your mentor of her role and responsibilities to you and the program.

As a mentee, you should not confront your mentor; allow the director to address your concerns with the mentor. After the conversation between the director and mentor, the director will inform you if you will remain with your current mentor or be reassigned to another mentor. If you keep your original mentor, you should work hard to convince her that you possess both the passion and skills to conduct research. On the other hand, if you are matched with another mentor you will still need to do the same.

I would recommend that you ignore your mentor's peculiar personality traits and quirks and focus more on whether you are receiving research opportunities. As a young scholar, you have to work effectively with professors who embody different personality characteristics. It is a humbling reminder that we all have traits that are problematic for other people. One sign of personal and professional development and growth is the ability to nurture meaningful relationships with people we perceive to be radically different from ourselves. The beauty of our humanity is our diversity.

Seeking Favoritism

Dear Dr. Mentor,

I am the first person in my family to attend college and I am enjoying my college experience. In fact, last semester I was invited to join a research team. My professor is well known in her field of criminal justice. I am lucky to work with her. She is the research mentor for three other undergraduate students. My mentor is nice but I think she likes the other three undergraduates better than me. The professor and the other three students seem to have a special bond. I do not know how this happened since we all joined the research team at the same time.

I know the other students have had opportunities to socialize with the professor and her family at her home. I was invited but I had to work on both occasions. I need to work as many hours as I can because I cannot depend on my family for financial support and I have already maxed out my student loans for this year. I want to hang out with my professor just like my peers, but what can I do when I am working when I am not in classes? Please help me, Dr. Mentor.

Seeking Favoritism

Dear Seeking Favoritism,

It is quite comforting to know that some students actually want to spend time getting to know their professors. My students try to avoid me like a bubonic plague. I even offer students candy to come see me during office hours but my students are too smart to be bribed. I sit in my lonely office and listen to my colleague next door engage in warm and friendly conversations with her students.

Well, I do not want to bore you with my problems, back to your letter. I understand your need to work many hours to pay for school. I was a first-generation college student a long time ago and I am still paying back my student loans. However, I also know that you need to devote more time to develop your relationship with your research mentor. I would encourage you to have a one-on-one conversation with your mentor about your family background and work situation. You should express how much you would like to participate in the social gatherings at her home if you did not have to work. Next, you could ask her if you could treat her to lunch within the next two weeks. She will be impressed with the kind gesture (most likely she will not allow you to pay for her lunch).

In addition to inviting your mentor to lunch, you could also send her a thank you card for serving as your research mentor. You could write a detailed message explaining what you learned by working on the project. You could also write a letter to your mentor's department chair to express your gratitude for her. I do not believe your mentor dislikes you; rather, I think she has not had the privilege to get to know you better.

Once you take the initiative to engage in an open and honest conversation with her about why you cannot attend many after school gatherings, I am sure you and your mentor will find other opportunities to get together and socialize with one another. You could also frequently visit your mentor during her office hours and talk about academic and non-academic matters. Remember, every time you meet with your mentor you have an opportunity to connect with her. In order to build social capital with your professor, you need to see her often and have meaningful conversations with her.

I believe it is only a matter of time before you win the favor of your mentor. Although earning favor with others is good, it is more important to enjoy the favor that comes from your creator and within yourself.

Positive Feedback

Dear Dr. Mentor,

I am writing because I do not know how to talk with my mentor about giving me positive feedback on my research proposal. I have rewritten the proposal three times and he is still not happy. At each meeting, he tells me I am making some progress but I am a long way from having a polished proposal. I am so tired of working on this proposal I just want to start the research project. I need to complete the research project by the end of this summer because I am applying to Ph.D. programs next year. The proposal is never going to be perfect in his eyes. I cannot win. It would help if he gave me a little encouragement along the way. He does not motivate me. I do not know if I can continue to work with him and his negative vibes. Please help me, Dr. Mentor.

Positive Feedback

Dear Positive Feedback,

This letter will probably not uplift your spirit. I have a well earned reputation for being pessimistic. Of course, I would describe myself as being a realist. I think of it as a special gift that I can see problems before other people experience the problem. I think it is a sixth sense. I hope you do not dismiss my advice because you think I am crazy (I am *special*, not crazy). The issue you have with your mentor is common. Most mentees desire a lot of praise regarding their work. It is not your generation's fault; you have been socialized to believe everyone is a superstar and winner. Therefore, when you have a professor tell you to rewrite a proposal, the comments are perceived to be harsh.

However, I would encourage you to rethink what constitutes positive feedback. You could ask yourself the following questions.

(1) Is the proposal stronger after each revision?
(2) Does the mentor provide detailed comments/suggestions throughout your proposal on how to improve it?

If you answered "yes" to both questions, I believe you have a good mentor who cares about your overall development as an academic writer. Trust me, if your mentor did not take a personal interest in you, he would not request multiple revisions. He is not being mean or trying to demoralize you. Rather, he is preparing you to become a successful writer in graduate school. I would encourage you to ask your mentor for sample research proposals that you could use as a model as you revise your paper again.

At your next meeting, you could thank your mentor for caring enough to take the time to help you become a better scholar. If you learn the techniques and skills of good academic writing as an undergraduate you will thrive in your Ph.D. program. The encouragement and positive feedback you desire from others should first come from within you. You should celebrate your achievements and remind yourself that your best days are yet to be lived. Thus, you should not quit the program, replace your mentor, and most importantly, never give up on yourself.

Acting White

Dear Dr. Mentor,

I am an African-American female college student at a large, predominantly white university. I was the valedictorian of my high school. I do not want to sound arrogant but I am brilliant. However, my high I.Q. does not protect me from being teased by White and Black peers as "acting white."

I am proud to be an African-American female so I am always angry when I hear those remarks. I wish I could laugh and say that the comments do not hurt me. However, those words do wound me at my core. Could you please provide me advice on how to respond to my peers?

Acting White

Dear Acting White,

In the past, I have had people make similar comments to me. Now, when someone accuses me of "acting white," I quickly take out my NAACP membership card to show them. It is my "get out of 'acting white' jail card." It works all the time.

Another approach you might take is to invite your peers to join a Black history book club with you. Hopefully, if they read some books about the numerous scholars and scientists within the Black community, they will learn that you are not an anomaly. Unfortunately, too many people still believe the myth that there are distinct "races" and that some races are intellectually superior to others. In fact, many scientists, based on sound research, now argue that there are no genetic markers found in one race that are not found in another race. Furthermore, a person's I.Q. is more influenced by his/her social class background than his/her socially constructed racial identity.

Well, I will get off my soap box regarding the social construction of race but remember that your peers are making comments that are not grounded in science. You should continue to excel in your academics and not get distracted by a few people who discourage you because of their lack of knowledge or jealousy.

In addition, you might want to invite some of your peers to join your study group. I have discovered that if you remain respectful and kind to people who make disparaging comments to you, you could win them over or expose them. You should not change your behavior or apologize for being smart. You are a young, intelligent, and gifted Black female scholar but you are not the first, nor will you be the last and that is something to celebrate. You should never allow negative comments to diminish your self-worth.

Too Busy

Dear Dr. Mentor,

I have a time management issue with my mentor. I am an active leader on campus. I am on the executive board of four major student organizations on campus. As a student leader, I have been afforded wonderful opportunities. I have also built social networks with faculty, staff, and administrators through my organizations.

I have never had a time management problem until last semester when I joined the mentoring program. I was assigned a mentor in my major. Initially, I was excited to work with the professor but now I am having second thoughts because we have conflicting schedules. My mentor is never available to meet with me at a time that works for me.

I would love to continue in the mentoring program but he is too busy to meet with me. Should I quit the program? What do you think, Dr. Mentor?

Too Busy

Dear Too Busy,

I will keep my response short because I do not have a lot of time to write a long letter. After all I am an extremely important faculty member, don't you know that? Unfortunately, some faculty members actually feel they are too busy to talk with students. I hope your mentor does not embody that attitude. It is more likely that you and your mentor are experiencing problems with finding a time to meet because of both of your hectic schedules.

Therefore, I recommend that you first reflect on why you joined the mentoring program. You could create a detailed list of the benefits for joining the program. You could ask yourself if the mentoring program could help you advance your overall academic and career goals. You could consider your needs and determine if the mentoring program is a good fit for you at this time. Hopefully, you would recognize the true value of the program and want to continue to participate in it.

If you decide you would like to stay in the program, you should immediately contact the program director and explain the situation to her/him. The director is the best person to evaluate whether you and your mentor are a good match. I am confident that you would easily find another mentor because most administrators, staff, and faculty in higher education are committed to mentoring young people. Many of us enter the profession with a passion for teaching, research, and empowering students to achieve their personal and academic goals. You are our top priority; please do not quit the program.

General Advice to Mentees

Dear Mentees,

I have enjoyed reading your letters. At this time, I would like to share with you some final thoughts on how you could build social capital with faculty, staff, and administrators. First, you have to recognize that developing strong trusting relationships take time and hard work but the rewards are worth it. In order to create a trusting mentoring relationship, you need to get to know your mentor as a person and let her/him get to know you. You must learn to be vulnerable and explicitly express your academic and social needs to your mentor. Your mentor cannot help you if you do not let her/him know the issues you are struggling with inside and outside of school. You have to make the commitment to learn the implicit and explicit expectations of all your professors. If you are unclear about the expectations, keep asking questions until you are clear about them. You need to develop a relationship with professors before there is a crisis. As a mentee, you have to trust your mentor and believe that she/he wants what is best for you.

In addition to establishing trust, good mentoring relationships require some form of reciprocity. As a mentee, you could think of creative ways to express your appreciation to your mentor (e.g., funny electronic thank you cards). You could also offer to share your expertise and knowledge in an area with your mentor (e.g., help mentors enhance their technological knowledge and skills). You could impress your mentor if you demonstrate genuine interest in her/his research projects and provide her/him with articles that relate to her/his research.

Third, you need to listen attentively to your mentor and make some changes in your behavior based on her/his recommendations. You do not have to agree with or implement all of your mentor's suggestions but you should demonstrate that you have heard and taken some of your mentor's feedback into serious consideration. Mentors do not expect their mentees to become "yes, sir" or "yes, ma'am" robots but it is reasonable for mentors to expect their mentees to show consistent and measurable progress toward their academic goals. If mentees do not show personal and academic development, it could lead to misunderstandings, frustration, greater emotional distance, and an overall negative mentoring experience.

Finally, I have included below a list of characteristics and skills I believe mentees should embody in order to understand and navigate the hidden curriculum and attract good mentors.

- Intellectually Curious

- Proactive

- Self-Motivated

- Reliable

- Self-Directed

- Open-Minded

- Honest

- Self-Reflective

- Teachable

- Demonstrates Good Listening Skills

- Demonstrates Sense of Humor

- Persistent

- Full of Integrity

- Committed

- Conscientious

- Respectful

- Grateful

- Responsible

- Accepts Critical Feedback

- Demonstrates Good Communication and Interpersonal Skills

- Demonstrates Effective Time Management Skills

- Demonstrates Effective Study Skills

- Confident

- Demonstrates Campus Engagement

If you do not currently possess all of these traits, do not worry; it is not too late to develop them within a strong mentoring relationship. I want you to know that Dr. Mentor believes in you and that no matter how difficult your journey might seem now, you will achieve success. Do not give up! Once you accomplish your goals it will be your responsibility to allow others to stand on your shoulders as they reach for their stars. The cycle of mentoring each generation cannot be broken.

Note

1. Some of the ideas presented in this chapter were shared with me by former students and mentees. I changed the stories to protect students' confidentiality. I am grateful to the following students for sharing their mentoring experiences with me Amy Westmoreland, Adam Baker, Clemon Dabney and Breanna Alston.

Chapter 6

Overcoming Mentoring Barriers: Do Not Give Up

The goal of this chapter is to provide encouragement and advice to mentors, mentoring program directors, and administrators. Dr. Mentor is back to help mentors and program directors successfully triumph over common challenges of the mentoring process. The strategies shared in this chapter are based on Dr. Mentor's and her colleague's experiences.[1]

I am Finished

Dear Dr. Mentor,

I am a faculty member at a large public university. I have been an informal mentor to several students. However, this year I decided to join the university's formal mentoring program. I was matched with a sophomore student who appears to be disengaged in our mentoring relationship. Our first meeting was at the mentoring orientation luncheon. I thought we had a good connection. I was eager to meet her for our one-on-one meeting. I emailed her the next day and it took us approximately three weeks before we could agree upon a date that worked for both of us. My mentee is an active student leader on campus.

During our meeting, she seemed disinterested and was constantly checking the time on her cell phone. I asked her if she had another important meeting to attend. She quickly replied that she would need to leave soon because she is the secretary of a student organization and the club meeting would start in twenty minutes. I was a little perturbed by her response and I asked her why she joined the mentoring program. She stated that many of her friends thought it was a cool program and it would look good on her résumé.

I could no longer take it, so I politely ended our meeting to allow her to attend her more important student organization meeting. I suggested we meet again soon. I informed her that I wanted her to take the initiative to contact me with the dates and times she is available to meet. Well, I have been waiting for approximately three weeks and she has not emailed me once. I know I should not say this but I am ready to end our formal mentoring relationship. I have never experienced these types of problems with my informal mentoring relationships. What are your recommendations for improving my formal mentoring relationship?

I am Finished

Dear I am Finished,

I appreciate your commitment, generosity, compassion, and the numerous selfless acts of kindness you express toward me. I am blessed to have an awesome and cool mentor, like you. You rock!

Now, that is what your mentee should say to you on a regular basis, but you probably will not hear those sentiments until your retirement party. I understand your frustration with your mentee's lack of engagement in your relationship. Unfortunately, many mentees do not recognize that mentoring is a partnership and that all participants are responsible for doing their part to create and maintain the relationship. I acknowledge that your partner is not carrying her weight but I plead with you to not give up on her.

I believe if you can extend your patience a little longer, you will be able to improve your relationship and teach her some valuable skills that will help her increase her social capital. My recommendations are the following:

(1) Email the mentoring program director and share your concerns with her and ask her for suggestions on fun activities you could engage in to build rapport with the student. You should also request that the director help encourage the mentee to make your mentoring meetings a high priority. In addition, the program director should remind the student of her responsibilities as a mentee.

(2) Email your mentee to schedule another meeting and let her know that you want to talk with her for approximately forty-five minutes on strengthening your mentoring partnership (you will use activities recommended by the program director).

(3) Once you meet with your mentee let her know at least two characteristics you admire about her and provide two reasons why you specifically want to serve as her mentor.

(4) You should tell your mentee that you are committed to her as a student and person. However, the one requirement you should request from her is that she meets with you once a month for at least one hour per meeting. You should also emphasize that you want your mentoring partnership to be strong, which would require your mentee to be equally dedicated to the mentoring process.

(5) During each meeting, you should first affirm your mentee's self-worth by actively listening and showing genuine interest in her overall physical, mental, and spiritual well-being. Next, you can address other concerns/issues and goals related to your mentee's overall academic success. If you build a strong trusting relationship with your mentee, you will be able to resolve whatever problem arises within the relationship.

Formal mentoring relationships are more problematic than informal relationships, but they are still rewarding. As a mentor, you should not give up on more challenging mentees because these students need you even more than your super engaged easy-going mentees. Remember, one of your tasks as a mentor is to help your mentee acquire social capital. If she is unable to establish social capital with you, how will she be able to build it with other administrators, staff, and faculty on campus? Your mentee needs you even if she currently lacks the social skills to express her needs and show appreciation.

Let us fast forward and imagine we are at your retirement party. Reflect on the range of emotions you would feel when your mentee brags about her wonderful mentor who never gave up on her even during the most difficult times of the relationship. I hope you finish the race you started as her mentor, you will never regret it and neither will your mentee.

Time Management Drill Sergeant

Dear Dr. Mentor,

I am an academic advisor and I have noticed a common problem among students of color on my campus, a predominantly white institution (PWI). I have observed that many of my advisees of color are student leaders within ethnically-centered organizations. Please do not misunderstand me, I believe it is wonderful that they are leaders in these important organizations but my fear is that the students are spending too much time on projects and events related to their student organizations and their academic grades are suffering as a result.

I have tried to warn them about the consequences of their poor time management skills but they do not seem to get it. I offer workshops on time management skills but they do not show up. I do not want to be known as the time management drill sergeant but these students are placing their social life at a higher priority than their academic life. Do you have any suggestions for what I could do to help my students?

Time Management Drill Sergeant

Dear Time Management Drill Sergeant,

I salute you! I think some students need to attend a time management boot camp. For instance, imagine if every time a student missed class without a valid documented excuse they would have to do fifty sit-ups, and when they did not turn in a homework assignment on time they would have to do fifty push-ups for everyday that it is late. It would certainly help them get into better academic and physical shape. However, I foresee many administrative and legal problems with creating a boot camp environment on college campuses. Therefore, we need to think of options that are more realistic.

Since the students do not attend your time management workshops, perhaps you could bring the workshops to them. In other words, you could volunteer to offer a time management and study skills workshop at one of their student organization meetings. In addition, I think you could give a mini-time management workshop to your advisees during your regular advising sessions. The two suggestions require more flexibility and creativity on your part as the advisor but sometimes that is necessary in order to effectively advise and mentor students.

It is important to remember that many students of color join organizations that celebrate their ethnic culture in order to feel less isolated and alienated on predominantly white college campuses. As an advisor and mentor, you should affirm their ethnic culture and encourage them to be actively involved in one or two student organizations.

You can be culturally sensitive and firm when you provide them strategies for improving their time management and study skills. It is okay to assertively remind them that their highest priority should be to excel in their classes. Your mission should you choose to accept it is to graduate your cadets with honors and prepare them with skills that will help them succeed in their careers and life. I hope you accept this important mission because if you do not your students could self-destruct without your intentional mentoring.

He Knows Everything

Dear Dr. Mentor,

I do not know if you have ever experienced this but I have a mentee who is beyond mentoring. My mentee knows everything; at least, that is his attitude. If I tell him to go left, he goes right; he does his own thing. I think it is a waste of my valuable time to work with a young person who does not listen to my advice. I am not being egoistical but I do know a little more than he does but he refuses to let me guide him. Do you have any strategies for how to handle a "know-it-all" mentee?

He Knows Everything

Dear He Knows Everything,

I can certainly relate to you. Yes, I have had several students like your mentee. In fact, I have grown a lot of gray hair dealing with students who resist my wisdom. Therefore, as mentors we need to be creative in how we interact with our "know-it-all" mentees.

The first strategy for how to handle your mentee is do not interpret his words and behaviors as a personal sign of disrespect to you. You have to remind yourself that you are not responsible for and you cannot control your mentee's opposition and defiance. As mentors, we can make a difference but we are not miracle workers. If a student does not want to be helped, you cannot help him, but do not internalize it as a personal failure.

The second strategy is to allow your mentee to have the freedom to disagree with your opinion on the path he should follow. It was very difficult for me to do this because I have some control issues. However, I had to learn that being a benevolent dictator is still a dictator and that does not foster healthy mentoring partnerships. Therefore, please make sure you empower your mentee to take full responsibility for his decisions, even the unwise ones, because it is probably the only way he will learn life lessons.

The final tip is do not write off your mentee just because he does not follow your advice. Your mentee has free will and as a mentor, you have to respect his free will and decisions. You should not harbor negative feelings toward your mentee because he disobeyed you. Remember he has the right to live his life on his own terms. We are mentors, not God, and we should respect our mentees' free will. I will end with a humbling thought I try to remember when I am advising my mentees who are sometimes very "strong-willed." They might actually know what is better for them than I do, so who am I to tell them how they should live their lives?

Also, I cannot give up on students who do not listen to my advice because I recall many occasions when I made big mistakes and people still gave me second, third, and fourth chances to find my way back to the "right path." It is my human duty to pay that kind of grace and forgiveness forward to the next generation. If we are honest with ourselves, we were all once that "know-it-all" student; it is part of our developmental growth as human beings. Thus, when our fellow brothers and sisters fall down we need to practice compassionate restoration as we help them get up and stand again.

Do Not Push Too Hard

Dear Dr. Mentor,

This is my first mentoring experience with a first-generation college student. My mentee has opened up to me about a lot of family issues she is having at home and she has to work more than 25 hours a week to help support her family because her mom is currently unemployed. She goes home every weekend to help her family with watching her little siblings. She is getting Cs and Ds in her classes. I do not know what I should tell her but she is not going to make it if she keeps her crazy work schedule and spends weekends babysitting instead of studying. I do not want to push her too hard due to her family circumstances. What should I do?

Do Not Push Too Hard

Dear Do Not Push Too Hard,

I understand your dilemma: you want to provide your mentee with emotional support and at the same time, you want to emphasize to her that she has to prioritize her academic life over her family issues. It is a tough conversation to have with your mentee but you have to do it soon. The longer you wait, the further she will get behind in her academic studies.

If you want to be a good mentor, you should not avoid difficult discussions regarding the struggle between your mentee's responsibilities at home and school. Your role is to help your mentee understand the distinction between short-term and long-term outcomes. For instance, in the short-term, your mentee might feel that she should help her family now even at the expense of her long-term academic goals. However, you should explain to her the difference between the limited economic resources she is able to provide to her family now without a degree compared to the larger economic contribution she will make to her family for a longer period of time when she graduates with a college degree.

In addition to sharing your insights with your mentee, you should inform the program director about her issues.

Of course, the ultimate decision should be made by your mentee; you are only responsible for presenting different options to her. It is important to remember if you ignore controversial topics because you do not want to offend your mentee, you are doing her a disservice by not providing her with alternative paths. If a mentor and mentee have not had disagreements in their relationship then that relationship has never been fully tested to see if it could endure and survive conflict. Therefore, I encourage you to hold your mentee to the highest academic standards and expect her to exceed those standards, and as long as you empower her with love and support, you could never push her too hard.

Trust Me

Dear Dr. Mentor,

I am a White, upper-middle class heterosexual man. I know these are socially constructed identities. I recognize that given my multiple social identities I enjoy a lot of privileges and power in the United States. I have studied systems of power, privilege, and oppression for a long time. I am an executive administrator at my school and my team is committed to increasing diversity. I am a strong supporter of our mentoring program and I have been a mentor to two underrepresented students for approximately six months. However, the problem I have is that my mentees always seem intimidated by me and I do not know why because I would do anything for my mentees. I want them to be able to trust me and not fear me, so what can I do to break down those barriers between our different social worlds?

Trust Me

Dear Trust Me,

I applaud you for your enlightened self-awareness of your social privileges. Many mentors do not reflect on how their social identities could influence their mentoring relationship. I believe if you have honest conversations with your mentees about what you perceive to be potential barriers (e.g., ethnicity, social class, gender, and administrator status) to your relationship, it could allow you and your mentees to address immediately those issues early in the relationship. Most researchers agree that age, culture, race/ethnicity, gender, and social class are not significant mentoring barriers. However, you will need to think about ways to create comfortable social settings when you meet with your mentees. You should not meet in your big corner office, which will only reinforce the aura of fear and intimidation. You should ask the program director for fun suggestions on how to foster trust within your mentoring partnership.

Your goal should not be to impress them but rather to relate to and connect with them. If you want your mentees to trust you, they have to get to know you and see you as another imperfect human being. The more honest and vulnerable you allow yourself to be with them, the more they will let down their guards and allow you into their world. It is important to be mindful that some mentees have also been hurt in previous mentoring relationships. For example, some mentees begin to trust their mentors with their true feelings but then they disengage from the entire mentoring process when their mentors do not trust them on the same level, or if the mentor prematurely ends the relationship when a difficult problem arises.

I believe you have a generous heart but you have to be patient and give your mentees time to see beyond your obvious social identities and see your heart and the genuine care you have for them. The high level of trust you seek from your mentees might take a longer time but it will be worth the wait. If you keep believing in them, they will eventually believe in and trust you.

Cannot Train Professors

Dear Dr. Mentor,

I am a mentoring program director and every year I have a difficult time getting new faculty members to attend our training workshops. In fact, we now call it orientation sessions because I was told that faculty prefer the word orientation versus training. I know I need professors to make the mentoring program successful but I do not understand why they resist training sessions. I thought we shared the same mutual goal, which is to serve students. As a staff member, it is hard to gain the respect of professors; I hate the hierarchy at my school. What would you suggest I do to attract more professors to our orientation/training seminars?

Cannot Train Professors

Dear Cannot Train Professors,

I sincerely apologize on behalf of all the challenging professors you have to interact with in your mentoring program. I believe it is hypocritical for professors to promote life-long learning and resist being trained themselves. It is ludicrous to think that having a Ph.D. and teaching for numerous of years automatically prepares a person to effectively mentor students. Yes, there are skills related to teaching that are similar to mentoring but teaching and mentoring are not the same. If your professors want to be exemplar mentors, they need some training. I encourage you to invite faculty members to join your advisory board. The faculty members of the advisory board could help you recruit professors who are held in high esteem on your campus and once these professors are invested in your program, other professors are more likely to join it.

Of course, I have no problem with you replacing the word training with orientation if that will appease the fragile egos of some professors but I think you could include the same type of information as you would in a typical training workshop. In addition, I think you could have a competitive application process (including interviews) with potential candidates. You need to market your mentoring program as a highly productive and prestigious university program (you need support from your top academic administrators). The mentoring program could reward mentors (e.g., certificates or gift cards) for their outstanding service. You should have a rigorous selection process and recruit only the best professors for mentoring; not all professors should be mentors. In fact, some of them should not be in the classroom. Remember the mentoring motto: "First, do no harm to mentees." This should be the motivating force in your selection process of mentors.

If you water-down your orientation session to avoid complaints by some professors you are not preparing your mentors with the crucial knowledge, abilities, skills, and resources they need to help their mentees achieve academic success. Therefore, I strongly encourage you to have all mentors attend a mandatory orientation session. Your decision to be firm about educating all new mentors might not increase your popularity with the faculty initially but you will be serving the needs of your students. I wish I could dismantle the hierarchy among administrators, staff, and faculty because it is a lose-lose situation; no one wins, especially our students.

Need Institutional Support

Dear Dr. Mentor,

I am the new mentoring program director at my community college. In the past three years, there have been two different directors (excluding me) for this mentoring program. I have many fresh ideas that I want to implement in the program but I do not have adequate office space, personnel, or funding for mentoring activities and programming events. I want to stay and turn this program around because I believe in the mission of mentoring but I need more institutional support. Please advise me, what should I do?

Need Institutional Support

Dear Need Institutional Support,

I do not know how to politely say this, but I think you should keep your résumé updated and start looking for other positions. I know this is probably not the response you would expect from me but I want to be honest with you. If your college does not provide you with adequate office space, personnel, or funding for mentoring activities and events, they are setting you up for failure. For instance, you cannot run a successful mentoring program without a full-time mentoring program director, full-time administrative assistant, a medium-size private office space that is designated exclusively for mentoring services (and no other programs), and a budget line that is comparable to similar programs at the college.

I am always amazed how colleges want all the desirable institutional mentoring outcomes (e.g., increased retention and graduation rates) without making reasonable investments in creating and sustaining successful mentoring programs. If you choose to fight for your program, you will need to increase your social capital with faculty, staff, administrators, and students. I would suggest you have one-on-one meetings with department chairs, program coordinators, administrators in academic and student affairs, and leaders of student organizations and tell them explicitly how they would benefit from a mentoring program. You will need the buy-in of the larger campus community to pressure top administrators to provide you with the institutional support you need to maintain a successful mentoring program.

If your marketing campaign is successful, you should get the resources and support you need but if it does not work, I suggest you start looking for another job. I admire your passion and commitment to mentoring but I do not think you should become a martyr for it because passion alone is not enough to manage and sustain a mentoring program; you need institutional support. I wish you mentoring success!

Community Mentor

Dear Dr. Mentor,

My mentee is required to serve as a community volunteer in my organization as part of his mentoring program. He is always late and he does not have the best work habits. Do you have any suggestions about how to motivate him?

Community Mentor

Dear Community Mentor,

For the record, I do not think young people are lazy because they have amazing multitasking abilities. For example, they can concentrate for extended hours on texting, watching television, and playing video games. I only wish I could get them to focus some of their energy on their homework assignments. Seriously, the few tips I can give you are the following:

(1) inform the mentoring program director of your mentee's poor work ethic and ask the director for advice on motivating him;

(2) remind your mentee that his service to your organization is a requirement of his mentoring program;

(3) establish and post your top ten rules for working in your organization and explain them to your mentee; and

(4) make sure there is a sanction associated with each rule and explain those sanctions to your mentee (consult with the mentoring program director before determining your sanctions).

Overall, I believe if you collaborate with the program director, you would both be able to help your mentee value community service and teach him the skills he needs to be successful in the labor market.

Family Mentor

Dear Dr. Mentor,

I have a son attending college and I have been asked by his mentoring program director to be his mentor. I attended the training session on how to be a family mentor but I still blur the boundaries between being his mom and being his mentor. Do you have any advice on how I could have a better mentoring relationship with my mentee/son?

Family Mentor

Dear Family Mentor,

I think it is a great idea that you serve as your son's mentor. The first strategy I would suggest for separating your parental role from your mentoring role is to refer to your son only as a mentee when you have your mentor hat on and make sure you review and comply with the Family Educational Rights and Privacy

Act (FERPA) policy. In addition, you should not ask your mentee questions about his social life, especially about, how often he goes out to parties; you know, questions that a mother would ask her children. Your focus as a family mentor is to encourage your mentee to form strong mentoring relationships with people at his school. You should also be supportive of your mentee by reminding him that his main priority is to do well in school and he should not worry about family issues. As a family mentor, your primary goal is to reassure your mentee that everything is okay at home, so that your mentee will be able to focus more on his academic career. Your role as a family mentor is important to the overall success of your mentee/son.

Peer Mentor

Dear Dr. Mentor,

I am a junior peer mentor for a first-year student. I was excited about joining the mentoring program because it would give me an opportunity to give back to a program I benefited from two years ago. However, my mentee does not listen to my advice and she has missed meetings without giving me proper notice. My mentee does not see me as a person with real authority. What should I do in this situation?

Peer Mentor

Dear Peer Mentor,

Welcome to my world! Many of my mentees do not listen to me or follow my advice. I might have a little more authority than you but I often receive the same level of respect (or lack of). I would encourage you to contact the program director and explain your situation to her because sometimes directors need to intervene to make sure your mentee fulfills her responsibility in the partnership. I do not know if this would make you feel better, but some research studies indicate that mentees have stronger relationships with peer mentors than with faculty and staff mentors. Therefore, do not get discouraged and internalize your mentee's disengagement as an indication that you are not a good mentor. Your mentee is probably going through some personal issues and that is another reason why it is important to reach out to your program director so that your mentee does not have to suffer in silence. I hope you continue to believe in the value of mentoring and do not give up on your mentee.

General Advice to Mentors, Mentoring Program Directors, and Administrators

Dear Mentors, Mentoring Program Directors, and Administrators,

I applaud you for supporting students through mentoring programs. You are making a difference in the lives of many students, one mentoring experience at a time. I want to leave you with a few thoughts about how you could improve your overall mentoring experience. As a faculty/staff mentor you have to train yourself not to internalize your mentee's behaviors and her educational outcomes. Your mentee has free will and she is entitled to make her own decisions even if you believe they are not in her best interest. You cannot impose your will on her and if she chooses not to listen to and follow through on your advice, you should not give up on her. Your role is to be there for her whenever she decides she is ready to hear your wisdom.

As a mentor, you also want to enter the relationship with a sense of humility and an open mind about learning from your mentee. You cannot have a top-down learning approach because mentoring is a partnership. If you feel a little awkward at the beginning of your relationship, that is normal, you have to become comfortable with being uncomfortable. Although the mentoring experience should be satisfying for both mentors and mentees, the needs of the mentees should be the highest priority. In order to maintain a strong relationship with your mentee, you must collaborate with the mentoring program director. You do not want to be perceived as a difficult know-it-all faculty member who is constantly asking for exceptions to mentoring policies (e.g., not attending mandatory training workshops).

It is essential that all mentors be trained on how to help mentees decode and interpret the hidden curriculum. Your mentee will not learn the hidden curriculum unless you develop a trusting relationship with her/him. The characteristics listed below are some of the common traits that mentees look for in their ideal mentors, which can help foster strong mentoring relationships. Do not worry; if you do not embody all the characteristics or skills you could still be an effective mentor if you maintain a willingness to learn from both the mentoring program director and your mentee. Remember, your mentee is a work-in-progress and so are you.

Here are some of the traits mentees are looking for in their mentors.

- Knowledgeable

- Personable

- Resourceful

- Motivating

- Helpful

- Reliable

- Open-Minded

- Honest

- Good Listener

- Sense of Humor

- Persistent

- Full of Integrity

- Committed

- Patient

- Respectful

- Culturally Competent

- Willing to Share Wisdom

- Willing to Share Personal Challenges

- Effective Good Communication and Interpersonal Skills

- Flexible

- Caring

- Available

- Demonstrates Empathy

Mentoring program directors have to embody some of these traits and be skilled diplomats because they have to build social capital with administrators, staff, faculty, and students. The directors could establish an advisory mentoring board composed of administrators, staff, faculty, and students who could help market the mentoring program to their peers, respectively. In addition, program directors could present empirical data to administrators on how institutional benefits of mentoring (e.g., increased retention and graduation rates) could have a positive economic impact on the school. Directors should require high academic standards for all of the mentees because the mentoring program needs to have a solid reputation for academic excellence. Although it is important to incorporate fun activities within the mentoring program, directors could emphasize to the mentees that they expect them to graduate with honors. Many faculty members would also be interested in joining a mentoring program that promotes academic excellence.

Finally, as administrators your support (or lack of support) could determine the overall success of the mentoring program. If you do not express the importance of mentoring to all the stakeholders at your school, the mentoring program is less likely to produce long-lasting institutional educational outcomes. You have a right to require assessments and evaluations of the program but only if you have fully funded and provided the necessary resources to make the mentoring program successful. I hope administrators will choose to transform mentoring programs and create a more equitable higher education system.

Note

1. Some of the ideas presented in this chapter were shared with me by colleagues. I changed the stories to protect students' confidentiality. I am grateful to the following colleagues and friends for sharing their mentoring experiences with me: Cynthia Fraction, Denise Dieffenbach, Sharon Howell, Ashley Booker, Lynda McDonnell, Victoria Svoboda, Susan Smith-Cunnien, Meg Wilkes Karraker, Peter Parilla, Tanya Gladney, Patricia Conde-Brooks, Tonia Bock, Monica Hartmann Kathleen Boyle, Elizabeth Dussol, Carolyn Holbrook, Mary Easter, Priscilla Gibson, Carla-Elaine Johnson, Aundria Morgan, Sherrie Fernandez-Williams, Latoya Beck.

Conclusion

Krista graduated from college within six years and she never developed strong mentoring relationships with her professors in the Communication and Journalism Department. She decided to major in English, like her mentor. However, today she is not pursuing her dream of becoming a writer; instead, she is a manager at a local retail store. She survived college with the help of her mentor but she could have had the opportunity to thrive in college if she had acquired earlier the institutional cultural capital and social capital she needed to navigate the hidden curriculum of higher education. The American Dream University failed Krista and so many other students like her when they did not unveil the hidden curriculum to all their students.

The findings in this book indicate that understanding the hidden curriculum is an integral component for achieving academic success.[1] Therefore, I posit that academic mentoring programs could be restructured to explicitly and systematically reveal the hidden curriculum to students. One approach to restructuring mentoring programs is to develop a mentoring curriculum that standardizes the types of institutional cultural capital and social capital that mentees receive within the program. Moreover, a mentoring curriculum provides mentors with a blueprint for how to successfully transmit to their mentees high degrees of institutional cultural capital and social capital.

I recommend three approaches for developing a mentoring curriculum. First, all the academic stakeholders (e.g., administrators, staff, faculty, and students) need to dialogue with one another about the academic culture of their institution and create several scenarios that identify and explain the major attributes of the hidden curriculum of their college or university. Second, these scenarios could be included in a handbook for mentors and mentees. Third, mentors could be required to discuss the scenarios in the handbook with their

143

mentees. It is important to emphasize that it is not necessary for mentors to have a standard teaching style or technique for transmitting institutional cultural capital and social capital to their mentees.

However, it is crucial that all the scenarios and other topics in the handbook be discussed in detail in order to ensure that all the mentees in the program have access to the same institutional cultural capital and social capital. If colleges and universities restructure their current mentoring programs to include a mentoring curriculum they could be one step closer to developing a mentoring institution. I strongly contend that mentoring institutions represent the next frontier of higher education.

Mentoring Institutions

There are two major structural problems with traditional academic mentoring programs. First, many traditional mentoring programs do not consider systematically teaching the academic culture of higher education to all students as an objective of their program. As a result, many White first-generation college students are excluded from traditional academic mentoring programs. If academic mentoring programs continue to focus exclusively on "at-risk" students and do not offer services that explicitly reveal the hidden curriculum of the college to all students, "at-risk" students in the program could feel stigmatized and alienated from the larger campus community based on their racial and social class backgrounds. Furthermore, many White first-generation college students could remain disadvantaged because they do not have access to the resources and services offered by traditional mentoring programs.

Second, most traditional mentoring programs incorporate one of two mentoring models within their programs: one-on-one mentoring or network mentoring. The problem with one-on-one mentoring is that it could lead to the "grooming effect" which only exposes the mentee to the institutional cultural capital and social capital of one faculty member, staff member, or administrator. Although network mentoring reduces the "grooming effect" it still has limitations because it only exposes the mentees to the institutional cultural capital and social capital of the mentors in that particular program. The problem with relying exclusively on the mentors who participate in a particular mentoring program is that students are not fully maximizing the quality or quantity of institutional cultural capital and social capital that they could receive if more stakeholders at the college or university participated in the mentoring process.

To address these two problems, I propose creating academic mentoring institutions. Mentoring institutions could develop a mentoring curriculum that incorporates the three cycles of mentoring—advising, advocacy, and apprenticeship. Mentoring institutions could be cost effective and improve students' understanding of the academic culture of higher education and foster civic responsibility among college students. Unlike traditional academic mentoring programs, mentoring institutions could accomplish the following three objectives. First, academic mentoring institutions could effectively, explicitly, and systematically reveal the hidden curriculum of higher education to all new and transfer students through a required credited course designed and taught by various teams of administrators, staff, faculty, and advanced students. Second, academic mentoring institutions could unveil the hidden curriculum of the university to all students and not just target "at-risk" students. Third, academic mentoring institutions could strongly encourage greater participation among administrators, staff, and faculty to share their institutional cultural capital and social capital with students through the credited course by rewarding mentors during their annual review process (e.g., some form of financial compensation).

I am not advocating for the creation of a bigger mentoring program. Instead, I am suggesting that the best practices of mentoring could be embedded within the academic culture of colleges and universities just like teaching and research. After all, mentoring is quintessentially a form of teaching that focuses on the hidden curriculum. Colleges and universities do not have to invest an exorbitant amount of financial resources to establish mentoring institutions. Rather, they primarily have to think of creative ways of efficiently and systematically tapping into the existing reservoir of institutional cultural capital and social capital embodied in staff, faculty, administrators, and students and encourage these stakeholders to share their institutional knowledge with one another.

Another reason for creating academic mentoring institutions is that they could foster more inclusive and cooperative learning environments, providing the best preconditions for promoting civic responsibility. Ideally, if mentoring becomes part of the academic cultural fabric of higher education, mentoring institutions could also improve relationships among administrators, staff, faculty, and students. More importantly, developing mentoring institutions could benefit students in two major ways: (1) student mentees who fail to establish personal connections with their assigned mentors still have access to the institutional cultural capital of the college; (2) teaching students how to navigate the hidden curriculum would no longer be the primary responsibility of their assigned mentors; rather, it becomes the responsibility of all faculty, staff, and administrators.

In sum, I have presented a case for why we should not think of academic mentoring only in terms of individual mentoring relationships; rather we should consider how academic mentoring can operate at the institutional level. Since acquiring institutional cultural capital and social capital do not naturally occur for all students because they come from diverse racial and social class backgrounds, it is the responsibility of colleges and universities to ensure that students have equal access to the different types of academic capital they need to thrive in college. If post-secondary institutions fail to provide all students with equal access to institutional cultural capital and social capital, they implicitly validate and reproduce structural inequalities within higher education. Colleges and universities could demystify the higher education process by explicitly and systematically revealing the unwritten academic expectations, norms, values, and behavioral codes of conduct to all students. Finally, if colleges could encourage academic stakeholders to make the hidden curriculum transparent for all students they would create a more equitable, meritocratic, and just higher education system.

Note

1. The ideas and information presented in the conclusion come from my unpublished dissertation. Buffy Smith, *Demystifying the Higher Education System: Rethinking Academic Cultural Capital, Social Capital, and the Academic Mentoring Process*, Unpublished Dissertation, University of Wisconsin-Madison, 2004.

Appendix A: Methodology

Recruitment

After the University of Wisconsin-Madison Human Subjects Committee approved my research project, I began the recruiting process in 2001. I initiated a meeting with the director of the Cleophus Mentoring Program. I served as a mentor in this program from 1998-2003. I also met with the director of another mentoring program, The Everlean Mentoring Program. I assured both directors that I was not interested in evaluating the respective programs, rather I was interested in the types of institutional cultural capital and social that were transmitted and acquired within mentoring relationships.[1]

In order to protect the identity of my respondents I changed their names and any other specific information that could be used to identify them. I also gave pseudonyms for the mentoring programs. The students in the Everlean Mentoring Program had to maintain a minimum of a 3.0 GPA, but there was not a minimum GPA requirement for the Cleophus Mentoring Program. One of the objectives of the Everlean Mentoring Program was to establish strong personal friendships between mentors (faculty and administrators) and students as a means to foster academic success among the students. The Cleophus Mentoring Program encouraged mentors (faculty, staff, administrators and graduate students) to serve as supportive allies to help students feel less isolated on campus as they worked toward their academic goals.

The directors of the mentoring programs matched mentors and mentees based on numerous characteristics such as shared academic interests, hobbies, and other personal attributes (including race and gender) that the directors thought might make the faculty member and student a good match. Both men-

147

tors and mentees volunteered to participate in the respective programs, except for the mentees in the Everlean Mentoring Program who were required to participate in the program as one of the stipulations for receiving their scholarship. Mentors and mentees were encouraged to meet on a regular basis (not specifically defined) and to make a two-year (Cleophus) or four-year (Everlean) commitment to participate in the mentoring programs.

After meeting with the two directors, they agreed to assist me with the project by allowing me to post an e-mail advertisement about the study to their membership e-mail listserv. I also placed an advertisement about the study in the faculty and staff newspaper for six weeks and posted flyers at the diversity center on campus. The newspaper ads and flyers indicated that I wanted to interview mentors and mentees for approximately two hours about their mentoring experience. The eligibility requirements were that they had to have participated in one of the targeted mentoring programs for at least one year and had at least three face-to-face meetings with their mentors/mentees. I provided a monetary incentive of $25 to both mentors and mentees.

There was a greater response rate from the mentees than from the mentors. As part of the screening process, I asked the mentees the name of their mentors and invited their matched mentors to participate in the study. The mentors referred to me by their mentees all refused to participate in the study. I did not have a prior relationship with the mentors (lack of social capital). Some of the reasons the mentors provided for declining my invitation for an interview were the following: (1) they could not make a two-hour commitment for an interview; (2) they were not interested in the study; (3) they did not have a positive mentoring experience and they did not want to talk about it; and (4) they did not like to be interviewed and were suspicious of participating in research studies. In fact, all of the mentors in the study, except for one faculty member, were administrators with whom I had developed a close professional relationship with during my tenure as an academic advisor (strong social capital).

Interviewing Process

I conducted interviews with eight mentors (faculty and administrators) and twelve mentees. The mentees included eleven undergraduate students and one law student who started the mentoring program when she was an undergraduate. Each respondent completed a survey at the beginning of the interview. The mentors and mentees provided background information about their race, gender, social class, and parents' educational attainment (see Appendix B). The survey also asked mentors and mentees to describe how often they communicated with one another, what types of topics they discussed, and what types of activities they engaged in on a regular basis during their mentoring relationships.

I completed the interviewing process when I had reached theoretical saturation. In other words, I stopped recruiting respondents once I noticed that the mentors and mentees were providing similar answers to the interview questions and not presenting "new" information. As a result, I was confident that no new categories would emerge from additional interviews. My pre-test included interviews with two mentees and two graduate student mentors; the interviews were very useful in helping me conceptualize and refine my questions, but I did not include their information with the final data. The interview guide (i.e., list of interview questions) was influenced by my three-pronged conceptual framework and consisted of open-ended structured questions (see Appendix C). I read each question verbatim to all the respondents and I followed-up with probing questions when it was necessary to obtain more specific examples and information.

Sample

The eight mentors I interviewed were seven administrators and one faculty member; however, two of the administrators also taught several courses on a regular basis at the university. As for the mentees, I had a semi-personal relationship with two of them prior to the interviews. We engaged in friendly conversations when we attended the same mentoring program events. The two students participated in the Cleophus Mentoring Program, the same program I had served in as a mentor for six years. The other six students participated in the Everlean Mentoring Program but I did not have a personal relationship with them prior to the interviews.

Coding Techniques

I transcribed all the interviews, which produced approximately 400 pages of transcripts. The transcripts served as my primary data source and my field notes and respondents' background survey information were my secondary data sources. At the initial stages of the coding process, I read the text of all the transcripts multiple times and compiled notes on the patterns that emerged during the readings of the text, in order to have confidence in the validity of the themes. Next, I began to code the text one question at a time. For example, I read all the responses for a particular question multiple times and recorded the themes that emerged from that particular question, and then I repeated the same process with the next questions. This process is known as opened coding because it allowed me to conceptualize and categorize the data free from any structural constraints of preconceived categories, and as a result new themes emerged from the data.[2] I employed the opened coding technique in identifying the themes that addressed the research questions: (1) what types of institutional cultural capital and social capital do students need in order to succeed in college (see figure 1.2), and (2) what types of institutional cultural capital and social capital are transmitted and acquired within mentoring relationships (see chapters 2 and 3)?

   In addition to opened coding, I also employed the closed coding technique to analyze my data. Closed coding allowed me to analyze the data through my three-pronged conceptual framework[3] that served as the building blocks for the three-cycle mentoring model: advising, advocacy, and apprenticeship. I constructed a series of interview questions that directly addressed each cycle of my mentoring model (see Appendix C).

Analysis

The sociological and educational concepts of cultural capital, social capital, and the hidden curriculum guided my analysis and interpretation of the detailed responses to the interview questions. In selecting the themes for each question, I made a concerted effort to use many of the exact phrases expressed by the respondents for the category names of the themes. If I could not use their exact words, I used words that would portray the same meanings. Likewise, when interpreting the selected quotations I kept my analysis close to the participants' words without speculating or coming to conclusions that would not be fairly self-evident to most readers. In fact, I cited longer quotations not only to show the richness of the data but also to ensure that the respondents' words, tones, and perspectives remained as authentic and powerful as the day they were first expressed during the interviews. I grounded all my interpretations within the data and literature.

   Moreover, I employed the method of analytic induction to interpret and analyze the data through the conceptual frameworks of cultural capital, social capital, and the hidden curriculum. The definition that best explains the analytic induction method is the following:

> We wish to suggest a third approach to the analysis of qualitative data—one that combines, by an analytic procedure of constant comparison, the explicit coding procedure of the first approach (analysis of data after coding) and the style of theory development of the second (the integration of data and theory). The purpose of the constant comparative method of joint coding and analysis is to generate theory more systematically than allowed by the second approach, by using explicit coding and analytic procedures.[4]

The importance of using this analytic induction method is that it allows the researcher to analyze the data after each new theme emerges through the coding process and then integrates the data with preconceived categories and with existing and emerging theories. This approach is different from pure grounded theory because pure grounded theory focuses on constructing new theories that are directly built upon emerging concepts and themes from the data. However, grounded theory does not include integrating the data with preconceived categories or with existing theories.[5]

In contrast, the analytic induction method allows researchers to enter the field with preconceived categories and then integrate the data with the preconceived categories and with existing and emerging theories. For instance, in this study, I went into the interviews with the preconceived categories of advising, advocacy, and apprenticeship. After comparing and analyzing the data with these categories, the categories developed into my three-cycle mentoring model, which was grounded in the conceptual framework of cultural capital, social capital, and the hidden curriculum.

Every theme that emerged from the coding process was analyzed through the lens of my theoretically driven three-cycle mentoring model and when a new theme did not "fit" into the model, I modified and refined my model to take into account all the new themes. This analytic procedure did not occur at only one particular point in the analysis process; rather, it was a continuous process that required me to reflect, refine, and reconceptualize the connection between my conceptual framework and the empirical data throughout the study.

Methodology Issues with Studying Mentoring Programs

Most academic mentoring programs have not undergone systematic and rigorous evaluations. Thus, it is difficult to ascertain the direct relationship between mentoring and academic success. The few empirical studies that examine the relationship between academic mentoring and academic success are all plagued by similar methodological flaws. Internal and external validity limitations are the two most common methodological problems with measuring the effects of mentoring on academic success.[6]

Many academic mentoring relationships are developed and supported through formal academic mentoring programs. These programs do not exist in a vacuum; in fact, many of them are nested within several academic support services (e.g., academic counseling, learning centers, and tutorial services). As a result, it is very difficult to isolate and measure whether actual mentoring relationships or academic support services directly affect students' academic success (e.g., GPA, retention rate). This institutional nesting illustrates the internal validity problem and correlation issues that affect our framing, understanding, and evaluation of mentoring programs.

Many scholars avoid stating that there is a direct or strong correlation between mentoring and academic success and instead emphasize that mentoring relationships are often by-products of academic success.[7] In other words, students who embody and display certain attributes associated with academic success (e.g., self-motivation and intellectual curiosity) are more likely to attract faculty and administrators who would want to serve as their mentors and help guide them through their academic career.[8]

External validity is the second most common problem associated with evaluating the relationship between mentoring and academic success. The findings from most studies on mentoring programs cannot be generalized to different student populations and types of colleges and universities, because these studies suffer methodological limitations such as small sample sizes, lack of diversity in the student population, and lack of multiple research sites.[9] For instance, many studies on mentoring programs only look at one program with a limited number of students participating in it and these studies usually do not examine the effects of mentoring on White students. Moreover, these studies do not investigate the differences and similarities in the relationship between academic mentoring and academic success across different community colleges, liberal arts colleges, comprehensive universities, and research universities.

In order to address these two major methodological problems, some scholars advocate for designing mentoring programs with cross-sectional and longitudinal components. Cross-sectional studies would examine the effects of mentoring on students' academic success by comparing students who participate in mentoring programs with students who do not participate in mentoring programs or any other academic intervention programs. On the other hand, longitudinal studies could collect information pertaining to academic achievement and the mentoring process from mentors and mentees at different times throughout their mentoring relationship. Longitudinal studies are crucial since some scholars suggest that the positive effects of mentoring may not be evident for several years.[10]

Limitations and Significance of the Study

There are some potential methodological limitations of this study. First one could argue that the study has a small sample size and an external validity problem because I conducted my research at only one university (i.e., a large public research university in the Midwest) and it is not representative of most colleges and universities. These two issues are legitimate criticisms and as a result, I was very cautious in my interpretations of the data. I do not claim that the findings are generalizable to larger and more diverse populations of students, faculty, staff, and administrators at different types of colleges and universities. However, the purpose of my study was to explore an area of research that has not been given a lot of attention by scholars in general and sociologists in particular about the types of institutional cultural capital and social capital that are transmitted and acquired within formal academic mentoring relationships. Since this was the objective of my research, having a small sample size or collecting data at only one university did not limit me from examining and illuminating the interconnection between mentoring and the hidden curriculum.

Moreover, some qualitative scholars argue that purposeful sampling or "information-oriented sampling" is more appropriate than "statistical sampling" when researchers are interested in gathering in-depth rich information about a social phenomenon.[11] Researchers also suggest that small sample sizes that are theoretically grounded are more "likely to replicate or extend the emergent theory."[12] Therefore, given the purpose of my research, the sample size was not a major disadvantage because it provided richer and deeper understanding of the theoretical and practical intersections among cultural capital, social capital, the hidden curriculum, and the mentoring process. Overall, the value of qualitative research is best articulated in the following statement:

> Qualitative research is not looking for principles that are true all the time and in all conditions, like laws of physics; rather, the goal is understanding of specific circumstances, how and why things actually happen in a complex world. Knowledge in qualitative interviewing is situational and conditional.[13]

In addition, I employed two triangulation methods to increase the internal validity and credibility of my research. The triangulation methods I implemented were at the levels of data (i.e., multiple sources of data, multiple perspectives) and theory (i.e., more than one theoretical framework to interpret the findings).[14] In other words, I collected data from multiple respondents who presented multiple perspectives (e.g., the matched mentors and their mentees) on the mentoring process. In addition, I utilized multiple theories (e.g., cultural capital, social capital, and the hidden curriculum) to analyze and interpret the findings from the data. Finally, the significance of my qualitative study is that it provides new insights into how faculty, staff, and administrators could transmit the institutional cultural capital and social capital that "at-risk" students need to understand and navigate the hidden curriculum of higher education.

Notes

1. Anselm Strauss and Juliet Corbin, *Basics of Qualitative Research: Grounded Theory Procedures and Techniques* (Newbury Park, CA: Sage Publications, Inc., 1990).

2. Maryann Jacobi, "Mentoring and Undergraduate Academic Success: A Literature Review," *Review of Educational Research* 61, no. 4 (1991): 505-532.

3. Strauss and Corbin, *Basics of Qualitative Research: Grounded Theory Procedures and Techniques*, 1990.

4. Bruce Berg, *Qualitative Research Methods for the Social Sciences*, 4th ed. (Boston: Allyn & Bacon, 2001).

5a. John W. Creswell, *Qualitative Inquiry and Research Design Choosing Among Five Traditions* (Thousand Oaks, CA: Sage, 1998).

5b. Berg, *Qualitative Research Methods for the Social Sciences*, 2001.

6a. Jacobi, "Mentoring and Undergraduate Academic Success: A Literature Review," 1991.

6b. W. Brad Johnson, Gail Rose and Lewis Z. Schlosser, "Student-Faculty Mentoring: Theoretical and Methodological," in *The Blackwell Handbook of Mentoring*, ed. Tammy D. Allen and Lillian T. Eby, Blackwell Reference Online, 2007, www.blackwell reference.com (accessed September 2, 2011).

7a. Maryann Jacobi, "Mentoring and Undergraduate Academic Success: A Literature Review," 1991.

7b. Johnson, Rose and Schlosser, "Student-Faculty Mentoring: Theoretical and Methodological," 2007.

8a. W. Brad Johnson, "Student-Faculty Mentorship Outcomes," in *The Blackwell Handbook of Mentoring*, ed. Tammy D. Allen and Lillian T. Eby, Blackwell Reference Online, 2007, www.blackwellreferece.com (accessed September 2, 2011).

8b. Clark D. Campbell, "Best Practices for Student-Faculty Mentoring Programs," in *The Blackwell Handbook of Mentoring*, ed. Tammy D. Allen and Lillian T. Eby, Blackwell Reference Online, 2007, www.blackwellreference.com (accessed September 2, 2011).

9a. Jacobi, "Mentoring and Undergraduate Academic Success: A Literature Review," 1991.

9b. Johnson, Rose and Schlosser, "Student-Faculty Mentoring: Theoretical and Methodological," 2007.

10a. Jacobi, "Mentoring and Undergraduate Academic Success: A Literature Review," 1991.

10b. Johnson, Rose and Schlosser, "Student-Faculty Mentoring: Theoretical and Methodological," 2007.

11a. Creswell, *Qualitative Inquiry and Research Design Choosing Among Five Traditions*, 1998.

11b. Eunjung Lee, Faye Mishna and Sarah Brennenstuhl, "How to Critically Evaluate Case Studies in Social Work," *Research on Social Work Practice* 20, no. 6 (2010): 682-689.

12a. Creswell, *Qualitative Inquiry and Research Design Choosing Among Five Traditions*, 1998.

12b. Lee, Mishna and Brennenstuhl, "How to Critically Evaluate Case Studies in Social Work," 2010.

13. Herbert J. Rubin and Irene S. Rubin, *Qualitative Interviewing: The Art of Hearing Data* (Thousand Oaks, CA: Sage, 1995), 38-39.

14a. Cynthia Franklin and Michelle Ballan, "Reliability and Validity in Qualitative Research," in *Handbook of Social Work Research Methods*, ed. Bruce A. Thyer (Thousand Oaks, CA: Sage, 2001), 273-292.

14b. Michael Quinn Patton, *Qualitative Research & Evaluation Methods* (Thousand Oaks, CA: Sage, 2002).

Appendix B. Mentor/Mentee Survey

BACKGROUND INFORMATION

1. What is your sex? (check one response).

    A. _____ Female
    B. _____ Male

2. Please mark the **one** race or ethnicity that you think applies to you best?

    A. _____Hispanic
    B. _____Asian or Pacific Islander
    C. _____American Indian/Native American/Alaskan Native
    D. _____African American/Black, not of Hispanic origin
    E. _____Middle Eastern (specify)_____
    F. _____Biracial (specify)_____
    G. _____White, not of Hispanic origin
    H. _____Race not included above (specify)_____

3. What occupation did your mother or female guardian, and your father or male guardian hold while you were growing up? Please Print.

Mother or Female Guardian's Occupation:

_____

Father or Male Guardian's Occupation:

_____

4. What is your current occupation? (if student, provide major) Please Print.

_____

5. Select the category that best represents your **family of origin social class** background as you were growing up? (Check one response).

Family of Origin Social Class

Upper class	A. _____
Upper-middle class	B. _____
Middle-middle class	C. _____
Lower-middle class	D. _____
Working class	E. _____
Lower class	F. _____

6. How did you select the above family of origin social class category? (Check one response).

A. Parents' income _____
B. Parents' education _____
C. Both A and B _____
D. Other (please specify) _____

7. What is the highest level of education **you** completed? (Check one response). (undergraduate students can skip this question)

    A. Associate's degree _____
    B. Bachelor's degree _____
    C. Some graduate or professional school_____
    D. Master's degree_____
    E. All but dissertation (ABD) _____
    F. Doctoral degree (Ph.D., Ed.D.)_____
    G. Professional degree (J. D., M.D.)_____

8. What is the highest level of education completed by your father or male guardian, and your mother or female guardian? (Check one response in **each column**).

Mother or Female Guardian	**Father or Male Guardian**
Highest Level of Education Completed	
Completed elementary school or less	
A._____	A. _____
Some high school	
B._____	B._____
High school diploma or equivalent	
C._____	C._____
Some college, business or trade school	
D._____	D._____
Associate's degree	
E. _____	E._____
Bachelor's degree	
F._____	F. _____

Some graduate or professional school
G._____   G. _____

Master's degree
H._____   H. _____

All but dissertation (ABD)
I._____   I. _____

Doctoral degree (Ph.D., Ed. D.)
J._____   J._____

Professional degree (J.D., M.D.)
K._____   K. _____

9. What is your mentee's/mentor's sex? (check one response).

   A._____Female
   B._____Male

.
10. Please mark the **one** race or ethnicity that you think best applies to your
    mentee/mentor.

   A.   _____Hispanic
   B.   _____Asian or Pacific Islander
   C.   _____American Indian/Native American/Alaskan Native
   D.   _____African American/Black, not of Hispanic origin
   E.   _____Middle Eastern (specify)_____
   F.   _____Biracial (specify)_____
   G.   _____White, not of Hispanic origin
   H.   _____ Race not included above (specify)_____

11. On average, how often do you communicate with your mentee/mentor? (Fill
    in all the blanks that apply)

   Phone _____times per month
   E-mail_____times per month
   Face to Face_____ times per month

12. On average, how long do you communicate with your mentee/mentor? (Fill in all the blanks that apply)

Phone _____ per minutes or _____ per hours
E-mail _____ 5 lines or less per message
_____ 6-12 lines per message
_____ 13-20 lines per message
_____ 21 lines or more per message
Face to Face _____ per minutes or _____ per hours

13. List three activities that you do with your mentee/mentor on a regular basis?

1. _____

2. _____

3. _____

14. List three topics that you discuss with your mentee/mentor on a regular basis?

1. _____

2. _____

3. _____

15. How long have you participated in the mentoring program? (Check one response)

_____ 1 year
_____ 2 years
_____ 3 years
_____ 4 years
_____ 5 years
_____ 6 and more years (specify how many years)_____

16. How many mentees have you mentored in this particular mentoring
    program?(how many mentors have you had in this particular program)
    (Fill in all the blanks that apply)

    _____total number of mentees/mentors
    _____number of mentees/mentors per year

17. What is the name of your mentoring program?

    _____

18. Please provide us with the name, phone number, and e-mail address of your
    mentee/mentor?

    Name_____

    Phone_____

    E-mail_____

Appendix C. Mentor/Mentee
Interview Guide Questions

GENERAL QUESTIONS:

1. Describe the purpose or goal of higher education. Probe: Give specific examples.

2. Describe the relationship between academic success and the goals of higher education. Probe: Give specific examples.

3. Describe the similarities and differences between academic advising and academic mentoring. Probe: Give three similarities and three differences.

4. What forms of knowledge or sets of skills do you think your mentee/mentor can offer you? Probe: Give specific examples.

5. What forms of knowledge or sets of skills do you think you can offer your mentee/mentor? Probe: Give specific examples.

6. Describe the forms of knowledge and sets of skills your mentee needs to know to be successful in college. (you learned from your mentor to be successful in college) Probe: Give specific examples of academic and social skills.

7. Describe how you teach your mentee the forms of knowledge and sets of skills she/he needs to know to be successful in college. (your mentor teaches you the knowledge and skills you need to be successful in college) Probe: Give specific examples of academic and social skills.

8. Describe your expectations of your mentee/mentor. Probe: Give specific examples.

9. Describe your obligations to your mentee/mentor. Probe: Give specific examples.

10. Describe the level of trust between you and your mentee/mentor. Probe: Give specific examples.

11. Describe some of the things you have received from your mentee/mentor. Probe: Give specific examples of material and nonmaterial things.

12. Describe some of the things you have given to your mentee/mentor. Probe: Give specific examples of material and nonmaterial things.

13. Describe the norms you and your mentee/mentor follow when you interact with each other. Probe: Give specific examples.

14. Describe how these norms change depending on the topic of your conversation. Probe: Give specific examples.

15. Describe the consequences for you if these norms are not followed in your mentoring relationship. Probe: Give specific examples.

16. Describe the consequences for your mentee/mentor if these norms are not followed in your mentoring relationship. Probe Give specific examples.

ADVISING QUESTIONS:

17. How would you describe the academic culture of this university? Probe: Give specific examples.

18. Describe how you teach the academic culture of this university to your mentee. (your mentor teaches you the academic culture) Probe: Give specific examples.

19. Describe your typical academic advising session with your mentee/mentor. Probe: Give specific examples.

20. In your opinion, what is the best academic advice you have given (received) to (from) your mentee (mentor)? Probe: Give specific examples.

21. Describe at least three academic programs or resources that you have discussed with your mentee. (your mentor has discussed with you) Probe: Give specific examples.

ADVOCACY QUESTIONS:

22. Describe your relationship with other faculty, staff, and administrators who interact with your mentee on a regular basis. (you interact with on a regular basis because of your relationship with your mentor) Probe: Give specific examples.

22a. How often do you interact with them?

22b. Describe some of the general conversations you have with them about your mentee's academic progress. (your academic success) Probe: Give specific examples.

23. How would you describe the way you help your mentee to network at this university? (your mentor has helped you network) Probe: Do you introduce your mentee to your colleagues? (does your mentor introduce you to his/her colleagues) Give specific examples.

24. Have you ever read a paper or essay exam written by your mentee? (has your mentor ever read a paper or essay exam written by you)

24a. If yes, describe the recommendations you have made to your mentee to help improve his/her writing skills. (your mentor has made to help you improve your writing skills) Probe: Give specific examples.

25. Describe the suggestions or recommendations you have made to your mentee to help improve his/her verbal communication skills. (your mentor has made to help you improve your verbal communication skills) Probe: Give specific examples.

APPRENTICESHIP QUESTIONS:

26. Describe the conversations you have with your mentee about how he/she should approach a TA or professor when earning a low grade on a test or paper. (your mentor has had with you about how to approach a TA or professor) Probe: What are the dos and don'ts of how to approach a TA or professor? Be specific, please give examples.

26a. How often do you have these conversations? Probe: How many times per month or per semester?

27. Describe the conversations you have with your mentee about how she/he should engage in classroom discussions. (your mentor has had with you about how to engage in classroom discussion) Probe: What are the dos and don'ts of how to engage in classroom discussions? Be specific, please give examples.

27a. How often do you have these conversations? Probe: How many times per month or per semester?

28. Describe the conversations you have with your mentee about how she/he should conduct an independent research project. (your mentor has had with you about how to conduct an independent research project) Probe: What are the dos and don'ts of how to conduct an independent research project? Be specific, please give examples.

28a. How often do you have these conversations? Probe: How many times per month or per semester?

CLOSING QUESTIONS:

29. Discuss at least three reasons why you wanted to be in a mentoring relationship. Probe: Give specific examples.

30. Would you like to make any final comments about your mentoring experience?

Bibliography

Apple, Michael. *Ideology and Curriculum*, 2nd ed. New York: Routledge, 1990.

——. *Education and Power*. New York: Routledge, 1982.

Arriaza, Gilberto. "Schools, Social Capital, and Children of Color," *Race, Ethnicity and Education* 6 (2003): 71-94.

A Shared Agenda: A Leadership Challenge to Improve College Access and Success, Boston, MA: Pathways to College Network: The Education Resource Institute (TERI), 2004. www.pathwaystocollege.com (accessed September 2, 2011).

Astin, Alexander. "Student Involvement: A Developmental Theory for Higher Education," *Journal of College Student Personnel* 25, (1984): 287-300.

——. *Four Critical Years: Effects of College on Beliefs, Attitudes and Knowledge*. San Francisco, CA: Jossey-Bass, 1977.

Aud, Susan, William Hussar, Grace Kena, Kevin Bianco, Lauren Frolich, Jana Kemp, and Kim Tahan. *The Condition of Education 2011* (NCES 2011-033). U.S. Department of Education, National Center for Education Statistics. Washington, DC: U.S. Government Printing Office, 2011.

Berg, Bruce. *Qualitative Research Methods for the Social Sciences*, 4th ed. Boston: Allyn & Bacon, 2001.

Bergquist, William. *The Four Cultures of the Academy: Insights and Strategies for Improving Leadership in Collegiate Organizations* (San Francisco: Jossey-Bass, 1992).

Beyene, Tsedal, Marjorie Anglin, William Sanchez, and Mary Ballou. "Mentoring and Relational Mutuality: Protégés' Perspectives," *Journal of Humanistic Counseling, Education and Development* 41, no. 1 (2002): 87-102.

Bourdieu, Pierre. "The Forms of Capital." In *Handbook of Theory and Research for the Sociology of Education*, edited by John G. Richardson, 241-258. New York: Greenwood, 1986.

——. *Distinction: A Social Critique of the Judgment of Taste*, Richard Nice (Translation). Cambridge, MA: Harvard University Press, 1984.

——. *Outline of a Theory of Practice*, Richard Nice (Translation). Cambridge, UK: Cambridge University Press, 1977.

———. "Cultural Reproduction and Social Reproduction." In *Knowledge, Education, and Cultural Change: Papers in the Sociology of Education*, edited by Richard Brown, 71-112. London: Taylor & Francis, 1973.

Bourdieu, Pierre and Jean-Claude Passeron. *Reproduction in Education, Society and Culture*. Beverly-Hill, CA: Sage, 1990.

Bourdieu, Pierre and Loïc J.D. Wacquant. *An Invitation to Reflexive Sociology*. Chicago: University of Chicago Press, 1992.

Bowels, Samuel and Herbert Gintis. *Schooling in Capitalist America: Educational Reform and the Contradictions of Economic Life*. New York: Basic Books, 1976.

Cabrera, Alberto and Steven La Nasa. "On the Path to College: Three Critical Tasks Facing America's Disadvantaged," *Research in Higher Education* 42, no. 2 (2001): 119-149.

Campbell, Clark D. "Best Practices for Student-Faculty Mentoring Programs." In *The Blackwell Handbook of Mentoring*, edited by Tammy D. Allen and Lillian T. Eby, Blackwell Reference Online, 2007. wwwwblackwellreference.com (accessed September 2, 2011).

Chickering, Arthur. *Education and Identity*. San Francisco, CA: Jossey-Bass, 1969.

Clashes of Money and Values: A Survey of Admission Directors, Inside Higher Ed, 2011. www.insidehighered.com (accessed September 22, 2011).

Coleman, James. *Foundations of Social Theory*. Cambridge, MA: Belknap Press, 1990.

———. "Social Capital in the Creation of Human Capital" *American Journal of Sociology* (Issue Supplement) 94 (1988): S95-120.

Collier, Peter and David Morgan. "'Is that Paper Really Due Today?' Differences in First-Generation and Traditional College Students' Understandings of Faculty Expectations," *Higher Education* 55 (2008): 425-446.

Collins, Nancy. *Professional Women and Their Mentors: A Practical Guide to Mentoring for the Woman Who Wants to Get Ahead*. Englewood Cliffs, NJ: Prentice Hall, Inc., 1983.

Collins, Randall. "Functional and Conflict Theories of Educational Stratification," *American Sociological Review* 36 (1971): 1002-1019.

Creswell, John W. *Qualitative Inquiry and Research Design Choosing Among Five Traditions*. California: Sage, 1998.

Cronan-Hillix, Terry, Leah K Gensheimer, W.A. Cronan-Hillix and William S. Davidson. "Students' Views of Mentors in Psychology Graduate Training," *Teaching of Psychology* 13 (1986): 123-127.

Delpit, Lisa. *Other People's Children: Cultural Conflict in the Classroom*. New York: The New Press, 1995.

DiMaggio, Paul. "Cultural Capital and School Success: The Impact of Status Culture Participation on the Grades of U.S. High School Students," *American Sociological Review* 47, no. 2 (1982): 189-201.

DiMaggio, Paul and John Mohr. "Cultural Capital, Educational Attainment and Marital Selection," *American Journal of Sociology* 90, no. 6 (1985): 1231-1985.

Dinovitzer, Ronit, John Hagan and Patricia Parker. "Choice and Circumstance: Social Capital and Planful Competence in the Attainment of Immigrant Youth," *Canadian Journal of Sociology* 28, no. 4 (2003): 463-488.

Dunphy, Linda, Thomas E. Miller, Tina Woodruff, and John E. Nelson. "Exemplary Retention Strategies for the Freshman Year." In *Increasing Retention: Academic and Student Affair Administrator in Partnership, New Directions for Higher Education*, ed. Martha M. Stodt and William M. Klepper, 39-60. San Francisco: Jossey-Bass, 1987.

Durkheim, Emile. *Moral Education*. New York: The Free Press, 1961.

Eby, Lillian T., Jean E. Rhodes and Tammy D. Allen. "Definition and Evolution of Mentoring." In *The Blackwell Handbook of Mentoring*, edited by Tammy D. Allen and Lillian T. Eby, Blackwell Reference Online, 2007. www.blackwellreference.com (accessed September 2, 2011).

Fagenson, Ellen A. "The Mentor Advantage: Perceived Career/Job Experiences of Protégés Versus Non-Protégés," *Journal of Organizational Behavior* 10 (1989): 309-320.

Farkas, George. "Cognitive Skills and Noncognitive Traits and Behaviors in Stratification Processes," *Annual Review of Sociology* 29, no. 1 (2003): 541-562.

Farkas, George, Robert Grobe, Daniel Sheehan, and Yuan Shaun. "Cultural Resources and School Success: Gender, Ethnicity and Poverty Groups within an Urban School District," *American Sociological Review* 55, no. 1 (1990): 127-142.

Farmer-Hinton, Raquel and Toshiba Adams. "Social Capital and College Preparation: Exploring the Role of Counselors in a College Prep School for Black Students," *The Negro Educational Review* 57 (2006): 101-116.

Franklin, Cynthia and Michelle Ballan. "Reliability and Validity in Qualitative Research." In *Handbook of Social Work Research Methods*, edited by Bruce A. Thyer, 273-292. Thousand Oaks, CA: Sage, 2001.

Freire, Paulo. *Pedagogy of Hope*. New York: Continuum Publishing Company, 1994.

———. *Education for Critical Consciousness*. New York: Continuum, 1982.

Friedman, Nathalie. *Mentors and Supervisors: A Report Prepared for the Institute of International Education*. New York: Columbia University, 1987.

Galbraith, Michael and Norman Cohen. *Mentoring: New Strategies and Challenges*. San Francisco: Jossey-Bass, 1995.

Gallien, Louis and Marshalita Peterson. *Instructing and Mentoring the African American College Student*. Boston, MA: Pearson Education, Inc., 2005.

Giroux Henry. *Border Crossings: Cultural Workers and the Politics of Education*. New York: Routledge, 1992.

———. "The Politics of Postmodernism," *Journal of Urban and Cultural Studies* 1, no. 1 (1990): 5-38.

———. *Theory and Resistance in Education: A Pedagogy for the Opposition*. New York: Bergin and Garvey, 1983.

Gofen, Anat. "Family Capital: How First-Generation Higher Education Students Break the Intergenerational Cycle," *Family Relations* 58, no.1 (February 2009): 104-120.

Gonzales-Rodriguez, Yvonne. "Mentoring to Diversity: A Multicultural Approach," *New Directions for Adult and Continuing Education* 66 (1995): 69-77.

Grove, Kathleen. *Building Bridges: The Use of Looping and the Development of Cultural Capital in an Urban Elementary School*. Dubuque, IA: Kendall/Hunt Publishing Company, 2005.

Haring, Marilyn. "Networking Mentoring as a Preferred Model for Guiding Programs for Underrepresented Students." In *Diversity in Higher Education: Mentoring and Diversity in Higher Education*, edited by Henry T. Frierson, 63-76. Greenwich, CT: JAI Press Inc., 1997.

Healy, Charles C. "An Operational Definition of Mentoring." In *Diversity in Higher Education: Mentoring and Diversity in Higher Education*, edited by Henry T. Frierson, 9-22. Greenwich, CT: JAI Press Inc., 1997.

Henningsen, Mary, Kathleen Valde, Gregory A. Russell and Gregory R. Russell. "Student-Faculty Interactions about Disappointing Grades: Application of the Goals-Plans-Actions Model and the Theory of Planned Behavior," *Communication Education* 60, no. 2 (2011): 174-190.

Horn, Laura J., Xianglei Chen, and Clifford Adelman. *Toward Resiliency: At-Risk Students Who Make It to College*, Office of Educational Research and Improvement Washington, DC: U.S. Department of Education, 1997.

Horvat, Erin. "The Interactive Effects of Race and Class in Educational Research: Theoretical Insights from the Work of Pierre Bourdieu," *Penn GSE Perspectives on Urban Education* 2, no. 1 (2003): 1-25.

———. "Understanding Equity and Access in Higher Education: The Potential Contribution of Pierre Bourdieu." In *Higher Education: Handbook of Theory and Research*, edited by John Smart, 207. New York: Agathon, 2001.

House, James. *Work Stress and Social Support*. Reading, MA: Addison-Wesley, 1981.

Jackson, Philip. *Life in Classrooms*. New York: Holt, Rinehart, and Winston, 1968.

Jacobi, Maryann. "Mentoring and Undergraduate Academic Success: A Literature Review," *Review of Educational Research* 61, no. 4 (1991): 505-532.

James, David P. "Developing and Designing a Mentoring Program in Higher Education." Workshop, annual meeting of the International Mentoring Association, Washington, DC, March 2001.

Johnson, W. Brad. "Student-Faculty Mentorship Outcomes." In *The Blackwell Handbook of Mentoring*, edited by Tammy D. Allen and Lillian T. Eby, Blackwell Reference Online, 2007. www.blackwellreference.com (accessed September 2, 2011).

Johnson, W. Brad, Gail Rose and Lewis Z. Schlosser. "Student-Faculty Mentoring: Theoretical and Methodological." In *The Blackwell Handbook of Mentoring*, edited by Tammy D. Allen and Lillian T. Eby, Blackwell Reference Online, 2007. wwwblackwellreference.com (accessed September 2, 2011).

Kalmijn, Matthijs and Gerbert Kraaykamp, "Race, Cultural Capital and Schooling: An Analysis of Trends in the United States," *Sociology of Education* 69, no. 1 (1996): 22-34.

Keller, Thomas E. "Youth Mentoring: Theoretical and Methodological Issues." In *The Blackwell Handbook of Mentoring*, edited by Tammy D. Allen and Lillian T. Eby, Blackwell Reference Online, 2007. www.blackwellreference.com (accessed September 2, 2011).

Knox, Pamela and Thomas McGovern. "Mentoring Women in Academia," *Teaching of Psychology* 15, no. 1 (1988): 39-41.

Kram, Kathy. *Mentoring at Work: Developmental Relationships in Organizational Life* Glenview, IL: Scott, Foresman & Co., 1985.

Laden, Berta. "Socializing and Mentoring College Students of Color. The Puente Project as an Exemplary Celebratory Socialization Model," *Peabody Journal of Education* 74 no. 2 (1999): 55-74.

Ladson-Billings, Gloria. "Toward a Theory of Culturally Relevant Pedagogy," *American Educational Research Journal* 32, no. 3 (1995): 465-591.

Lareau, Annette. *Unequal Childhoods: Class, Race, and Family Life*. Berkeley: University of California Press, 2003.

———. "Linking Bourdieu's Concept of Capital to the Broader Field: The Case of Family-School Relationships." In *Social Class, Poverty, and Education: Policy and Practice,* edited by Bruce J. Biddle, 77-100. New York: Routledge Falmer, 2001.

Lareau, Annette and Elliot Weininger, "Cultural Capital in Educational Research: A Critical Assessment," *Theory and Society* 32 (2003): 567-606.

Lee, Eunjung, Faye Mishna and Sarah Brennenstuhl, "How to Critically Evaluate Case Studies in Social Work," *Research on Social Work Practice* 20, no. 6 (2010): 682-689.

Lee, John M. Jr., and Anita Rawls. *The College Completion Agenda 2010 Progress Report.* College Board Advocacy & Policy Center. 2010. www.collegeboard.com (accessed August 26, 2011).

Lee, Wynetta. "Striving toward Effective Retention: The Effect of Race on Mentoring African American Students," *Peabody Journal of Education* 74, no. 2 (1999): 27-43.

Lewis, Dawn and David James. "Using Faculty Members to Ensure Academic Success for Community College Students through Mentoring Best Practices: Benefits of the Faculty-Student Mentoring Program." Workshop, annual meeting of the International Mentoring Association, Orlando, Florida, March 2012.

Liang, Belle and Jennifer West, "Youth Mentoring: Do Race and Ethnicity Really Matter?" *Research in Action* 9, 3-22 (Alexandria, VA: Mentor/National Mentoring Partnership, 2007).

Lorde, Audre. *Sister Outsider: Essays and Speeches.* Trumansburg, NY: Crossing Press, 1984.

Margolis, Eric, Michael Soldatenko, Sandra Acker, and Marina Gair. "Peekaboo: Hiding and Outing the Curriculum." In *The Hidden Curriculum in Higher Education,* edited by Eric Margolis, 1-19. New York: Routledge, 2001.

Matthews, Dewayne. *A Stronger Nation through Higher Education.* Lumina Foundation for Education, Inc. 2010. www.luminafoundation.org (accessed August 26, 2011).

McCormick, Theresa. "An Analysis of Five Pitfalls of Traditional Mentoring for People on the Margins in Higher Education." In *Diversity in Higher Education: Mentoring and Diversity in Higher Education,* edited by Henry Frierson, 187-202. Greenwich, CT: JAI Press, Inc., 1997.

McDonough, Patricia M. *Choosing Colleges: How Social Class and Schools Structure Opportunity.* Albany: State University of New York Press, 1997.

Merriam, Sharon. "Mentors and Protégés: A Critical Review of the Literature," *Adult Education Quarterly* 33 (1983): 161-173.

Moore, Kathryn M. and Marilyn J. Amey. "Some Faculty Leaders are Born Women." In *Empowering Women: Leadership Development Strategies on Campus, New Directions for Student Services,* edited by Mary Ann D. Sagaria, 39-50. San Francisco: Jossey-Bass, 1988.

Mulholland, Zachary J. *The Value of Education: A Comprehensive Look at the Benefits Associated with Higher Education.* Indiana University Public Policy Institute, no. 11-C16 (June 2011).

Mullen, Carol A. "Naturally Occurring Student-Faculty Mentoring Relationships: A Literature Review." In *The Blackwell Handbook of Mentoring,* edited by Tammy Allen and Lillian Eby, Blackwell Reference Online, 2007. www.blackwellreference.com (accessed September 2, 2011).

Musoba, Glenda and Benjamin Baez. "The Cultural Capital of Cultural and Social Capital: An Economy of Translations." In *Higher Education: Handbook of Theory and Research,* edited by John Smart, 24. New York: Agathon, 2009.

Nakamura, Jeanne, David Shernoff and Charles Hooker. *Good Mentoring: Fostering Excellent Practice in Higher Education.* San Francisco, CA: Jossey-Bass, 2009.

Nora, Amaury. "The Role of Habitus and Cultural Capital in Choosing a College, Transitioning from High School to Higher Education, and Persisting in College among Minority and Non-Minority Students," *Journal of Hispanic Higher Education* 2, no. 3 (2004): 180-208.

Nora, Amaury and Alberto F. Cabrera. "The Role and Perceptions of Prejudice and Discrimination on the Adjutment of Minority Students to College," *Journal of Higher Education* 67, no. 2 (1996): 119-148.

Oakes, Jeannie, Amy Wells, Makeba Jones, and Amanda Datnow. "Detracking: The Social Construction of Ability, Cultural Politics and Resistance to Reform," *Teachers College Record* 98, no. 2 (1997): 482-510.

Oliver, Melvin and Thomas Shapiro. *Black Wealth/White Wealth: A New Perspective on Racial Inequality.* New York: Routledge, 1997.

Osterman, Paul. *College for All?: The Labor Market for College-Educated Workers.* Washington, DC: Center for American Progress, 2008.

Otto, Mary. "Mentoring: An Adult Developmental Perspective," *New Directions for Teaching and Learning* 57 (1994): 15-24.

Packard, Becky, "Student Training Promotes Mentoring Awareness and Action," *Career Development Quarterly* 51, no. 4 (2003): 335-345.

Pascarella, Ernest. "Student-Faculty Informal Contact and College Outcomes," *Review of Educational Research* 50, no. 4 (1980):545-595.

Pascarella, Ernest, Christopher Pierson, Gregory Wolniak, and Patrick Terenzini. "First-Generation College Students: Additional Evidence on College Experiences and Outcomes," *Journal of Higher Education* 75, no. 3 (2004): 249-284.

Patton, Michael Quinn. *Qualitative Research & Evaluation Methods.* Thousand Oaks, CA: Sage, 2002.

Pearson, Richard. *Counseling and Social Support: Perspectives and Practice.* Newbury Park, CA: Sage, 1990.

Perna, Laura W. "Precollege Outreach Programs: Characteristic of Programs Serving Historically Underrepresented Groups of Students," *Journal of College Student Development* 43 (2002): 64-83.

———. "Differences in the Decision to Attend College among African Americans, Hispanics, and Whites," *Journal of Higher Education* 71, no. 2 (2000): 117-141.

Philip, K. and Leo Hendry. "Making Sense of Mentoring or Mentoring Making Sense? Reflections on the Mentoring Process by Adult Mentors with Young People," *Journal of Community & Applied Social Psychology* 10 (2000): 211-223.

Portes, Alejandro. "Social Capital: Its Origins and Applications in Modern Sociology," *Annual Review of Sociology* 24 (1998): 1-24.

Pulsford, David, Kath Boit and Sharon Owen. "Are Mentors Ready to Make a Difference? A Survey of Mentors' Attitudes towards Nurse Education," *Nurse Education Today* 22, no. 6 (2002): 439-446.

Putnam, Robert. *Bowling Alone.* New York: Simon & Schuster, 2002.

Quinnan, Timothy W. *Adult Students "At-Risk": Culture Bias in Higher Education* Westport, CT: Bergin & Garvey, 1997.

Rendón, Laura I. "Validating Culturally Diverse Students: Toward a New Model of Learning and Student Development," *Innovative Higher Education* 19, no. 1 (1994): 33-50.

Riley, Richard W., Marshall S. Smith, Terry K. Peterson, Adriana de Kanter, Diana Phillips, and Judy Wurtzel. *Yes, You Can: Establishing Mentoring Programs to Prepare Youth for College.* Washington, DC: U.S. Department of Education, 1998.

Roscigno, Vincent and James Ainsworth-Darnell. "Race, Cultural Capital and Educational Resources: Persistent Inequalities and Achievement Returns," *Sociology of Education* 72, no. 3 (1999): 158-178.

Rubin, Herbert J. and Irene S. Rubin. *Qualitative Interviewing: The Art of Hearing Data.* Thousand Oaks, CA: Sage, 1995.

Scandura, Terri A. and Ekin K. Pellegrini. "Workplace Mentoring: Theoretical Approaches and Methodological Issues." In *The Blackwell Handbook of Mentoring,* edited by Tammy Allen and Lillian Eby, Blackwell Reference Online, 2007. www.blackwellreference.com (accessed September 2, 2011).

Schaefer, Richard. *Racial and Ethnic Groups.* Upper Saddle River, NJ: Prentice Hall, 2011.

Schockett, Melanie and Marilyn Haring-Hidore. "Factor Analytic Support for Psychosocial and Vocational Mentoring Functions, *Psychological Reports* 57 (1985): 627-630.

Sedlacek, William E., Eric Benjamin, Lewis Z. Schlosser and Hung-Bin Sheu. "Mentoring in Academia: Considerations for Diverse Populations." In *The Blackwell Handbook of Mentoring,* ed. Tammy D. Allen and Lillian T. Eby, Blackwell Reference Online, 2007. www.blackwellreference.com (accessed September 2, 2011).

Shapiro, Thomas. *The Hidden Cost of being African American: How Wealth Perpetuates Inequality.* New York: Oxford University Press, 2004.

Shultz, Eileen, George Colton and Cynthia Colton. "The Adventor Program: Advisement and Mentoring for Students of Color in Higher Education," *Journal of Humanistic Counseling, Education and Development* 40, no. 2 (2001): 208-218.

Smith, Buffy. "Accessing Social Capital through the Academic Mentoring Process," *Equity and Excellence in Education* 40, no. 1 (2007): 36-46.

———. "The Great Hope of Academic Mentoring Programs: The Unfulfilled Promise," *African American Research Perspectives* 11, no. 1 (Summer 2005): 169-181.

———. *Demystifying the Higher Education System: Rethinking Academic Cultural Capital, Social Capital, and the Academic Mentoring Process,* Unpublished Dissertation, University of Wisconsin-Madison, 2004.

Spencer, Renée. "Naturally Occurring Mentoring Relationships Involving Youth." In *The Blackwell Handbook of Mentoring,* edited by Tammy D. Allen and Lillian T. Eby, Blackwell Reference Online, 2007. www.blackwellreference.com (accessed September 2, 2011).

Stanton-Salazar, Ricardo. "A Social Capital Framework for Understanding the Socialization of Racial Minority Children and Youths," *Harvard Educational Review* 67 (1997): 1-40.

Stanton-Salazar, Ricardo and Sanford Dornbusch. "Social Capital and the Reproduction of Inequality: Information Networks among Mexican-American High School Students," *Sociology of Education* 68 (1995): 116-135.

Steele, Claude. "Stereotype Threat and Black College Student," *About Campus* (May/June 1999): 2-4.

Steelman, Lala and Brian Powell. "Acquiring Capital for College: The Constraints of Family Configuration," *American Sociological Reviews* 54, no. 5 (1989): 844-855.

Strauss, Anselm and Juliet Corbin. *Basics of Qualitative Research: Grounded Theory Procedures and Techniques.* Newbury Park, California: SAGE Publications, Inc., 1990.

Terenzini, Patrick T., Alberto F. Cabrera, and Elena M. Bernal. *Swimming Against the Tide: The Poor in American Higher Education*, College Board Research Report No. 2001-3. New York: The College Board, 2001.

Thayer, Paul B. "Retention of Students from First Generation and Low Income Backgrounds," (ERIC ED446633). *Opportunity Outlook* (May 2000): 2-8.

The American Heritage College Dictionary, 3rd edition. Boston, MA: Houghton Mifflin Company, 2000.

Thomas, Russell, Patricia Murrell, and Arthur Chickering. "Theoretical Bases and Feasibility Issues for Mentoring and Developmental Transcripts." In *Mentoring-Transcript Systems for Promoting Student Growth*, edited by Robert Brown and David DeCoster, 49-65. San Francisco: Jossey-Bass, 1982.

Tierney, William. "Models of Minority College-Going and Retention: Cultural Integrity versus Cultural Suicide," *Journal of Negro Education* 68 (1999): 80-91.

Tingson, Connie R. and Jennifer McGowan. *University Mentorship Program Guidebook*. Office of New Student Programs, University of Michigan, 2000.

Tinto, Vincent. *Leaving College: Rethinking the Causes and Cures of Student Attrition*, 2nd ed. Chicago: University of Chicago Press, 1993.

———. "Dropout from Higher Education: A Theoretical Synthesis of Recent Research," *Review of Educational Research* 45 (1975): 89-125.

U.S. Census Bureau, Statistical Abstract of the United States, 2011, Table 228, 150. www.census.gov/population (accessed September 1, 2011).

Vance, Connie. *Fast Facts for Career Success in Nursing*. New York: Springer Publishing Company, 2011.

Vargas, Joel H. *College Knowledge: Addressing Information Barriers to College*, Boston, MA: College Access Services: The Education Resources Institute (TERI), 2004. www.teri.org (accessed September 2, 2011).

Walpole, MaryBeth. "Emerging from the Pipeline: African American Students, Socioeconomic Status, and College Experiences and Outcomes." *Research in Higher Education* 49, no. 3 (May 2008): 237-255.

———. "Socioeconomic Status and College: How SES affects College Experiences and Outcomes," *Review of Higher Education* 1, no. 27 (2003): 45-73.

Warburton, Edward, Rosio Bugarin, and Anne-Marie Nunez. *Bridging the Gap: Academic Preparation and Postsecondary Success of First-Generation Students* (NCES Report 2001-153). National Center for Education Statistics. Washington, DC: U.S. Department of Education, 2001.

Wilson, Reginald. "Negative Mentoring: An Examination of the Phenomenon as it Affects Minority Students." In *Diversity in Higher Education: Mentoring and Diversity in Higher Education*, edited by Henry Frierson, 177-185. Greenwich, Connecticut: JAI Press Inc., 1997.

Winkle-Wagner, Rachelle. "Cultural Capital: The Promises and Pitfalls in Educational Research," *ASHE Higher Education Report*, 36, no. 1, 2010.

Wunsch, Marie. "New Directions for Mentoring: An Organizational Development Perspective," *New Directions for Teaching and Learning* 57 (1994): 9-13.

Zelditch, Morris. "Mentor Roles in Graduate Studies." In *Diversity in Higher Education: Mentoring and Diversity in Higher Education*, edited by Henry Frierson, 23-37. Greenwich, Connecticut: JAI Press Inc, 1997.

Index

academic culture, 25-27
academic knowledge and skills, 27-29
acculturation and assimilation, 100-101
Apple, Michael, xiv, 22, 25, 60, 72-73
Arriaza, Gilberto, 23, 61
Astin, Alexander, 56, 72
at-risk, xii-xiii, 2-4, 17-19

Berg, Bruce, 150
Bergquist, William, 91
Beyene, Tsedal, 35, 36
Bourdieu, Pierre, xiv, 18, 19, 20, 21,
    22, 25, 33, 55, 58, 60, 61, 76
Bowels, Samuel 17, 22, 60

Cabrera, Alberto, 20
Campbell, Clark, 6, 7, 151
Chickering, Arthur, 57
Coleman, James, xiv, 22, 25, 33, 34,
    35, 39, 42, 58
college enrollment, xi
college graduation rates and rank, xii,
    2, 3, 17-18
Collier, Peter, 23, 25, 61
Collins, Nancy, 6, 91
Collins, Randall, 18
conflict perspective, 18-19, 60
Creswell, John, 150, 152-153
critical resistance perspective, 60
Cronan-Hillix, Terry, 4
cultural capital, 18-25, 58
cultural favoritism, 19-20, 55

definitions of major concepts, 46-48
Delpit, Lisa, 97

DiMaggio, Paul, 20
Dinovitzer, Ronit, 33
Dr. Mentor's advice: building strong
    relationships, 127-129, 133-134;
    community mentors, 136-137;
    earning low grades, 116-117; en-
    couraging mentees, 132-133;
    family mentors, 137-138; general
    advice to mentees, 123-125; gen-
    eral advice to mentors, directors,
    and administrators, 139-141; insti-
    tutional support, 135-136; inter-
    preting feedback, 120-121; match-
    ing issues, 117-118; mentees
    know everything, 131-132; peer
    mentors, 138; problems with
    classmates, 115-116; race issues,
    111-112, 112-114, 121-122; re-
    search assistant issues, 114-115,
    118-119; time management issues,
    122-123, 129-130; training issues,
    134-135
Dunphy, Linda, 6
Durkheim, Emile, 59

Eby, Lillian, 4, 5
educational attainment and earnings, 2

Fagenson, Ellen, 4
Farkas, George, 22, 25, 76
Farmer-Hinton, Raquel, 33
field, 20
formal curriculum, 5, 9, 22
Franklin, Cynthia, 153
Freire, Paulo, 60

Friedman, Nathalie, 90
functionalist perspective, 18, 59-60

Galbraith, Michael, 90
Gallien, Louis, 97
Giroux, Henry, 17, 60 72-73
Gofen, Anat, 89, 99
Gonzales-Rodriguez, Yvonne, 92-93
Grove, Kathleen, 20

habitus, 20
Haring, Marilyn, 36, 91 92-94
Healy, Charles, 4, 90
Henningsen, Mary, 23, 25, 61
hidden curriculum, 5, 7, 9, 22, 59-60
Horn, Laura, 3
Horvat, Erin, 20, 25
House, James, 56

Jackson, Philip, 22, 59
Jacobi, Maryann, 7, 56, 97, 149, 151-152
James, David, 89, 95-96
Johnson, W. Brad, 6, 7, 151-152

Kalmijn, Matthijs, 25
Keller, Thomas, 5
Knox, Pamela, 92
Kram, Kathy, 90
Krista, xiii-xiv, 11-13, 42-46, 80-85, 106, 143

Laden, Berta, 33
Ladson-Billings, Gloria, 97
Lareau, Annette, xii, 3, 10-11, 20, 23, 25, 58-59, 61
Lee, Eunjung, 152
Lee, Wynetta, 36
Lewis, Dawn, 89, 95-96
Liang, Belle, 97

Margolis, Eric, 22, 59
Matthews, Dewayne, xii, 2
McCormick, Theresa, 91
McDonough, Patricia, xii, 3, 6, 10-11, 20
mentoring: benefits, 96; curriculum, 101-104, 143-144; definition, 4-5, 90; evaluation process, 104-105; four theories, 56-58; grooming

model, 92-93; history, 5-6; informal and formal, 4-5; matching, 96-97; mission statement, 94-95; network model, 93-94; phases and functions, 90-91; positive and negative outcomes, 91-92; previous studies, 7; purpose 6, 89; recruiting, 95-96; research questions, 9-10; roles and responsibilities, 98-100; training process, 97-98
mentoring cycles: advising, 63, 66-68; advocacy, 63-64, 68-72; apprenticeship, 64-65, 72-79; model, 10-11, 60-63
mentoring institutions, 144-146
meritocracy, 17
Merriam, Sharon, 4, 6, 90
methodology: analysis, 150-151; evaluating programs, 151-152; interviewing process, 148-149; limitations and significance, 152-153; recruitment, 147-148; sample and coding techniques, 149-150
Moore, Kathryn, 4
Mullen, Carol, 4
Musoba, Glenda, 18, 19, 55

Nakamura, Jeanne, 89, 95-96
Nora, Amaury, 3, 10-11, 20

Oakes, Jeannie, 22, 76
Oliver, Melvin, 25
Osterman, Paul, 2-3, 18
Otto, Mary, 92

Packard, Becky, 42
Pascarella, Ernest, 20, 56
Patton, Michael, 153
Pearson, Richard, 56
Perna, Laura, 2, 25
Philip, K., 33
Portes, Alejandro, 32
Pulsford, David, 42
Putnam, Robert, 33

Quinnan, Timothy, xii, 3

Rendón, Laura, 10-11
Riley, Richard, 89, 95-96

Roscigno, Vincent, 20
Rubin, Herbert, 153

Scandura, Terri, 6,
Schaefer, Richard, 18, 100
Schockett, Melanie, 91
Sedlacek, William, 6
Shapiro, Thomas, 25
Shultz, Eileen, 33
Smith, Buffy, 9, 25, 32, 33, 34, 36, 65,
    89, 90, 96, 143-146
social capital: closure, 39; concept, 22,
    33, 58-59; establishment of norms,
    34-38; information channels, 40-
    42; institutional cultural capital,
    32-34; sanctions, 38
Spencer, Renée, 4
Stanton-Salazar, Ricardo, 23, 32, 61
Steele, Claude, 97

Steelman, Lala, 20
Strauss, Anselm, 25, 147, 150

Terenzini, Patrick, 2
Thayer, Paul, 3, 89
Thomas, Russell, 57
Tierney, William, 20, 23, 25, 61
Tingson, Connie, 89
Tinto, Vincent, xii, 3, 6, 56
transmission of academic knowledge,
    29-32
Vance, Connie, 89, 95-96
Vargas, Joel, 3
Walpole, MaryBeth, xii, 20
Wilson, Reginald, 90, 91, 92
Winkle-Wagner, Rachelle, 20
Wunsch, Marie, 91
Zelditch, Morris, 4, 90

About the Author

Buffy Smith, Ph.D., is a sociologist, educator, and consultant. She is an Associate Professor in the Department of Sociology and Criminal Justice at the University of St. Thomas. She earned her B.A. in Sociology at Marquette University and a M.S. and Ph.D. in Sociology at the University of Wisconsin-Madison. The courses she teaches include Social Problems, Race & Ethnicity, Social Stratification, and the Sociology Senior Seminar. Dr. Smith's primary research interests include examining racial and class disparities within the higher education system. She also writes on policy issues dealing with mentoring, access, retention, equity, and diversity in higher education. She has over 10 years of experience researching how colleges and universities can assist underrepresented students with understanding and navigating the institutional culture of higher education in order to achieve academic success. Dr. Smith has received several awards and grants that recognize her research on diversity issues in higher education. Dr. Smith's publications have been featured in research and practice oriented journals such as *African American Research Perspectives* and *Equity & Excellence in Education.* She can be reached via email at bsmith@stthomas.edu.